of a Poter My Child
died in the Doctors hands.
My health since then has
been very bad. They then took
away my Child 8 years and
a halfe now Old, and it is
for asking to see him that
I have been imprisoned, it is
onely by trying to baffel Justice
that they are trying to put me to
a Madhouse. May it please
your Excelency. to see me
Justified you will have
The prayers of your humble
Servant Ellen Hinchey
C.

TELEX 70155 LIME EI

' subject

A REMARKABLE STORY

PETER TAIT
A Remarkable Story

John E Waite

Milnford Publications

First published in Great Britain in 2005 by
Milnford Publications

Hardback ISBN 0-9550379-0-5
Paperback ISBN 0-9550379-1-3

Cover design by Dick Barnard
Printed and bound in Great Britain by
Creative Print and Design Group

Milnford Publications
Leigh House
Little Norton
Stoke sub Hamdon
TA14 6TE
www. milnford-publications.com

Contents

Illustrations

Between pages 114 and 115

Between pages 242 and 243

Illustration acknowledgements

The author is grateful to the following for permission to reproduce illustrations:

The late Lady Viola Tait, 2;
Jim Kemmy Municipal Museum, Limerick, 4, 5 and 9;
Canadian War Museum (© AC 19800020-028), 7;
The family of James Tait, 11 and 15;
National Archives, Dublin, 12;
National Library of Ireland, 14 (Tait's Arms);
Jeanette Pearson, 14 (Sir Peter and Lady Tait); and
Ottoman Bank Archives and Research Centre, Istanbul, 18.

The photographs of the uniform buttons, 8, were taken by ikon studios; that of the Tait Clock, 10, by John O'Brien; and that of the staircase at 27 Rue Venedik, 16, by Monica Fritz.

The photograph of Cannocks, 6, was found for me by John O'Brien and that of the Hôtel de France in Batoum, 17, by Irina Goshkheteliani.

Acknowledgements

Of the great many people who have helped to make this book possible, my thanks are due particularly to Phil Astley, Michael Barrett, Lorans Tanatar-Baruh, Aylin Beşiryan, John Booker, Eileen Brooks, Rick Burton, Shane Campbell, René Chartrand, Jean Clapham, Fiona Clark, Isabel Donnellan, John Dundon, Christine Durrant, Kakha Dzotsenidze, Edhem Eldem, Conor Farrell, Eric Fernberg, Melanie Golder, Irina Goshkheteliani, John Hannafin, the late Kevin Hannan, Rita Hughes, Mary Johnson, Lucy Johnston, Berdia Kamarauli, Merab Kezevadze, Margaret McBride, Carolyn McInnes, Mike McNamara, Mike Maguire, Teimuraz Mamatsashvili, Brendan Martin, Brian Maund, Mike Musick, John O'Brien, Leonard O'Brien, Chris O'Mahoney, Natasha Parker, Jeanette Pearson, Brendan Pender, Les Riley, the late David Scott, Karen Sampson, Lady Sandilands, Jon Sheedy, Brian Smith, Susan Snell, Andrew Soundy, the late Lady Tait, Father Michael Wall, Larry Walsh, Thelma Watt and Susan Webster.

My grateful thanks for their advice and encouragement are also due to Isla Baring, the late Jim Kemmy TD, Caroline Finkel, Elena Frangakis-Syrett, Godfrey Omer-Parsons, the late David R Pearce, Hedley Westerhout, Christopher Zimmerli and, most of all, to Frank Tetlow.

Preface

Writing a biography of Peter Tait has not been an easy task. It has in many respects needed the skills of a detective rather than those of an author. And although he was my grandmother's father, I have no greater claim to write his biography than would a complete stranger, so entirely was his memory, together with every written record of his life, consigned to oblivion by his family.

But outside his family he is, even today, remembered in the city of Limerick, in Ireland, where, by the age of forty, he had risen from modest beginnings, as a counter-hand in a drapery store , to become a Deputy Lieutenant of the city, its Mayor for three successive years, and had received the honour of knighthood from the Lord-Lieutenant.

The Limerick years were a relatively easy part of his life to write about, not least because others have trodden the same path before me.

The first to attempt the story of Peter Tait seems to have been J F Walsh, who read a paper to the Old Limerick Society in 1954. Much later, in 1988, Jim Kemmy wrote an article for the *Old Limerick Journal*; and in 1989 Kevin Hannan wrote a brief article for the *Limerick Leader* and in 1994 an article for the *Old Limerick Journal*.

In addition, Frances Twomey described Peter Tait's involvement in Cannock Tait & Co, in her thesis on that company, as did Finbarr Crowe in an article in the *Old Limerick Journal* in 1985.

But these all dealt with Tait's years in Limerick up to the end of 1868. They did not deal at all with the subsequent years when he was living in London or in Constantinople; not least because virtually nothing was known, in Limerick or elsewhere, about those later years. Also, what was written about the Limerick years was often based on contemporary newspaper reports, or just on myth; both inspired to a great extent by their subject himself. And he was a master of 'spin'. This, I have found, frequently produced a somewhat distorted view of events, which I have endeavoured to correct.

But writing the story of the next twenty-two years of Tait's life was far from easy, as there were no markers to follow. Yes, there had been stories that he had ventured into shipping, and vague rumours of a failed attempt to establish a cigarette factory in India, or possibly Turkey, but there was no flesh on the bones. However, I found a few clues here and there and by following these a coherent and remarkable story has emerged.

There are, nevertheless, a few questions to which I have not found answers, but they do not interfere with the flow of the story, and I expect that others may well be able to fill in some of the gaps. There must surely be papers of which I am unaware, or to which I have not had access, for example in Turkey, that could shed more light on Tait's life.

Almost throughout, Tait's career was composed of a succession of quite distinct episodes. Although these to a greater or lesser extent overlapped each other in time, I have nevertheless in most cases followed each one through from start to finish, rather than follow a strict chronological order. However, I have included in each chapter heading an indication, broadly speaking, of the years covered by that chapter. I hope this method of writing will make the story easier to read.

Risking the criticism that a great many of my words are other people's, I have included, frequently verbatim, not only much of what Tait himself is reported to have said, but also what others are reported to have said about him; in the belief that, in the absence of more direct evidence, this is the closest we shall come to an understanding of the man.

Since it has proved impossible to give more than a glimpse of Tait's private life, the emphasis is on his business career; its remarkable successes and its no less remarkable failures.

To appreciate the magnitude of these successes and failures, it will be helpful to bear in mind the difference in the purchasing power of money between the time the events I describe took place and the present day.

The following figures are based on an index prepared by the Bank of England and show approximately how much it would cost in today's money to buy something which cost £1 in each of the years shown -

1845	£52
1855	44
1865	45
1875	43
1885	55

Thus, for example, something which cost £1 in 1865 would cost £45 in today's money. As a help to the reader, I have sometimes shown this comparison in the text, in italics within square brackets, following the sum of money to which it refers; in the case of foreign currencies, having first converted them into sterling at the rate of exchange current at the time.

1

The Early Years
1828-1859

The Shetland Islands, where this story begins, had become the property of the Scottish Crown in 1469 as the dowry of Margaret, daughter of Christian I of Norway and Denmark, on her marriage to James III of Scotland. They comprise a group of some ninety islands, the southernmost of which is almost ninety miles north of the Scottish mainland. In midsummer the sun barely sets, whilst in midwinter it rises above the horizon for only a little over five hours. The islands are almost treeless.

Peter Tait was born in 1828 at Lerwick, the capital of the Shetland Islands. His ancestry can be traced back with certainty only to the early years of the eighteenth century, although it is probable that his distant ancestors were of Scandinavian extraction. His great grandfather, who was born in about 1720, lived in Hoove, on the west coast of Mainland, the principal of the islands. The family may well have been engaged in fishing, which from earliest times was the chief occupation of the Shetlanders; much of the catch being salted for export.

However, by the beginning of the nineteenth century the economy of Shetland was undergoing change and a class of small shopkeepers had grown up. Peter Tait's father, Thomas, was one such. At the time of the 1841 census he was living in what is now Reform Lane in Lerwick, when he was described as a net manufacturer, but by 1851 the family had moved to Albert Court and Thomas was then a draper and greengrocer. Both Reform Lane and Albert Court are small lanes on the western side of Commercial Street in the centre of Lerwick; Albert Court being opposite the Market Cross. Lerwick is situated on the east coast of Mainland at a latitude of 60° 9′ north and a longitude of 8′ west.

Thomas Tait had been born in 1792, the third of four children; two girls, two boys. He married, in 1817, Margaret Linklater, two years his junior. Thomas and Margaret had four sons and five daughters between 1818 and 1838. One of the sons and one of the daughters died in infancy; another of the daughters was, in the crude terminology of the day, 'an imbecile from birth', although she lived to a good age, cared for by one of her mother's sisters. Peter, born on 8 August 1828, was the second of the three sons who survived to adulthood. The others were James, the eldest of the three, born in 1824 and Robert Thomas, the youngest, born on 11 December 1838. Robert was to play a significant part in the story of Peter Tait.

Little is recorded about the upbringing of the children but it is unlikely that things were easy. Because of the seasonal nature of the fishing, shopkeepers had to provide extended credit to many of their customers, four to six months being not unusual, and so survival was sometimes precarious. However, we know that, in his infancy, Peter had a wet-nurse, Barbara Irvine, and she may have attended the other children as well. Later, after the move to Albert Court and when all but three of the children had left home, there was a house servant.

Nothing is recorded of James's education, but Peter and Robert attended the Sabbath School under Robert Sinclair[1] and, later, the Lerwick Parochial School. There, Peter was taught by James Barclay[2], and Robert by John G Glass, who had the responsibility for teaching reading, writing, arithmetic, book-keeping, English grammar, mathematics and navigation, as the basic courses, with, in addition, the elements of Latin, Greek, French and German.[3] However, the fees depended upon the subjects taken and we do not know how many of these subjects Thomas was able to afford for Robert.

Barbara, Peter's eldest sister, born in 1820, was the first of the siblings to leave home; she married in 1841 Alexander Nicoll, who was Sheriff Clerk Depute of Zetland. They had four children, three sons and a daughter. Alexander Nicoll died in 1848 at the early age of 31, and on 16 May 1854 Barbara married, secondly, Balfour Logie, who was some nine years her junior, with whom she had a further five children; three sons and two daughters.

Logie was from Orkney; his family home being at Trenabie on the island of Westray.

Only two of Barbara's nine children were to play parts in the story of Peter Tait; Thomas Nicoll, born in 1843, and Laurence Nicoll, born in 1847. However, Logie was to become a major player.

James was probably the next to leave home, going first to Aberdeen, where he established a drapery business. It was there that he met, and in 1850 married, Barbara Leslie. In 1851 James opened a branch of the business in Kirkwall in Orkney, where he was helped by his widowed sister Barbara, and by Jane, one of his younger sisters. He engaged Logie as storekeeper. By the time of his marriage to Barbara in 1854, Logie had become a partner in the business, which was then known as Tait & Logie.

Peter Tait leaves home for Limerick in Ireland

Peter left the family home in Lerwick in 1844 for Limerick in Ireland; a substantial city port on the River Shannon. He was only sixteen, and although there is nothing to suggest that he did not travel on his own, it seems unlikely that Thomas would have allowed a sixteen-year-old to embark on such a journey without a travelling companion and without making some arrangements for his reception on arrival.

In the event, Peter obtained employment as a counter-hand with Cumine & Mitchell, also Scots, who had a drapery business in Georges (now O'Connell) Street. Doubtless this is what had been arranged by Peter's father beforehand; Cumine & Mitchell were probably known to him as customers of his own business in Lerwick.

Although it has been suggested that one of Peter's sisters was already living in Limerick in 1844, having married Martin Honan who had been mayor of the city in 1842 and 1843, this was not so; no other member of Peter's family went to Limerick until after Peter himself was established there.

The work at Cumine & Mitchell was seasonal, although why this should have been so is not clear. Perhaps sales were concentrated in the months when the summer goods and the winter goods first came into stock in the spring and autumn. The counter-hands were laid off out of season and during these periods, when he was out of paid work, Peter is supposed to have bought shirts which he hawked round the docks in a basket and sold to visiting seamen. Many years later the basket hung in the hall of his home in Limerick as a reminder of his humble beginnings.

Famine in Ireland

Peter Tait had barely established himself in Limerick before the onset of the great Irish famine, which lasted from 1845 to 1849. The history of the famine has been told and retold. It does not reflect well on the British Government of the time, although it is possible that the Government thought it was acting in the wider interest of the nation as a whole. But the results were appalling.

Before the famine almost the whole of the Catholic population of Ireland subsisted entirely on potatoes. Other forms of food were virtually unknown to them. Although grain was grown on a large scale it had always been exported and continued to be so during the famine years; the Government taking the view that it should not interfere with private trade.

The cause of the famine was a blight which, in certain weather conditions, attacked the potato plants and caused the potatoes to rot, either in the ground or after they had been dug, with fearful rapidity. The cause of the blight, a fungus *phytophthora infestans*, was only identified many years later and it was many years more before its control by Bordeaux mixture was discovered.

In 1845 a large part of the potato crop was destroyed by blight; in 1846 the failure was almost complete, there was no alternative food available, or made available by the Government in London; the Irish population faced starvation.

It is difficult for us today to imagine the conditions which prevailed in Ireland at that time, but the following letter, an eloquent plea for help addressed by Mr N M Cummins, a Cork Magistrate, to the Duke of Wellington on 17 December 1846 and published in *The Times* newspaper on the 24th, conveys well how desperate the situation had become.

Cummins wrote –

My Lord Duke,

Without apology or preface, I presume so far to trespass on your Grace as to state to you, and by the use of your illustrious name, to present to the British public the following statement of what I have myself seen within the last three days.

Having for many years been intimately connected with the western portion of the County of Cork, and possessing some small property there, I thought it right personally to investigate the truth of the several lamentable accounts which had reached me, of the appalling state of misery to which that part of the country was reduced.

I accordingly went on the 15th inst. to Skibbereen, and to give the instance of one townland which I visited, as an example of the state of the entire coast district, I shall state simply what I there saw. It is situated on the eastern side of Castlehaven harbour, and is named South Reen, in the parish of Myross [a place only some eighty miles south of Limerick]. Being aware that I should have to witness scenes of frightful hunger, I provided myself with as much bread as five men could carry, and on reaching the spot I was surprised to find the wretched hamlet apparently deserted. I entered some of the hovels to ascertain the cause, and the scenes that presented themselves were such as no tongue or pen can convey the slightest idea of.

In the first, six famished and ghastly skeletons, to all appearance dead, were huddled in a corner on some filthy straw, their sole covering what seemed a ragged horse cloth, their wretched legs hanging about, naked above the knees. I approached with horror, and found by a low moaning they were alive - they were in fever, four children, a woman and what had once been a man. It is impossible to go through the detail. Suffice it to say, that in a few minutes I was surrounded by at least 200 of such phantoms, such frightful spectres as no words can describe. By far the greater number were delirious, either from famine or from fever. Their demoniac yells are still ringing in my ears, and their horrible images are fixed upon my brain. My heart sickens at the recital, but I must go on.

In another case, decency would forbid what follows, but it must be told. My clothes were nearly torn off in my endeavour to escape from the throng of pestilence around, when my neckcloth was seized from behind by a gripe which compelled me to turn. I found myself grasped by a woman with an infant just born in her arms, and the remains of a filthy sack across her loins - the sole covering of herself and babe. The same morning the police opened a house on the adjoining lands, which was observed shut for many days, and two frozen corpses were found, lying upon the mud floor, half devoured by the rats.

A mother, herself in fever, was seen the same day to drag out the corpse of her child, a girl about 12, perfectly naked, and leave it half covered with stones. In another house, within 500 yards of the cavalry station at Skibbereen, the dispensary doctor found seven wretches lying, unable to move, under the same cloak. One had been dead many hours, but the others were unable to move either themselves or the corpse.

To what purpose should I multiply such cases? If these be not sufficient, neither would they hear who have the power to send relief and do not, even 'though one came from the dead'. Let them, however, believe and tremble, that they shall one day hear the Judge of all the earth pronounce their tremendous doom, with the addition, 'I was an hungered and ye gave me no meat, thirsty and ye gave me no drink, naked and ye clothed me not'.

But I forget to whom this is addressed. My Lord, you are an old and justly honoured man. It is yet in your power to add another honour to your age, to fix another star, and that the brightest in your galaxy of glory. You have access to our young and gracious Queen. Lay these things before her. She is a woman. She will not allow decency to be outraged. She has at her command the means of at least mitigating the sufferings of the wretched survivors in this tragedy. They will soon be few indeed in the district I speak of, if help be longer withheld.

Once more, my Lord Duke, in the name of starving thousands, I implore you to break the frigid and flimsy chain of official etiquette, and save the land of your birth, the kindred of that gallant Irish blood which you have so often seen lavished to support the honour of the British name, and let there be inscribed on your tomb 'Servata Hibernia'.

I have the honour to be, my Lord Duke,

Your Grace's obedient humble servant,

N.M.Cummins,

Justice of the Peace.

Ann Mount, Cork, Dec.17.

The Duke of Wellington, who had been born in Ireland, where his family, although of English stock, had been settled for at least two hundred years, was an intimate friend and confidential adviser of the young Queen Victoria. But, in spite of this and of the efforts of Cummins, and many others, to bring about a change in attitude in London, little or nothing improved the lot of the destitute, although as time went on auxiliary workhouses were established in an attempt to provide shelter for the homeless. The Military Barracks in Prospect Row at Boherbuoy in Limerick became one such. It was destined some years later to become Peter Tait's army clothing factory.

Peter seems not to have suffered during the famine years; he had seasonal employment and his out of season business of selling shirts had presumably been sustained by whatever activity there was in the docks. Indeed, by about 1850 he had rented number 4 Bedford Row and engaged a woman to make the shirts he sold.

However, before considering further the progress of Tait's shirt making activities, or the establishment of his army clothing factory, which were to form the basis of his fame and fortune, it may be useful to look briefly at various family and personal matters.

The death of Peter Tait's uncle at Walster

In October 1850, one of Peter's uncles, his father's brother Peter, died in Shetland, aged sixty-one. Although not a wealthy man by any means, he had some property; a small farm at Walster on Mainland and several houses in and near Lerwick. He left a life interest in all his property to his widow, Barbara, then aged only forty-one. To his nephew Peter he left the freehold of the farm at Walster, subject to a mortgage of £300, and three houses in what is now Reform Lane in Lerwick. Besides the properties left to Peter, two other houses were left to Charles and John Turnbull Tait, sons of Peter's aunt, Catharine, née Tait, the widow of James Tait. Catharine herself was left an annuity of £2, although she did not live long to enjoy it; dying in 1853. There were various legacies; Barbara, Peter's eldest sister, was left £10 and Peter's other sisters were left £3 each, as were his aunt Catharine's daughters.[4] These amounts seem to us today exceedingly small, even allowing for the fact that the standard, and therefore the cost, of living was far lower then than now.

John Turnbull Tait

The John Turnbull Tait who, with his brother Charles, inherited property from their uncle in 1850, emigrated to Australia in 1862 when he was thirty-two. There, he married Ann Sarah Leeming and they had five sons, Charles, John, Edward, Nevin and Frank, who were to become one of Australia's most remarkable theatrical families. Their story was told by Frank's widow, Lady Viola Tait, in her book *A Family of Brothers*.[6]

Financial difficulties experienced by Tait & Logie

There are no records to tell us what young Peter's inheritance was worth, but we do know that he disposed of the properties quite soon, although on what terms is not recorded. The farm at Walster was registered in the name of his father in 1852, but disposed of by him in 1854. The freehold of the houses in Reform Lane was registered in the name of Peter's brother James, in 1854.[5]

These transactions may have been connected with the financial difficulties encountered by the firm of Tait & Logie in 1854. The firm was unable to meet its commitments, owing more than £3,000 [*about £130,000*], a considerable sum, which must have related to the main business in Aberdeen as well as to the branch in Kirkwall. The problem was evidently overcome, on this occasion, by the creditors agreeing to a composition of their claims.[7] But both Peter and his father may have helped.

There was then an extraordinary episode in the affairs of the Kirkwall branch of the firm, which was by now being run by Logie; James Tait being in Aberdeen, where he lived with his family. In October 1854 the firm of Tait & Logie issued a summons against William Sharp, a tailor in Kirkwall with whom they had considerable dealings, alleging he owed them £60 19s 10d.[8]

It was Tait & Logie's practice to enter transactions with their customers, both sales and payments made, in pass books which were retained by the customers. When they sent an account to Sharp for what they alleged he owed them, Sharp produced his pass book which showed a much lesser debt. But Tait & Logie said that Sharp had fraudulently mutilated his pass book to support his version of events. It was all very unpleasant. Sharp, on the other hand, said that he had on occasion settled accounts in ready money and that this had not been taken into account by Tait & Logie. He also accused Logie's wife, Barbara, of denying having received cash which Sharp had paid her 'in her parlour'. He also produced a letter sent to him by Logie on 4 May 1854, only twelve days before his marriage to Barbara, asking Sharp to 'oblige me with a few pounds' as he had 'a great lot of heavy payments ...

and am some short'. Sharp also hinted darkly that he knew more than he cared to say. Did this perhaps strike home, as the Court action seems not to have been pursued by Tait & Logie.

Years later, Logie told his family that Peter Tait was responsible for the bankruptcies in which they were both involved. One wonders.

Then, in 1860, by which time the shop in Kirkwall had been closed and Logie was working with Peter Tait in Limerick, James Tait again found himself in financial difficulties. On 20 April he petitioned the Court for the Sequestration of his Estate.[9] The petition was supported by Peter Tait & Co of Limerick, whose claim was of sufficient amount for this purpose. The State of Affairs ultimately showed a deficiency of £2,130. The involvement of Peter Tait & Co suggests that the Sequestration may have been engineered between the two brothers to avoid the possibility of one of the 'outside' creditors seeking to have James arrested and imprisoned for civil debt.

The inventory of the Estate shows that the freehold reversion of the properties which James acquired from Peter Tait in 1854, and which were let for a total of £30 4s per annum, was valued at £273, from which was deducted half, representing the value of Barbara Tait's life interest, leaving a net value for the freehold of £136 10s. In the event Barbara bought this from the Estate for £100. The creditors received dividends amounting to about one shilling (or 5%) in the pound.

James Tait received his discharge on 28 June 1861, following which he went to London, where, together with his brother Robert, he established the firm of Tait Bros & Co in premises at 190 Union Street, Southwark. But more of that later.

While these events were taking place in Scotland, things had been moving forward in Limerick.

Peter Tait's marriage to Rose Abraham

On 23 June 1853, in the Independent Chapel at 6 Bedford Row,[10] Peter Tait had married Rose Abraham, daughter of William Abraham, a nurseryman, and his wife Elizabeth, of Fort Prospect, Limerick. Rose was six years younger than Peter; having been born in 1834.

The Independent Chapel, where William Tarbotton had been the Minister since 1848, belonged to the Congregational Union of Ireland, a relatively small non-conformist sect.

Rose not only married into a man's world but to a man whose consuming passion was his work. And although there is nothing to suggest that the marriage was not happy and successful - it certainly seemed to survive the vicissitudes of Peter's career - there is almost nothing recorded about the private lives of the couple, beyond the knowledge of their having had nine children and where they lived over the years. Indeed, in the whole of the story which follows, there is only a handful of passing references to Rose.

Their first child, Elizabeth Anna, was born in 1854. She was followed by Margaret in 1856, Rose in 1857, Mary Jane in 1859, Peter jnr in 1860, Barbara Isabella in 1862, Thomas William in 1864, Evelyn Rosina in 1865 and, lastly, Alice Emily in 1867.

At some time before September 1854, Peter's brother Robert had joined Peter in Limerick as what Peter later described as 'clerk and assistant to me'.[11] Robert was then only fifteen years old. His addition to Peter's household was to have far reaching consequences.

Robert's leaving home was probably prompted by the fact that his parents moved from Lerwick to Kirkwall at about this time, to be near their daughters, Barbara, and Jane, who had married Hugh Pearson in Kirkwall in 1853.

Also clerk and assistant to Peter in Limerick by 1854 was John Thomson, a native of Kirkwall. John Thomson was to marry a local girl in Limerick in 1860. He became one of the managers in Peter Tait's factory before, much later, moving with his family to Canada.

Robert Tait fathers a child

And then came the bombshell that was to cause no end of trouble. In January 1859, Ellen Hinchy, a nurserymaid in Peter Tait's household, gave birth to a child. The father was Robert Tait, then only just twenty years old; Ellen being about twenty seven. Father O'Brien, of St Michael's Church in Limerick, baptised the child, a boy, into the Roman Catholic faith on 17 January. He was named James and sponsored by Margaret Hinchy, who was perhaps Ellen's mother. The birth was doubly unfortunate; not only was the child illegitimate, but the relationship between Robert and Ellen was akin to master and servant. Furthermore, Robert was a Presbyterian, Ellen a Catholic. I will return much later to the 'Hinchy affair' as it came to be known, when, towards the end of the 1860s, it became a significant embarrassment to Tait.

Tait acquires South Hill House

Until 1859 Peter and his family were still living at 4 Bedford Row, but on 26 April of that year he acquired a 100 years' lease of South Hill House on Roxborough Road, in Rathbane South, just outside the southern boundary of the County Borough, in the County of Limerick. It was to remain his Limerick residence until 1870.

The main house had been built by Lord Carbery in about 1820 and the freehold was still owned by his family. It had about eighteen rooms of modest size on basement, ground and first floors; there was a gate lodge, outbuildings, and a spectacular cast iron conservatory close to the house. The gardens extended to about five acres. In addition there was a smaller house, known as the Garden House, with its own outbuildings and small garden. There were about twenty six acres of parkland to the south and west of the main house, with extensive views over the County of Limerick.

Bearing in mind that Peter's mother-in-law, Mrs Eliza Abraham, owned Fort Prospect Nurseries in Limerick, it is perhaps not surprising to find that while Peter was living at South Hill House he became a leading member of the Limerick Horticultural Society and a frequent exhibitor at its shows. For example, the Society's catalogues for the years 1867 to 1870 show that he won first prizes for such varied entries as pelargoniums, ericas, cucumbers, exotic ferns, azaleas, achimenes, and gloxineas, as well as numerous second prizes, including one for peaches.

The erstwhile young counter-hand had slipped easily into the part of a leading member of Limerick society.

2

Tait's Army Clothing Factory
1853-1858

Once Tait was established in Bedford Row with one, and probably as time went on more than one, woman making shirts for him, there was to be no further record of his shirt making activities until on Saturday 29 January 1853, when he inserted the following notice in the *Limerick Chronicle*:

NOTICE
To Shirt Makers
PERMANENT EMLOYMENT
for
500 Shirt Makers
Apply to
MR. TAIT
Bedford-Row,
Limerick, Jan 29

From a woman in Bedford Row making shirts to be hawked in a basket, to five hundred shirt makers, was a sudden and startling expansion. Of course, it is most unlikely that Tait actually employed five hundred people; he had a gift for exaggeration. However, such a sudden requirement for a large number of shirt makers must mean that he had obtained, from someone, a large order for shirts. It was not the Government; his first Government order did not come until later.[1] But shirts there certainly were; as evidenced by two incidents which took place in April 1854. On the fifth of that month Denis Maloney and Wm Griffin appeared before the Limerick City Magistrates for the larceny of shirts from Mr Tait. And three days later seven young lads, formerly inmates of the Boherbuoy auxiliary workhouse, appeared before the City

Petty Sessions charged with stealing a quantity of shirts from that establishment, the property of Mr Tait.[2] Thus, it seems that not only was Tait making shirts at 4 Bedford Row, but that he was doing so in the old auxiliary workhouse as well, certainly as early as 1854.

Limerick lore

In 1950, the Limerick Clothing Factory Limited, as Tait's factory at Boherbuoy had by then become, published a booklet to celebrate its centenary. This event was based on the mistaken belief that Tait had acquired premises and started his factory in Chapel Street, off William Street, in the centre of Limerick in 1850, whereas Tait's interest in the Chapel Street premises did not arise until 1860, and then almost certainly only as mortgagee.[3] He seems to have been involved in the making of several relatively small loans as mortgagee in the 1860s and into the 1870s, either on his own account or possibly as trustee for the Pery and Jubilee Loan Society.

On the other hand, deeply embedded in Limerick lore, is the story that the troops of the 8th King's Royal Irish Hussars who took part in the charge of the Light Brigade on the heights between Balaclava and Tchernaya in the Crimea on 25 October 1854, were wearing shirts made by Tait. Had Tait received an order to supply shirts for the troops going to the Crimea, not direct from the Government, but from a contractor, perhaps Neville & Co, who had received such an order? Is it also possible to see, working behind the scenes, the hand of William Monsell, who was not only the Clerk of the Ordnance, a post about to be abolished along with the Board of Ordnance in the reforms of 1855 referred to below, but also one of the Members of Parliament for the County of Limerick. He was to be a good friend to Tait over the years; they both did much to further the interests of the people of Limerick.

Tait becomes a member of the Chamber of Commerce in Limerick

As might be expected, Tait became a member of the local Chamber of Commerce; being admitted in 1857. He had been proposed by Francis Spaight, seconded by Robert Rodgers, and had received sufficient support in the ballot of members held on

20 November. The subscription was £5 a year and, although the records of subscriptions paid do not survive beyond September 1865, it is likely that Tait remained a member of the Chamber at least until the early 1870s.

However, he seems to have played only a marginal role in the Chamber's affairs, although he did lend his support to a request to the Lords of the Admiralty in 1859 for the establishment of a naval school on board a training ship in the Shannon, similar to one then existing at Cork; perhaps a sign that, even then, his thoughts were turning to the possibility of Limerick and the Shannon becoming a gateway to the Americas.

The framework within which army clothing was supplied to the British Government

In all that follows in relation to the supply to the British Government of army clothing made by Tait in Limerick, the term 'army clothing' refers to clothing for the men in the ranks; privates, sergeants, bandsmen etc.

Officers' clothing continued to be made individually by tailors, as it had been before the introduction of the changes in which Tait played a part.

It may be helpful at this point to look at the framework within which outside contractors supplied army clothing to the Government over the years, and also at the way in which the Government itself increasingly took over the manufacture of army clothing from outside contractors.

The clothing for the Army in the years up to 1855 was supplied by the Colonel of each Regiment in accordance with patterns selected, sealed and issued by a Board of General Officers; what was known as the off-reckoning system. The Colonel received a fixed allowance for each man on the authorised establishment (without reference to the number of men actually in service, which might be substantially less than the authorised establishment, so that the Government was frequently paying the Colonels to clothe men who did not exist) and the Colonel nominated his own clothier. The clothing obtained by the Colonel, either when received at the regiment, or, later, on the clothier's premises, was inspected and compared with the patterns sealed by the Board of

General Officers. The clothing for the embodied Militia was also obtained, under various arrangements, by the Colonel.

Parliamentary Committees in 1833, 1849 and 1850 had considered the system but had not recommended any changes.

But, in 1854, when the war with Russia necessitated large augmentations to the Army, the Secretary at War considered it necessary in the interests of the public to cease the financial arrangements under which the Colonels provided clothing. Instead, although the Colonel continued to be responsible for the supply, the Government paid the cost price charged to the Colonel for the actual number of men in his regiment. The Board of General Officers was maintained. But, in spite of these changes, it was found that the public still derived no advantage by competition in the trade, which remained a virtual monopoly of a number of established suppliers. Therefore, by Royal Warrant of 21 June 1855, the Colonels were relieved of all duties connected with clothing, and the Board of General Officers was abolished; its functions being transferred to a Director-General of Army Clothing. All engagements already entered into by the Colonels for the supply of clothing for the year 1856-57 were taken over by the Government. Thereafter, clothiers were awarded contracts only following the submission by them of competitive tenders. The sealed patterns were held at the Tower of London, where contractors could examine them before tendering, and all completed supplies had to be submitted to Inspectors there for comparison with the patterns and specifications 'as the contract is entirely governed thereby'.[4]

However, it was under the old system that Tait received his first Government order, either towards the end of 1855 or more likely early in 1856; to furnish 3,000 suits of clothing (tunics and trousers) to the Royal Limerick County Regiment, a regiment of militia, for the year 1856-57. All subsequent contracts obtained by Tait were placed under the new system.

Nevertheless, the firms which had monopolised the supply of clothing to the Government prior to the introduction of the new arrangements, which they opposed, had considerable influence, and succeeded, in 1856, in having a Select Committee of the House of Commons appointed to inquire into the new system.

No changes were made to the new system following the Committee's deliberations, but it is interesting to note that one of the questions raised before the Committee, in response to complaints by a number of Irish contractors, had to do with the additional burden to be borne by contractors distant from London, who had to pay freight on cloth sent to them for making up and also on the return of finished goods; an expense not incurred by contractors resident in London. The answer was that this was something the contractor had to take into account in his price and indeed Tait, who had made no complaint, seems to have taken it in his stride.

The Royal Commission of 1858

Subsequently, in 1858, a Royal Commission was appointed to enquire into the administration of the Army Clothing Depots, and although the Commissioners pointed out certain defects in the management, the principle of the new system was upheld. Tait was examined by the Commissioners on 7 December 1858 and the record makes interesting and at times entertaining reading. The minutes of Tait's examination are reproduced in full as Appendix A. However, some of his evidence, in which he expressed his views as an army clothier, is referred to below.

Tait said that he used Thomas's sewing machines. Although other clothiers had tried using machinery, it was Tait's impression that they did not know how to use it and it turned out a failure. He said he took pains to ascertain the perfection of the sewing machine. Early in 1856 he had bought one, fastened it up in his own study and taken it all to pieces, and satisfied himself that machine sewing was better than hand sewing. He said he would have had a difficulty getting on with sewing machines, had he not made himself practically acquainted with them and able to work them himself. And in a dig at one of the clothiers who were part of the old monopoly referred to above: 'it is a good thing for the country that we have more persevering tradesmen to supply our army now'.

The sewing machines referred to by Tait had been invented by an American, Elias Howe, and patented by him in 1846, but were manufactured in England by William Thomas, to whom Howe had sold the patent-right for Great Britain. They were the first commercially viable machines to create a lock-stitch.

Although it is sometimes thought that Tait was the first person to use sewing machines for the manufacture of clothing, Barthelemy Thimonnier, a Frenchman, who had invented a sewing machine capable of creating a chain stitch, but not a lock-stitch, had opened a factory in 1841 in which he employed eighty of his machines in the manufacture of uniforms for the French army. However, the project was short-lived as the machines were destroyed by workers fearful that they would be put out of work by the introduction of the machines; an aspect which was also in the minds of the members of the Royal Commission in 1858.

Tait went on to tell the Commissioners that if the Government were to give him an order, he could clothe the whole of the British army; calculating that he could make about 250,000 suits a year. If the Government were ever in an emergency, using steam power he could then supply 10,000 suits a week. I have already remarked upon Tait's gift for exaggeration. Modesty, on the other hand, was not one of his strengths. Or was it just youthful enthusiasm; at the time of this enquiry he was still only thirty years old.

In fact, between 1856, starting from scratch, and the end of 1858, Tait had supplied 120,000 suits of clothing for regiments of the line; or total sales for those three years of some £250,000.

When asked 'Does not the use of the sewing machine throw a great many people out of work?' Tait said not; he employed about 1,000 people and was able to pay them superior wages. He employed no man at lower wages than a guinea a week and paid about 30% more than was paid in London. Although it does not appear in the Royal Commission's published Minutes of Evidence, it was reported in *The Times* that Tait had also told the Commission that his annual business returns, meaning presumably what today we should call his sales, amounted to £200,000 [*about £9,400,000*][5] and that he was quite independent of Government.

Again, 'You think that for the bulk of the supply of army clothing it would be much wiser for the Government to trust to the commercial and manufacturing enterprise of the country, than to manufacture the whole of the clothing themselves?'. To which

Tait replied: 'That is my decided opinion. I believe however, that clothing supplied by public contract is the true principle. If there is competition and the enterprise of Great Britain is brought to bear upon one branch of trade it ought to be done pretty perfect', (forgetting his grammar in the excitement of the moment?).

In answer to a later question Tait said that he had laid out £4,000 on machinery 'although I have no claim upon the Government' to receive future contracts. He believed that 'the Government are the trustees of the public money and whoever will supply them with the best and cheapest article has a right to the business'. This money spent on machinery was not all.

On 1 November 1858 Tait had formalised his occupation of the old auxiliary workhouse at Boherbuoy by entering into a lease of the premises for 999 years at a fixed rent of £160 per annum. The land on which the premises stood had a frontage to Edward (now Lord Edward) Street of about 230 feet and an average depth of about 1,300 feet; an area of just over six and a half acres. The buildings were on the part of the land nearest to Edward Street and occupied over three acres; the remainder of the land being fields. It was a term of the lease that Tait was entitled to 'rebuild or wholly take down the stores' forming the central part of the buildings and replace them with 'useful and permanent improvements'. This indeed Tait did, and continued to do, over the years.

Although Tait's acquisition of the lease of the premises at Boherbuoy in November 1858 was a logical step, since he had been occupying them for some time before that, it seems that some difficulty may have arisen which made it possible that his negotiations for the lease might not succeed. In May of the previous year he had acquired, for £500, from the National Bank, 19 Brunswick (now Sarsfield) Street, on the corner of Brunswick and Henry Streets in the centre of Limerick, which, before its acquisition by the National Bank, had been the residence of Sir David Roche Bart who was MP for Limerick from 1832 to 1844. The property was considerably larger than 4 Bedford Row. Did Tait perhaps intend to use it in addition to Bedford Row if he failed to acquire the lease of the Boherbuoy premises?

In the event, Tait never occupied the property, but he was to improve it by the addition of an extension on the Henry Street frontage and in 1866 sold it to the Union Bank for £1,500.

Some idea of the impression Tait had made on the members of the Royal Commission may be obtained from one of the questions asked of Mr David Ludlow, who was the next witness after Tait and had some knowledge of the use of sewing machines by Hebbert & Co, one of the largest suppliers of army clothing at the time, but who did not have any success with them. Mr Ludlow was asked 'Is not the real difference, between Mr Tait's experience and Messrs Hebbert's, that Mr Tait has thrown his whole soul into the working of this system, and carried it out with spirit, and Messrs Hebbert did it under difficulties, and never entered very heartily into the adoption of machine sewing?'.

That may have been a major factor, but the more significant point was that Tait's operatives worked in his factory, which enabled him to operate the sewing machines by steam power, whereas the other clothiers, not least Messrs Hebbert, relied extensively on the use of operatives in their own homes and, of course, the application of steam power was not possible in those circumstances.

The Government establishes its own clothing factory

Although, after 1863, a number of further changes were made in the administration of the Army Clothing Department, these did not have any significant effect on the firms supplying the clothing.

However, in about 1856 the Government had taken the first tentative steps towards the establishment of what was to become its own manufacturing facility; it was decided that the clothing for the Foot Guards should be made under the Government's own supervision. A small building was hired for the purpose in Westminster, but the clothing was only cut on the premises and given out to be made by operatives in their own homes in the same way as was done by the London clothiers. In 1859 the premises in Westminster were closed and the operations formerly carried on there were transferred to new buildings in Pimlico.

During this year, also, the Government decided to use sewing machines in its factory at Woolwich, where clothing for the

Artillery and Engineers was made, and to employ female operatives inside the building.

By 1861, reports had been received into the saving effected at Woolwich by the use of sewing machines, and officers were sent to Paris to inspect the premises of M. Godillot, which had just been fitted up for the manufacture of clothing by machinery. Tait might have wondered why the Government did not visit him in Limerick, where he had been using sewing machines operated by steam power with conspicuous success since 1856; indeed it is often said that Tait was the first clothier in Europe to install power-driven sewing machines for the mass production of clothing. But perhaps a visit to Paris at public expense proved more alluring than a visit to Limerick. In any event, the visit to Godillot resulted in the erection of the new Government factory at Pimlico, which was completed in 1863, with accommodation for 1,200 female operatives.

From then on, an increasing proportion of the clothing required for the Army was made at Pimlico. This, combined with the fact that between 1861, which saw the Trent Expedition of troops to Canada, and the Ashantee War in 1873, Britain was not engaged in any military activity, meant that there were some very lean years to come for the army clothing trade. For example, in 1870-71 the value of the garments produced at Pimlico was £273,000, while the value of clothing obtained from the trade was only £30,000. But, as we shall see later, during this period of inactivity at home, Tait was quick to take advantage of opportunities elsewhere.

3

Government Contracts for Army Clothing
1856-1864

Tait's first contract from the Government, to supply suits of clothing for the Royal Limerick County Regiment, I have referred to in the previous chapter.

Although information about the contracts obtained by Tait in the following years is very incomplete, there are some records for the financial years 1857/58 and 1858/59.

For example, in August 1856 he received a contract to supply chacos for the year 1857/58. A chaco is a military cap of cylindrical shape, with a peak, worn mostly by infantry, and generally with a plume at the front. For the same year he received contracts for supplying tunics and trousers for regiments of the line and rifle regiments.

And in April 1857, for the year 1858/59, he received various contracts for supplying clothing for regiments of the line and rifle regiments serving in India.

The prices paid for these items by the Government are recorded and they show that the Government effected considerable savings in the cost of army clothing at the time of the change to competitive tendering, although, in the next chapter, I refer to other possible factors to explain this effect.

In addition, some of the reports of the Inspectors at the Tower survive for these two years. These show that between September and December 1857 Tait submitted, for inspection, chacos for three battalions of the Rifle Brigade. However, chacos do not seem to have been one of his successes. Out of some thirty-six samples submitted, twenty four were rejected; either the bodies or the peaks were too light, or too soft, or not sufficiently bevelled at the brow; or the chin straps were too narrow. In one case the bands were found to be made of seal skin instead of calf. Or the samples were just 'badly made'.

With his clothing he was on much firmer ground. Of the clothing he submitted for inspection barely a handful was rejected.

In the case of supplies for years after 1858/59, the Inspectors' records become much less detailed and do not give much useful information about Tait's activities.

I have included as Appendix B a copy of the scale of sizes current in 1858 for an infantry regiment of 800 men, which shows that the tunics, allowing for the variation in waist size within each chest size, had to be made in sixty-nine sizes; the trousers in forty-two sizes.[1] In addition to the completed uniforms supplied, a number were supplied basted, or loosely tacked together, to be made up by the regimental tailor to fit any men not fitted by the standard sizes.

Most importantly, it is not possible, with the exception of his very first order, to say from the Government records what quantity of uniforms Tait supplied in any year, although he had of course told the Royal Commission in 1858 that he had supplied 120,000 suits of clothing in the three previous years. Rather later, in February 1864, Tait said in a letter to Sir Thomas Larcom, Under-Secretary for Ireland, that he had a contract for clothing fifty battalions of the line.[2]

At the end of 1862 Tait obtained a contract for 50,000 uniforms to be supplied in 1863/64; the only contract awarded by the Government to an outside contractor for that year.

This event occasioned extraordinary scenes on Tait's return to Limerick from London on 23 December with the contract in his pocket. He had telegraphed ahead with news of it, and to say that he intended to give three days' wages to all in his employment the following day as proof of his attachment to, and of his affection for, the people he employed.

Tait's welcome had been arranged by the Congregated Trades, a body comprising most of the old craft trade unions in Limerick. It did not at this time include the general operatives or labourers; these came later. The Congregated Trades, like its counterparts elsewhere, was rather localised in its focus and was described as somewhat paternal in its attitudes. Its work was mainly concerned with the promotion of Limerick trade and industry. Tait himself was President of the Congregated Trades in 1865.

The following extracts are taken from the report of the proceedings surrounding Tait's arrival which appeared in the *Munster News*, a more independently minded paper than the *Limerick Chronicle*.

The Trades met at the Mechanics' Institute ... about half-past five o'clock, where they were joined by a large number of Mr Tait's Operatives, bearing bannerets of many and varied hues, and preceded by two large and handsome flags, the word "Success" printed on one, and "Welcome" on another. After a short delay the entire body set out for the Railway Terminus, accompanied by an excellent brass band, a fife and drum band co-operating with them. On their route the Trades were joined by the Mayor, who accompanied them to the Terminus, ... and now let us state a few words in reference to the occasion of the proceedings. During the past two years Mr Tait has held an army contract, for clothing forty thousand men, ... All the work was executed in the Boherbuoy concerns, which were visited by the Lord-Lieutenant, ... when his Excellency complimented Mr Tait personally on the arrangements of his Factory, and the perfections of the productions issued from it. Mr Tait employed in the manufacture of the army clothing alone, last year, between ten and eleven hundred persons weekly, and they were capable of turning out five thousand suits a month. ... The hands in the factory are nearly all females, and those only who are most conversant with the society of this city, can appreciate the beneficial industrial results of such continuous and extensive employment. Many an humble family is supported by the earnings of its female members, and many were the households to which the news of Mr Tait's success introduced rays of comfort, making their Christmas hearths happier and brighter.

The clanging of the signal bell announced the approach of the half-past six o'clock train, and the sound was blended with the hearty cheers which arose from the people and which were continued after the train stood still. When it stopped, the Mayor, with ... a deputation from the body of the Trades, received Mr Tait on the platform, and accompanied him to the front entrance of the Terminus, where his appearance was the signal for a burst of cheering. No less than twelve or fourteen tar barrels were blazing in a trice, and twice as many flambeaux, whilst brilliant pyrotechnic, starlike and other lights were illuminating the air.

A carriage drawn by four greys with outriders was in attendance, but Mr Tait declined to enter it, declaring he stood out for the working classes, and would, like them, proceed on foot. The procession then advanced in the following order; the Band, the Bearers of the colours with the mottoes, "Welcome" and "Success", the Bearers of the large platform conveying tar barrels, clearly alight and borne before the Mayor, Mr Tait, officers of the Trades, with bearers of flambeaux at each side; then the following guilds - coopers, masons, tobacconists, tailors, painters, carpenters, boot-makers, plasterers, sawyers, brush-makers, cork cutters, ship-wrights, chandlers and smiths.

When the procession arrived at the Mechanics' Institute, the Mayor, Mr Tait, and the large number of friends who accompanied him, were conducted to the hall, where, when the repeated cheers had somewhat subsided, several members of the Trades called on the Mayor to take the chair.

That done, the secretary of the Trades read the following -

ADDRESS TO PETER TAIT, ESQ.

Sir,

We, the Congregated Trades of Limerick, beg most respectfully to tender you a sincere and cordial welcome. We hail your return amongst us with no ordinary degree of gratification, and fully appreciate your efforts on all occasions for the advantage of the working classes of Limerick. We feel that we cannot communicate our sentiments in language sufficiently expressive; but with the warmest pulsations of our hearts we tender you our regard and respect, as a true patron of labour, and a friend of local industry. We wish we could convey our gratitude to you in a more signal way than this, but at least it will place on record our thankfulness for the good you have achieved for a large portion of the working classes of our city, and for the welfare of the community at large. Allow us, at the same time, to give utterance to the admiration we entertain for the liberality by which you are personally characterised in your relations with all in your employment, for your ever gentlemanly demeanour, and kind deeds to all in your establishments, and for the generosity with which you have always contributed to the relief of our poor.

Mr Tait, who was received with prolonged and enthusiastic cheering, then said -

Mr Mayor, my friends, and fellow labourers, I certainly am not able tonight to give expression to the feelings which your great kindness has excited within me. Whatever I have done, I have done quietly, and for the benefit of the people of Limerick (cheers). I feel quite satisfied that the people of this city possess that spirit of gratitude which prevails in the breast of every true Irishman (cheers). I knew they would feel thankful to me, but I had no idea I would receive such a manifestation as this tonight for my humble exertions (continued cheering). I could not expect it. You know my habits are more retiring than otherwise; and your great demonstration coming on me, as it has tonight, completely overwhelms me, and makes me feel that the exertions of a life on your behalf could not sufficiently repay your kindness (great cheering). It has always given me the utmost pleasure to do all in my power for all in my employment, and the working classes, in general, of Limerick (hear, hear).

On my arrival in London, I found that, in consequence of interest being expressed in my favour, to the Government, by His Excellency, the Lord-Lieutenant, the Right Hon Mr Monsell, and Col Dickson, that fair play would be given to Ireland - that an impression had gone abroad that it was desired to raise an Irish cry in the matter. I considered it my duty immediately to write to Her Majesty's principal Secretary of State, for the War Department, and to inform him that all my transactions with his Department were the result of honourable competition alone (hear, hear). I desired no change from that principle and considered I could offer him no greater slight as a guardian of the public purse, than to suppose he would give any contracts connected with the public service, to any except those who supplied the best articles, and at the lowest price (cheers). And *such was the fact* (hear, hear). I resolved to make every fair effort to gain the contract, and I succeeded in my determination to go in and win (cheers and cries of bravo!). I reflected on the gratification it would be to many in this city if I succeeded, and I also knew what cheering news my success would be to those who are I may say dependent on me for their support (hear, hear).

But I must conclude by reference to the contract matter. When I found that a cry such as I have alluded to, was sought to be raised against me, I resolved to seek no favour; I determined to present no contract as a petitioner from this country, and put it in as an independent employer of the independent workmen of Limerick (great cheering).

I went to the manufacturing districts of England; I explored everything that my contract told me would need to be ascertained. I filled in my tender, put it in competition with those of the first men of the day - men who doubtless could buy you and me out. I waited and I obtained the tender, and here it is - signed, sealed and delivered (great cheering).

I can do without this contract, but it shall never leave me for any firm elsewhere as long as I have power to compete for it, and execute it when received (cheers).

I have only, in conclusion, to repeat that I cannot sufficiently express my thanks to you for the honour you have paid me. I will now, with your permission, retire to my quiet and happy home. I did not go beyond your city to seek a partner to share it with me, meet for me in every respect (cheers). I beg to thank you again and to assure you that I will never forget your kindness (cheers).

Following a brief address by the Mayor of Limerick, Tait then said that he would try to have the order which he had obtained executed as quickly as possible. There would, however, be some delay, but he would endeavour to make arrangements for the employment of the working classes as soon as possible. He would be looked upon with a jealous eye in the matter, because during the last years the contract had been shared with English firms, but this year they had retreated the field. He hoped the order would be executed to the satisfaction of the Government and to the credit of themselves.

Eighteen months later, in July 1864, there was a debate in the House of Commons on the subject of the Government manufacturing establishments. So far as the supply of clothing was concerned, there were those who supported the idea that it should all be manufactured in the Government's factories, and those who thought it should be entirely in the hands of outside contractors. The Marquis of Hartington, supporting the then present position as the best that could be adopted, said that 'At Pimlico clothing is made for forty battalions of the line, and shell jackets and trousers for the rest. The contractors still make the clothing of fifty three battalions, besides all the clothing for the Post Office officials, for the Metropolitan Police, and others, which, however, is passed through the army establishment to be inspected. There is only one contractor for the clothing still existing, and I believe he is a constituent of the right hon. Member for Limerick. He has succeeded in driving every other contractor out of the field, and it seems to me that if we were to relinquish our manufactory we should be left entirely in the power of this one contractor, or one or two others'.[3] That one contractor was Peter Tait and that was the significance of the contract with which he had returned to Limerick in December 1862.

As it is difficult to establish with certainty the extent of the orders received by Tait from time to time, so it is difficult to be certain how many people Tait employed. In his evidence to the Royal Commission in 1858 he had said that he then employed about 1,000 people, made up of 'perhaps 800 girls and women; no children', 'about 40 men indoors' and 'a great many men' working out of doors; that is, at home. One wonders where the line came between 'girls' and 'children'; perhaps above and below the age of consent, which at that time was twelve. It is said that a little girl from Boherbuoy, Annie Neville, then fourteen, was one of the first to work a sewing machine in Tait's factory.

The Address by the Trades quoted above suggests that in 1862 Tait was still employing much the same number; ten or eleven hundred, although Tait implied in his closing remarks that not all his employees were in work as he spoke, since he refers to his endeavour to make arrangements for the employment of the working classes as soon as possible. This was probably because his Government contracts tended to be seasonal, as clothing was ordered for financial years, April to April and there was an idle period between the completion of the clothing for one year and the ordering of the clothing for the next. This is something Tait sought to address, but not always with success.

Clothing for the Irish Constabulary

At the beginning of 1864 Tait proposed to the Director General of Clothing at the War Office that a new system should be adopted for the clothing of the Royal Irish Constabulary Force.

Until then, the method for providing the Constabulary with clothing was for it to be roughly cut out with the linings and garniture basted, or tacked, together ready for making up at the force's several stations.

Tait's proposal was that the cloth, linings and garniture should be supplied to him in bulk, for him to make up into uniforms, which he would then deliver to the headquarters or principal station in each County. The idea was hardly new, since this was how the clothing of the British army had been supplied for several years, except that by 1864 the contractor himself almost always supplied the cloth, the linings and the garniture. However, a significant difference was that the members of the Constabulary were scattered over Ireland in about 1,500 separate locations, which was to make the fitting of the individual members of the force very difficult. Perhaps this was the root cause of the problems which were to arise.

The Director General agreed to Tait's proposal, subject to the concurrence of the Irish Government.

Tait therefore wrote the letter to Sir Thomas Larcom in February 1864, already referred to, seeking the agreement of the Irish Government to what was proposed. This was an interesting move, because one would perhaps have expected someone from within Government to be seeking this approval. But it well illustrates Tait's propensity for dealing only at the very top and his inability to brook any kind of delay in getting things done.

In his letter to Sir Thomas, Tait explained (and this was the crucial point) that his object in submitting the proposal was that the making of the clothing for the Constabulary would give employment to his workpeople 'during the interval between the completion of one year's clothing for the line and the commencement of another, which occurs during the early part of the year when the want of employment is most severely felt'.

The agreement of the Irish Government was presumably forthcoming, since on 19 April a contract embodying Tait's proposal was entered into. Already two months had gone by since Tait had written to Sir Thomas Larcom. The whole of the clothing, 40,000 to 50,000 suits, was to be delivered to the District Headquarters and fitted to the satisfaction of the Commanding Officers by 15 August 1864.

However, Tait & Co considered the scale of sizes submitted to them with the contract to be unsuitable; a view in which they were supported by the Superintendent of the Royal Army Clothing Factory at Pimlico. They had therefore prepared and submitted a simple form, which they had asked should be completed with the number of uniforms of each size required by the force, and returned as soon as possible. However, the Inspector-General of Constabulary, Col Wood, initially refused to do this and the forms were not eventually sent out for completion until towards the end of July. When they were returned, completed, to Tait & Co is not recorded, but presumably not until some time in August.

It was by now no longer the early part of the year 'when the want of employment is most severely felt', but just coming up to the busiest.

The result was that delivery of the uniforms was delayed long past the contract date for completion, which Tait & Co explained was due entirely to the delay in the return to them of the forms indicating the sizes of the uniforms required.

The Inspector-General of Constabulary, whose fault this was, commented that 'a repetition of the serious inconveniences that had been sustained in the current year might be avoided by returning to the previous system', whilst expressing a desire 'to disclaim, in the strongest manner, any wish to throw obstacles in the way of a change of system, were such change conducive to the advantage of the public service'.[4]

It was to be some years before Tait was again given a contract to supply clothing to the Irish Constabulary.

Shirts for the Navy

Another of Tait's initiatives at about this time is recorded in the annals of the Sisters of Mercy in the Diocese of Limerick. He gave a lot of work to St Mary's Convent to be done in the Orphanage. It consisted of the making up of shirts for the Navy, for which Tait evidently had a contract with the Government.

He delivered the shirts to the Convent ready cut out and the children made them up; for which Tait paid 'very fairly' and which 'made the children very expert at sewing'; the exploitation of child labour or a youth training scheme, depending on your point of view.

However, the arrangement ceased in 1867, by which time the amount of work had increased considerably. Not only the children in the Orphanage, but also the girls in the House of Mercy, and poor women outside the Convent, had become involved, all of whom were well paid; in addition, a debt of £500 due from the Orphanage was repaid from the profits. It is not known why Tait terminated the arrangement, but it may have been because by then the Government no longer allowed contractors to use outworkers; requiring all work to be carried out in a factory and therefore subject to the Factory Acts.

4

Cannock Tait & Co
1858-1869

In the last two chapters I have followed the story of Tait's army clothing factory from its beginnings in 1853 up to 1864.

It is necessary now to go back to 1858, the year in which Tait formalised his occupation of the premises at Boherbuoy, and look at an entirely separate venture which he embarked upon in that year.

In 1850, Cumine & Mitchell, Tait's first employers in Limerick, who had been there since 1840 with premises in Georges Street, had sold their business to John Arnott and George Cannock, who carried on the business under the name Arnott Cannock & Co. Arnott and Cannock already had a substantial drapery outlet in Henry Street, Dublin, which they retained.

Then, on 11 November 1858, only ten days after entering into the lease of the premises at Boherbuoy, in a remarkable reversal of fortune, Tait bought Arnott's share in Arnott Cannock & Co in Limerick; forming a new partnership of himself, Cannock and Peter Thom, and renaming the business Cannock Tait & Co.

Of George Cannock we shall hear more later. Peter Thom was Tait's brother-in-law; having married Rose's sister Mary Anne in 1852. Tait and Thom became the active partners, the former more active than the latter. Cannock took no part in the day-to-day management; devoting himself to the running of the Dublin business which he and Arnott continued to own. He lived in Dublin until his retirement in 1865, when he moved to London; acquiring 23 Aberdeen Park in Highbury Grove, Islington.

In spite of his acquisition of an interest in Cannocks, Tait continued to own and run the clothing factory at Boherbuoy as an entirely separate enterprise.

When Tait entered on the scene, Cannocks owned properties fronting Georges Street and Honan's Quay, in the block of properties bounded by those two streets on the east and north, and by Brunswick Street on the south. The properties had been acquired by Cannocks piecemeal over the years and were badly in need of rationalisation and expansion to cater for the increase in business foreseen by Tait. He therefore embarked upon a major rebuilding programme at the end of 1858. He engaged William Fogerty of the Dublin architects Gribbons & Co to design an imposing new building on the Georges Street frontage. It had three main storeys as well as a mezzanine floor between the ground and first floors. The building was divided into eight bays; a further three bays and a clock tower being added by subsequent owners much later, in the 1880s.

The ground floor of the new building was retail space. The upper floors were used for the manufacture and polishing of furniture, and for upholstering and mattress making, for which horsehair was used; the mattress cases were also made on the premises, using sewing machines.

In addition, accommodation was provided for the large number of apprentices who lived on the premises; as well as dormitories, there were sitting rooms, a library, a dining room and kitchens provided for them.

Behind the frontage on Georges Street, the space was single storey with roof lights.

The whole establishment was lit by gas: electricity was not to come until 1878.

It was estimated that the project cost £9,000 [*about £415,000*] and is said to have been accomplished in just over three months, opening in time for the start of the summer season on 1 May 1859.

How was all this paid for?

It is not known how much Tait paid for Arnott's share in Cannock's, but it must have been a considerable sum. One can only speculate, in the absence of any direct evidence, as to where Tait obtained the money for this and for the ambitious re-building which followed, particularly as, at the same time, he was financing the rapid expansion of the army clothing factory, where, even though the premises at Boherbuoy had not yet cost any capital, he had spent £4,000 on machinery.

There is no doubt that, particularly in the early years of Tait's involvement, the supply of army clothing to the Government was very profitable. During the debate in the House of Commons in July 1864, already referred to, the Marquis of Hartington indicated, as an example, that between 1859 and 1862, following the setting up of the Government's own clothing factory at Pimlico, the average price charged by outside contractors for an infantry tunic, excluding the price of the cloth, had fallen from 12s 10d to 9s 6d, a reduction of twenty-six per cent.

But was Hartington right in ascribing the fall in the average price to the setting up of the Government's own factory? Might it not, instead, have been largely due to Tait's entry into the market and the breaking of the monopoly held by a limited number of contractors before the introduction of the reforms of 1855? If Tait, in the early years, had undercut the prices quoted by these other contractors by only enough to obtain the business for himself, he might well still have been making very considerable profits, derived largely from the economies afforded by his use of machinery as well as his methods of mass production. Walter Bagehot, the great economist of the period writing about the development of the London money market in the 1860s and early 1870s, indicates a further possibility – [1]

> In every district small traders have arisen, who 'discount their bills' largely, and with the capital so borrowed, harass and press upon, if they do not eradicate, the old capitalist. The new trader has obviously an immense advantage in the struggle of trade. If a merchant have £50,000 all his own, to gain 10% on it he must make £5,000 a year, and he must charge for his goods accordingly; but if another has only £10,000, and borrows £40,000 …, he has the same capital of £50,000 to use, and can sell much cheaper. If the rate at which he borrows be 5%, … and if, like the old trader, he make £5,000 a year, he will still, after paying his interest, obtain £3,000 a year, or 30%, on his own £10,000. As most merchants are content with much less than 30%, he will be able … to forego some of that profit, lower the price of the commodity, and drive the old fashioned trader – the man who trades on his own money – out of the market. … there is a steady bounty on trading with borrowed capital, and a constant discouragement to confine yourself solely or mainly to your own capital.

Could a combination of these various factors have been what enabled Tait to acquire his share in Cannocks, and pay for the new building; to purchase 19 Brunswick Street, and set up his new clothing factory at Boherbuoy?

Tait takes control at Cannocks

Having acquired his interest, Tait took a firm grip of Cannocks and under his energetic management great changes were to take place over the next ten years; a period which coincided with a great increase in the prosperity of Limerick and the surrounding areas. Under Tait's management the number of employees increased from about 100 to 150; of whom about 100 were apprentices.

Much later, in October 1865, Cannocks advertised their new winter goods in the *Limerick Chronicle* and the advertisement gives a good idea of the variety of goods in which they dealt; new French silks, sealskin jackets, mantles, fancy dresses, real Aberdeen winceys, French merinos, shawls, hosiery, gloves, millinery, furs, umbrellas, shirts, scarves and, in the tailoring and outfitting departments, new Himalaya tweed for suits, hunting and livery cloths, mackintoshes and the North British Co's waterproof coats and leggings.

Cannocks were not only retail drapers, but had a wholesale department as well, and Tait had expanded the latter greatly, to supply the increasing number of small retail outlets in the surrounding areas.

As well as expanding the existing business, Tait reintroduced glove making to Limerick; a trade for which the city had once been famous. In the eighteenth century a glover named Lyons is said to have received orders for his gloves from the Court at St Petersburg as well as from other European Courts; his gloves being so fine that a pair could be fitted into a walnut shell.

Tait remained the most active partner in Cannocks until 1865 when Peter Thom took over the day-to-day management, assisted by Tait's nephew, Thomas Nicoll.[2]

In March 1868 an attempt was made to set fire to the premises of Cannock Tait & Co. The fire was started early in the evening by a bottle containing some flammable liquid being thrown through a window of the calico department on the lower floor at the rear of the main building. Fortunately, the fire was noticed by two girls walking along the street at the side of the building, who called for help, and the fire was soon extinguished before much damage had been done. The incident caused some alarm at the time, not so much for the damage that was done, but for the realisation of what could have happened if the fire had taken hold; bearing in mind the large number of apprentices living on the premises.

As we shall see in a later chapter, Tait's interest in Cannock Tait & Co came to an abrupt end in 1869.

5

Clothing for the Volunteer Militia of Canada
1863-1880

The background to the ordering by the government of Canada of uniforms for the Volunteer Militia of Canada has been described as follows - [1]

> In 1861 Canadian security still depended on the British garrison. However, in 1855 provisions for a 5,000-man Volunteer force, composed mostly of rifle companies dressed in rifle green, had been started. By 1862 the force had grown to 25,000. Most were then reorganised into numbered battalions, the majority as infantry dressed in scarlet. Schools of Military Instruction for officers were organised in 1864, and in December of that year three "Administrative" battalions were called up on active winter duty.
>
> The Militia Act of 9 June 1862 decreed that the government would supply volunteers with "uniform clothing". It was the first time a Canadian government took over the issue of uniforms on a permanent basis. Adjutant General Walker Powell was sent to England to purchase 20,000 uniforms ...

On 20 March 1863 there was a debate in the House of Commons in London on the question of the Government's army clothing factory at Pimlico. During this debate Lieut-Col S A Dickson, one of the Members for the County of Limerick, protested against the gradual increase of clothing operations by the Government, the effect of which was to injure trade and to shut up those great establishments which were necessary, he believed, to the efficient supply of the service. He was informed that arrangements were being made to manufacture at Pimlico the clothing of the Canadian Militia regiments and of the officers of the Customs, while he had heard that day that the Government establishment at

Pimlico had offered estimates for making the uniforms of the Militia.

Dickson contended that, if the manufacture of army clothing were thus to be concentrated in the hands of the Government, it would be impossible to turn out all the clothing which might be required at a moment of exigency. A certain amount of clothing ought to be made by contract, while the Government factory should act as a check on the contractors. He wished particularly to call attention to the fact that the clothing made up at Pimlico was not subjected to the same inspection as that supplied by contract. He contended that the Government Inspector ought to inspect the clothing from the Government factory as well as that sent in by the contractors. The result of the first system was that faulty clothing had occasionally been sent from Pimlico. A large contractor at Limerick had recently supplied 800 tunics for a regiment of the line. On their arrival the shoulder straps and buttons had been cut off and placed on tunics made at Pimlico, which had then been sent down to the regiment, and had turned out to be defective. These defects had been complained of, but the matter had been hushed up.

There is no record of the prices quoted to Lieut-Col Walker Powell, Deputy Adjutant-General, who was acting on behalf of the Canadian Government, by Pimlico, and referred to by Dickson, but on 16 and 20 March Powell received estimates from Hebbert & Co for all the various items he required. One suspects there was then an intervention by Dickson or by Tait, or perhaps by both, because on 27 March, in a letter to the Under- Secretary of State for War at the War Office in London, Powell said that he had entered into a contract, on behalf of the Government of Canada, with Tait & Co, Limerick, for his total requirement of 20,000 tunics for the use of the Volunteer Militia of Canada.[2] He said Tait & Co had already ordered the cloth for the manufacture of these garments and had agreed to deliver 5,000 tunics on 10 April and the remainder on or before 2 May, 'the Government of Canada being anxious to have the whole of the Volunteer force completely uniformed prior to HM's Birthday (24 May), that being the day on which the Militia of Canada are inspected each year.'

He went on to say that Tait & Co could manufacture 10,000 tunics prior to 10 April, provided 6,500 yards of scarlet cloth, in addition to the quantity they now had in stock, could be obtained. It was therefore arranged that this quantity of cloth should be supplied to Tait & Co from Pimlico on condition that it would be paid for, or replaced, by 15 May.[3]

However, there must have been some delay somewhere, because it was later reported that, following delivery into the Provincial stores in Quebec, distribution to the newly organised corps of Volunteers did not commence until 23 May. It is not clear whether the first 10,000 tunics were ready for despatch on 10 April, and if they were, why distribution did not start until 23 May. Perhaps the trousers, which were being made in Canada, were not ready until then.

On 7 April 1863 the following piece appeared in the *Limerick Chronicle,* surely inspired by Tait, in an exaggerative mood as usual -

Mr Tait's Army Clothing Establishment - This large and extensive manufactory is now in full working operation, nearly 2,000 females being at present daily employed, and at extra time, completing the very superior clothing which is being made up for shipment to Canada for the militia there. On the first of the ensuing month 30,000 suits will be sent off by the enterprising proprietor, who is unceasing in his superintendence of the factory from morning 'till night. A visit to the vast emporium affords gratifying proof of the abundant employment given to the females of Limerick, through the medium of the Army Clothing contracts, which it is hoped will long continue. The various departments under Mr Logie, Mr McFarlane, Mr Thomson etc are carried out and conducted in a highly creditable manner - systematically arranged and judiciously apportioned. For the next fortnight the factory will be open for inspection of all respectable visitors, with permission of Mr Tait, and the treat will, no doubt, be gladly availed of.

This was followed on 23 May by another article -

The Clothing for the Canadian Volunteers - It is satisfactory to know that Peter Tait Esq of this city has with strict punctuality, completed within the short time specified, the large contract for clothing of the

Canadian Volunteers. He left for Liverpool on Tuesday for the purpose of personally witnessing the shipment thereof for their destination.

The promptitude with which this extensive order was completed reflects credit not only upon the contractor but upon the Limerick operatives, male and female, employed at the factory, demonstrating what can be accomplished in Ireland under a spirit of enterprise, as the Government Army Clothing Establishment at Pimlico, and some of the largest private manufacturers in England and Scotland declined to take the contract unless the time for executing it was doubled.

Col Powell, Canadian representative in this matter, highly eulogised the working capabilities of our Limerick operatives, and was highly pleased with the style and manner in which the clothing was made up.

There was of course a basis of truth in these articles. But, for example, it is difficult to believe that it could have taken 2,000 females, at extra time, to make 20,000 tunics only, not suits, in some seven weeks, when in 1858 1,000 employees could make 5,000 complete suits in a week. And there is a good deal of difference between 20,000 tunics and 30,000 suits. It is well to notice these points at this stage because much of the Tait myth in Limerick is unfortunately found, on examination, to be based on similarly inspired articles.

However that may be, once the connection had been established, Tait's factory continued supplying the Canadian Government with clothing until about 1880.

A banquet at the Clothing Factory

On 28 May, following the completion of the contract for the clothing for the Volunteer Militia of Canada, Tait gave a banquet at the Clothing Factory for over one hundred and forty people. The company consisted of the Mayor of Limerick, what the *Southern Chronicle* of 30 May described as 'a number of respectable guests', thirty delegates from the Congregated Trades, and a large number of the assistants and members of the firm of Cannock Tait & Co. The catering was arranged by Patrick Lynch, the proprietor of the George Hotel in Georges Street, of whom we shall hear more later, as also of his wife.

This was the first of a number of similar events put on by Tait over the years. The excuse on this occasion was the formal presentation by the Congregated Trades of their congratulatory address to Peter Tait, originally read out following his return to Limerick from London in the previous December, but which had now been 'printed on satin, beautifully framed, and ornamented with several well-executed designs' intended to make it one 'to which Mr Tait and his children could look in years to come as a proud testimonial of the good feeling he won from the Trades'.[4]

A tribute by the Bard of Thomond

The presentation of the address was followed by the reading of a tribute to Tait by Michael Hogan, the self-styled Bard of Thomond –

This beautiful offering is laid at the shrine
Of thy bold enterprise and thy manly spirit;
And long in the home of thy heart may it shine
A tribute of friendship and love to thy merit.
Thou hast won the warm hearts of the children of trade,
Thou hast shown how their native industry may rise,
If others, whose wealth is idleness laid
Would give nerve to their efforts in reaching the prize.

Yes, they may yield thee the laurel of honour, for thou
Hast nobly to earn its lustre come forth;
And the wreath of their love, that encircled thy brow,
Would never be thine if not won by thy worth.
For thou art all goodness and kindness to those
Who toil in the sphere of thy liberal employ;
While thy breast with a generous anxiety glows
To encourage their toil and reward it with joy.

Advance! – May the beams of prosperity lead
The march of thy enterprise still to its aim;
It is thee – such as thee – that deserves the high meed
Which merit and worth from a people must claim.
Advance – perhaps others, ashamed of their sloth,
May follow thy shining example and know
That wealth has no virtue, nor honour, nor growth,
Till put in the streams of industry to flow.

In the soul of our city thy memory shall live,
Thy name shall be honoured in cottage and hall;
And trade and her children shall gratefully give
A blessing to him so beloved by them all.
And in life's future day, when their sons shall pursue
The proud path of toil that to fortune aspires.
Oh! May they be blest with some spirit like you,
To show them the name thou hast shown to their sires.

It may be helpful at this stage to say something about Hogan, who became somewhat of an institution in Limerick. Born in 1832 at Thomondgate, just across the River Shannon from the centre of the city, he took to writing and became known particularly for his satirical ballads, which were the scourge of many local politicians and members of the clergy, and which shocked Limerick.

However, although Michael Hogan was probably genuine in his appreciation of what Tait did for his employees, and for the poor of Limerick, it was probably also because Tait paid him a retainer that the Bard wrote ballads supportive of Tait. Possibly the earliest of these was that just quoted, but, as we shall see, others followed.

Hogan died in 1899.

6

Attempted Revival of the Flax Industry
1864-1865

In 1864 Tait became very much involved in promoting the revival of the flax industry; not for his own account but in an attempt to enable small farmers to make a living from their land, which, in the years since the famine in the 1840s, had become well nigh impossible due to the low price of corn; with the result that large numbers were continuing to emigrate.

A public meeting was held in Limerick on 23 January 1864, at which Col Dickson was the principal speaker.

He had this to say - [1]

that no person except those who in the course of their professional avocations are brought into immediate contact with the inhabitants of the lower purlieus of a great town like Limerick ... can form the slightest idea of the misery that exists among the poorer classes. During the changes which have been taking place for the last 20 years, since the potato failure, there can be no doubt, but that the produce of the land has so depreciated in value that profit cannot be made of land now, like that which was made of it in those days. ... And in such times how are the people to live? What would support the small farmers and labouring classes? These were the very people they ought to look to.

One answer to this rhetoric came later when, at the City Police Court, a man was sent to goal for seven days for stealing, off the streets, manure belonging to Limerick Corporation.

There was discussion as to the merits or otherwise of the cultivation of flax, for which the climate in the South and West of Ireland was held to be particularly favourable. Although flax growing had been tried before, it was held to have failed because there were no, or at least insufficient, facilities for the preparation of the crop for market. This required the provision of scutching and dressing mills.

Councillor Synan, feeling that they should do something practical, suggested the formation of a committee to consider the costs of introducing skilled labour to teach the farmers how best to grow the flax, of erecting steeping and scutching mills, and of the establishment of a home market for the sale of flax; the Committee to report to a general meeting of the County. He proposed the formation of a joint stock company with limited liability; the shareholders in which to be the members of the committee he proposed.

Tait told the meeting that for some time back he had given much of his time and attention to the subject of the growth of flax. He had visited Belfast to look at the industry there and from what he had learned there and from his own knowledge of the growing demand for linen fabric he was satisfied that, if entered into with spirit and carried on with perseverance and determination, the cultivation of flax would to a large extent promote the prosperity of the country and the happiness of the people.

Tait supported the formation of a company as proposed by Councillor Synan but felt that it should be formed at once for the purpose of erecting scutching and dressing mills, where all these operations could be performed for the farmer at a stated charge per ton. This amended proposal was agreed to and the Limerick Flax Company Limited was duly formed and its capital fully subscribed; Tait being appointed Chairman. Tait probably foresaw that by the time a committee had considered the matter and reported, it would be the following year at least before any action was taken.

But not everyone agreed with the outcome of the meeting. The Earl of Donoughmore, a substantial landowner, had written to his agent with these words of caution - [2]

I wish you to let my tenants know that I have great doubts whether this crop is advantageous to them, and to warn each of them that if he sows it, he does so at his own expense, and contrary to my advice. Some years ago I tried an experiment upon six Irish acres [a little less than ten imperial acres], and kept an accurate account of the profits. They amounted to just 34s 1d, allowing nothing for the rent and taxes of the six acres of land. The present high price of flax, caused by the American war, is a great temptation; but I am confident, that when the war is over, prices will return to their former levels and the crop will not be remunerative. In any case, impress upon my tenants, that it would be wise for them to reserve their little capital for that style of farming which they understand, and can manage, and let lords and gentlemen farmers make experiments upon flax, if they think proper. When these experiments succeed, it will be time enough for the farmers to imitate them.

On the other hand, Lord Annally - [3]

intended to introduce and encourage the extensive cultivation of flax on his large estates in Clare and Limerick, to furnish instructions to his tenantry, erect scutching machinery, and provide the seed required for the first year or two.

Although the Government in London turned down a suggestion that it should pay for up to twenty practical Instructors for two or three years to visit the parts of Ireland where the cultivation of flax was being considered, to give advice, it agreed in March to put £2,000 at the disposal of the Lord-Lieutenant for promoting the cultivation of flax. The Government also provided a further £3,000 in 1865, but said that 'the renewal of the grant another year must not be expected'.[4]

However, the Earl of Donoughmore was most nearly right. All the initial enthusiasm really came to nothing, mainly because, following the end of the American Civil War, when cotton once more became plentiful and cheap, the price of flax fell as well, and its cultivation once more uneconomic, at least on the scale that had been contemplated.

7

Tait and the American Civil War
1864-1865

That Tait supplied uniforms to the Confederate forces during the American Civil War has always captured the imagination of those in Limerick who have spoken or written about Tait's army clothing factory. Mr J F Walsh, in his paper read to the Old Limerick Society in 1954, said that Tait -

> directed his attention to the Civil War in America and managed to supply uniforms to the Confederate troops. This was an ambitious undertaking, as distance and transport had to be overcome. However, he solved the problem by purchasing three steamboats, the *Evelyn,* the *Elwy* and the *Kelpie* .... .

Scarcely an article about Tait has appeared since then, which has not repeated this story. In more recent times it has even found its way into publications in the United States dealing with the Civil War. Tait certainly did supply uniforms to the Confederacy, but the story is not quite as it has been told.

Although Tait acquired an interest in the *Evelyn,* this was not until just before the end of the war. I will come to that later.

The *Elwy,* which was built in 1866, was chartered, not owned, by Tait during the summer of 1867 to run a passenger service between Limerick and Kilrush, a town about thirty-seven miles down-river from Limerick. As to that also, more later. How it came to enter the Tait story as a blockade runner during the Civil War it is not possible to say.

The *Kelpie* was owned by William Durgan. I have seen no evidence to suggest that Tait ever had any interest in her. The *Kelpie* had been built on the Clyde in 1857 by Tod and MacGregor and had been intended to run between Glasgow and Rothesay. However, she was bought in 1858 by Durgan, who had recently built the railway from Limerick to Foynes, a port twenty miles down river from Limerick. Durgan bought the *Kelpie* to run between the newly completed station at Foynes and Tarbert and Kilrush; the last two places being further down-river than Foynes. It was said to have generated £80 a week in its first summer, a figure which constituted 30% of the new railway's income for the period. However, in 1862, the *Kelpie* sailed from Limerick for Nassau on New Providence Island in the Bahamas, probably for employment as a blockade runner, a use for which her build made her well suited. Whether Durgan was intending to sell her on arrival at Nassau or whether he intended to use her on his own account, is not recorded. The *Kelpie* had left Limerick on 25 September but having called at St Thomas in the Virgin Islands, she was variously reported as having been sunk in a collision or an engagement some 50 or 80 miles east of Nassau on about 25 November.[1]

The American Civil War

The Declaration, by the former British colonies in north America, of their Independence of the British Crown, was signed on 4 July 1776. A Convention assembled at Philadelphia in 1787 to draw up a Constitution and in 1789 George Washington became the first President of the United States of America. From the first there were differences between the northern and the southern states of the Union; the South supported free trade, the North protection. But it quickly became apparent that slavery had to be the test question in the political differences between them; the North was against slavery, the South in favour. And because of this North/South divide, as more States were admitted to the Union, the question of slavery became one of overwhelming political importance: if slavery were permitted in the new States they would throw in their lot with the South, if not they would side with the North.

The problem festered until 1858, when the Supreme Court ruled that negroes, though free, could not be citizens of the Union, that Congress had no power to forbid slavery in any State or territory;

and that slaves if bought in a slave State, could be removed to a free State, and still remain slaves. This decision, known as the Dred Scott decision, strengthened the desire of the North for radical reform of the Constitution with regard to slavery, and matters came rapidly to a head.

In 1860 South Carolina seceded from the Union, rapidly followed by Alabama, Florida, Mississippi, Georgia and Louisiana, and then Texas. In February 1861 a Confederacy was formed, to be known as the Confederate States of America. Jefferson Davis of Mississippi was elected the first President. Virginia, North Carolina, Tennessee and Arkansas soon joined the Confederacy, and active preparations for war were made on both sides. The American Civil War had begun, and was to rage for four years; until, with the fall of Richmond in Virginia, the Confederate capital, on 2 April 1865 and the surrender of General Robert E Lee, the commander of the Southern forces, on 9 April, the defeat of the Confederacy was all but complete.

Economic importance of cotton

But to go back to 1861. Broadly speaking the economy of the Confederate States was based on the production of cotton. At that time the South produced some four-fifths of the cotton needed by the mills in Britain. Against this, industry was concentrated in the North. The South early made the mistake of placing an embargo on the export of cotton in the belief that Britain, because of its dependence on Southern cotton, would induce the North to accept the secession of the Southern States.

This proved to be a miscalculation, if only because the start of the war coincided with a period of overproduction, which had left more than 300 million pounds of manufactured cotton, and over one million bales of raw cotton, in stock in Britain. It was not until well into the following year that cotton became short in the English and Scottish mills.

But, more importantly, the South needed to import huge amounts of both food and materials to support the war effort and their only means of payment was by the export of cotton.

On 19 April 1861, Abraham Lincoln, then the President of the United States, realising this necessity, proclaimed a naval blockade of the Confederate ports; both those on the Atlantic coast and those on the Gulf of Mexico. Initially the physical blockade was not effectively enforced but as time went on the net was drawn tighter and it became increasingly difficult, as well as dangerous, for vessels to run the blockade.

However, there was also the legal position to consider. In international law even a vessel sailing under a neutral flag, and Britain had declared its neutrality on 13 May 1861, could be held to be in breach of the blockade, and liable to seizure as soon as it left its home port with the intention of delivering goods to a blockaded port. One of the devices resorted to in order to avoid this risk, was for one vessel to carry the cargo to a point as near as possible to the eventual destination and for its cargo to be transhipped to another vessel for the last part of the voyage.

This was not entirely disadvantageous, as it meant that the main voyage across the Atlantic could be undertaken by large vessels; their cargoes being transhipped into very fast vessels of shallow draft for running the blockade. As the war progressed the British shipyards built very large numbers of these fast blockade runners. They were capable of running close to the shore to evade the larger vessels enforcing the blockade. But even this advantage was eventually eroded, as the US Navy became better at its work and employed smaller inshore craft to give support to its larger ships.

The principal places where transhipment took place were Bermuda, Nassau, and Havana in Cuba. From Liverpool to Bermuda is about 2750 miles; to Nassau about 3450 miles and to Havana 3800 miles. Smaller vessels crossing the Atlantic also called at St John in New Brunswick, Halifax in Nova Scotia, and Madeira, presumably for coaling or as a feint to confuse the enemy.

The two principal Confederate ports used by blockade runners were Wilmington on the Cape Fear River in North Carolina, about eighteen miles upriver from Fort Fisher which commanded the entrance to the river, on the Atlantic coast, and Galveston at the mouth of the Trinity River in Texas, on the coast of the Gulf of Mexico. Wilmington is about 700 miles from Bermuda and 600 miles from Nassau; Galveston about 900 miles from Havana.

Successful blockade running was the lifeline of the South and it had to be made worthwhile for those engaged in it: the rewards had to be commensurate with the risk. Indeed the rewards offered to owners were such that a single successful voyage by a new blockade runner in 1863 or 1864 might not only pay for the cost of the vessel and its running expenses, but yield a very large profit as well.

The crews also had to be well paid. In a typical case in 1863 the amounts paid for a round trip into one of the blockaded ports, half before starting and half on return, were - [2]

Captain	£1,000
Chief Officer	250
2nd and 3rd Officers	150
Chief Engineer	500
Crew and Firemen, about	50
Pilot	750

Alexander Collie

One of the the principal British merchants to be involved in the trade between Britain and the Confederacy was Alexander Collie. He had been born in Scotland in about 1823, the son of an Aberdeen merchant. He started business in Manchester in about 1850 and by 1863 he had also established a warehouse in London. His business was the import and export of cotton and cotton goods. His brother William was in partnership with him as Alexander Collie & Co; William looking after the business in Manchester, while Alexander looked after that in London. A William Every was the firm's Manager in London. There was another brother, George, who had a separate firm, George Collie & Co, in Liverpool.

It was not until 1864 that Tait seems first to have become involved with Collie, who went on to play a very significant part in Tait's affairs over the next eight or more years. In order to try and understand their relationship, it is necessary to digress for a moment from Tait's own story, and look at that of Collie.

It was during the American Civil War that Collie made his fortune; in a few short years transforming himself from a merchant in a modest way of business into a City magnate, or at least so it appeared, and his credit became unquestioned. Towards the end of the Civil War he had bought, for a reputed £30,000, Sir Morton Peto's London house, 12 Kensington Palace Gardens, which he demolished and built for himself an imposing mansion in its place. He is supposed to have spent another £30,000 on his picture gallery.

But by the end of the Civil War, with the fall in the price of cotton, he had lost much of what he had gained, and endeavoured to recover his losses by gambling increasingly large sums of money, frequently misappropriated from others, on a recovery in the price of cotton, which never came, or at least came too late to save Collie.

The bankruptcy of Collie

It was not until 1875 that Collie went spectacularly bankrupt, taking with him a large number of those individuals and firms whose money he had misappropriated.

However, I include here, and not in its proper chronological order, a brief outline of this event and its consequences to give the reader the benefit of hindsight, not given to Tait, before I come to Tait's dealings with Collie, which were the proximate cause of Tait's own financial difficulties, which came to a head in 1869.

Collie's bankruptcy was heralded by a brief statement issued on 15 June 1875 by his solicitors, Hollams, Son, and Coward -

> We are desired by Messrs Alexander Collie and Co of 17 Leadenhall Street, London, and of Manchester, to inform you that they, with much regret, feel it their duty to suspend their payments.
> Messrs Turquand Youngs and Co, of Tokenhouse Yard, London, have been instructed to prepare a statement of affairs, which will be submitted to a meeting of creditors as soon as practicable.

A Receiver and Manager, John Young of Turquand Youngs & Co, was appointed by the Court of Bankruptcy on 2 July, but what was to become the focus of attention was not to be the bankruptcy proceedings, but the appearance at the Guildhall Police Court on 21 July of Alexander and William Collie on a charge of obtaining large sums of money from the London and Westminster Bank by false pretences.

Counsel for the bank explained that the bank had discounted bills of exchange for bill brokers, who had themselves discounted them for the Collies. The bank had believed that the bills were genuine trade bills, accepted by customers of Collie in respect of genuine transactions. The bills stated that they were 'for value received' and bore on the face of them certain marks and numbers purporting to refer to the bales of goods sold, and the accounts in Collie's ledger in respect of which they were drawn; whereas in truth they were largely accommodation bills and did not represent any transactions in goods at all; the words 'for value received' were false, and the marks and numbers equally so. On 15 June the bank held such bills on which it had advanced about £500,000 [*£21,000,000*], although it hoped, without justification as it turned out, that it would recover about half that amount.

Young, who had examined Collie's books, said that he had found that there were £1,500,000 to £1,750,000 worth of such accommodation bills in circulation, but they were supported by only between £63,000 and £100,000 worth of actual goods.

At the end of the day's hearing, the Court agreed that the prisoners, for that is what they now were, should be released on bail to appear at a later date, following further enquiries. Bail was fixed at £8,000 each, two sureties in £2,000 and each prisoner himself in £4,000, to reflect the gravity of the charges. However, the necessary sureties had not been approved by the time the Court rose and the prisoners were remanded to Newgate gaol. The Collies' solicitor asked the presiding Magistrate, Sir Thomas White, for the prisoners to be allowed to be taken to Newgate in a cab. Sir Thomas refused, saying that he could not see that there was any difference at present between the Collies and poor people who were charged with a similar offence, only for a smaller amount; the two prisoners must, therefore, go in a prison van. The Collies remained in Newgate gaol for three days until their bail was finally accepted by the Court and they secured their release. The sureties in the case of Alexander Collie were Josiah Radcliffe, of 3 Kensington Palace Gardens and Manchester, and William Frederick Wigg, of 17 Philpot Lane; those for William Collie being George Yule, of Palmerston Buildings, Bishopsgate Street, who had been a partner in Alexander Collie & Co until 1870, and

Theodore Andreae, of 110 Cannon Street, who had featured prominently in Alexander Collie's American Civil War ventures.

The Court next met on 29 July, when further evidence, of a largely technical nature regarding the operation of the market in bills of exchange, was taken. Just as the Court needed to understand the operation of the market in Bills of Exchange, so it would be helpful for the reader of this chapter and certain of the later chapters of this work to have at least a basic understanding of that market. I therefore include, as Appendix C, a very brief explanation of the nature of, and the operation of the market in, Bills of Exchange.

But of more interest, on 29 July, was the first meeting of the creditors of Alexander Collie & Co at which Young produced details of the extent of the firm's assets and liabilities. The assets were estimated at £250,500 and the liabilities at £1,890,000, a deficiency of £1,639,500 [*about £69,000,000*]. The figure for assets did not include the value of cotton which Collie had purchased for his own account during the course of the Civil War, and which was stored at Savannah, in Georgia at the mouth of the Savannah River. This cotton, 3,096 bales of upland and 1,757 bales of sea island, had been seized by the Federal forces when they took Savannah in December 1864. It was sold by them in New York for nearly $1 million [*about £4,200,000*], much less than half what it would have fetched in England, which sum was paid to the United States Treasury. Young later tried, without success, to recover this sum from the United States Government.[3] Looking ahead somewhat, by the time the bankruptcy proceedings were eventually completed in 1889, the unsecured creditors had received dividends totalling only one shilling and ten pence three farthings in the pound (or less than 10%).

Evidence as to the nature of Collie's fraud

On 5 August the Court heard further evidence, and it is worth repeating part of it, which illustrates not only the nature of Collie's frauds but also what seems to have been the extraordinary gullibility of those who lost money as a result. The bills in this instance were perhaps not strictly speaking accommodation bills, since they had been drawn originally in respect of what the accepting firm thought were genuine transactions; but the effect was the same.

Mr Rainbow was a partner in the City firm of Rainbow, Holberton & Co, merchants and official agents. The firm had first had a business relationship with Collie in 1872. Rainbow was shown ten bills drawn by Collie; part of those discounted by the London and Westminster Bank. He said that the bills referred to specific purchases of cotton by Collie for the joint account of Rainbow, Holberton & Co and Collie. The first two purchases were in February 1873, in respect of which Rainbows accepted bills for about £18,000. These were followed by two further purchases, bringing the total purchases to 3,900 bales of cotton at a total cost of £65,000, by which time Rainbow's firm had accepted bills drawn by Collie totalling a little over £50,000.

Rainbow confirmed that the bills held by the London and Westminster Bank in June 1875 were renewals by succession of the original bills accepted following the purchases of cotton in 1873. He said that all the bills were paid by his firm with money provided by Collie, who drew upon them again for the same amount, with interest and bill stamps. Rainbow said that he had no reason to doubt that, in the first instance, there was cotton purchased, but he never had any account of the purchases.

Rainbow had repeatedly asked Collie for, but never received, an account of the joint venture. When he asked about the disposition of the cotton, Collie advised against selling and said to hold on, giving as a reason the state of the Eastern market and the likelihood of a short crop in America.

And so it went on, with Rainbow asking Collie for information, but not getting any, until 14 June 1875, the day before the Collie bankruptcy, when Rainbow had an interview with Alexander Collie at Collie's office. Rainbow told the Court – [4]

I made enquiry as to my cotton. I enquired the state of the cotton market, and urged that our joint account transactions should be closed. Mr Collie replied that August would be the best month to sell. I said I wished the cotton to be realised immediately, and he promised that it should be done in the month of June. I was then speaking of all the cotton we held on our joint account - the £65,000 worth - nothing was said by Mr Alexander Collie at that interview which would cause me to believe it had been sold. On the next day Messrs Collie suspended payment. In consequence our house suspended. On the 18th June I saw Mr Alexander Collie again at his office, following our receipt of a communication from George Collie & Co of Liverpool. I informed Mr Alexander Collie of my intention of going to Liverpool to look after our interests with respect to the cotton, and he told me that his brother, Mr George Collie, was away in Scotland, and that if I went I should not see him. I reiterated my intention of going, and Mr Alexander Collie then informed me that something very wrong had been done. These are his exact words. He said our cotton had been sold and replaced and resold again, that the account had not been good, and that all trace of our interest in the cotton had been lost.

A similar story was told later in the Court of Bankruptcy by a John Adamson.

He said that in 1872 an arrangement had been made between himself, when he was carrying on business as a merchant and manufacturer, and Alexander Collie & Co for the purchase of cotton on joint account, and that he, Adamson, undertook to provide the capital from time to time required for that purpose, on which he was to receive interest at the rate of five per cent per annum; the net profits of the ventures being equally divided. The cotton purchased was to be stored in Liverpool on the joint account of Adamson and Collie & Co, and, from the early part of 1872 down to the date of Collie & Co's suspension, Adamson received letters from Alexander Collie stating what purchases had been made or contracts entered into on the joint account and the particulars of the bills necessary to be drawn for the purposes of the different ventures.

Adamson alleged that he accepted bills drawn by Collie & Co in the full belief that, in accordance with the continued representations of Collie contained in the correspondence, the money was required as capital for the different ventures, and that it would be applied either in the purchase of cotton for the joint account or in payment of cotton already purchased. He had perfect confidence in the Collies.

But he had lately discovered that the greater part of the invoices sent to him were fictitious, and that the cotton stated in the invoices to have been bought had not, in fact, been bought at all, and that such cotton as had actually been purchased had been resold or pledged by Alexander Collie or by his firm.

He saw Alexander Collie the day after his firm's suspension and inquired where the cotton was, and Collie said it was all gone. Adamson then said it was a case of fraud, which Collie admitted. Adamson had lost £120,197 [*more than £5,000,000*].[5]

A sensation in Court

The next meeting of the Guildhall Police Court was held on 9 August, when a great sensation was caused by the failure of Alexander Collie to surrender to his bail, the whole of which was forfeited.

A reward of £1,000 was offered by the City of London Police for his re-apprehension. The notice included a description of the fugitive - 'Age 52 years, height six feet, hair reddish brown (turning grey, cut short), whiskers reddish, and complexion florid, high cheek bones, eyes small, has a deep scar on upper lip extending towards the cheek, dresses well in dark clothes, tall hat, walks erect, square shoulders, rather thin build, a native of Scotland'.[6] Alexander Collie was never seen again. But, on 16 August 1879, the *Investigator*, which described itself as a journal in the interest of investors, and an exponent of joint stock company law, reporting an alleged sighting of Collie, suggested that the London and Westminster Bank was deliberately hindering the police in their attempts to arrest him; the bank not daring to allow him to be tried, since 'they would not figure well in the examination that would follow'.

William Collie remained, but it was generally felt that he had played a relatively minor part, and that, in the absence of Alexander, it would not best serve the ends of justice that his trial should go ahead, although a further charge was added to the indictment; the obtaining of about £150,000 from the Union Bank of Scotland by false pretences.

On 28 August 1875 *The Times,* reflecting on the several substantial failures that had occurred during the previous three months, said that the Collie failure was the worst; Alexander Collie & Co and other firms connected with their ventures having failed with deficiencies totalling more than £3,000,000, quite apart from the losses of those firms which had lost, but which had not failed, such as the London and Westminster Bank and The Union Bank of Scotland. The figure of £3,000,000, as such, may not seem very large to us, but convert it to today's monetary equivalent and it amounts to about £126,000,000.

Collie's involvement in the American Civil War

During the course of the American Civil War Collie had entered into arrangements, both with agents of the Confederacy, and with a large number of private firms and individuals by way of joint venture.

In the early part of 1863, Crenshaw & Co, of Richmond, North Carolina, reached agreement with the War Department of the Confederacy under which the War Department purchased a three-quarters interest in a number of blockade runners, the remaining quarter to belong to Crenshaw & Co. The vessels were to be employed to bring commissary and quartermaster stores into, and take cotton out of, the Confederacy. Three quarters of the cargo space in and out was available to the War Department; one quarter to Crenshaw & Co. For their one-quarter interest, Crenshaw & Co entered into a partnership with Collie. Whether Collie retained his share himself or sold his interest to others I do not know.

Collie's agreement with the State of North Carolina

Then, in October of the same year, Collie, on his own account, entered into an agreement with John White, a special commissioner in England for the State of North Carolina.[7] Under this agreement, Collie provided four steamers, in which a one-quarter interest was bought by the State and a three-quarters interest was retained by Collie. Collie put his share into a number of joint ventures with others; arrangements which were not disclosed to the State. This agreement ran concurrently with the agreement between Crenshaw & Co and the War Department.

The State was to pay for its quarter share of the cost of purchasing and fitting out the steamers in North Carolina cotton warrants (Manchester issue) at par; the working expenses to be payable by the owners in their respective shares. The first two steamers acquired were the *Hansa* and the *Don*, already owned by, and working for, Collie (or one or more of his joint ventures with private interests). He based the State's share of the cost on a price of £20,000 for each vessel, which he said was the estimated cost of each at Nassau, and considerably under the estimated market value. Who could tell? These two steamers were followed by the *Edith* and the *Elsie*.

The chief objects for which the agreement was entered into were stated to be 'to supply railway iron and rolling stock and such other articles as may be needed by the State, at a moderate rate of freight, and in regular quantities' and 'to run out regularly a quantity of cotton for the State, to enable it to benefit from the very high prices ruling in England'.

The agreement dealt *inter alia* with the arrangements for the actual operation of the ships, as follows -

In order to secure the greater economy, and the more efficient working facilities, the working management of the steamers will rest in the hands of Alexander Collie & Co, who, as representing the larger proportion, will appoint the captains and officers; but no important steps, such as disposing of any of the steamers, or replacing any of them, or adding to their number, will be undertaken without the full knowledge and consent of Mr White, the special commissioner here. Under this arrangement, the parties interested will have the benefit of a well-trained and experienced staff of men, at all points, and the government of the State, on its part, will give all the aid in its power to the efficient working of the business now inaugurated. It will give all the aid it can do to get transportation of cotton from the interior when required, and it will guarantee the undertaking from any restrictions or impediments being thrown in the way of full cargoes being obtained for each steamer of cotton or other produce with the least possible delay. The inward carrying-power of the steamers from the islands will be at the service of the State, at the rate of 5 per ton, payable at the islands, for railway iron and rolling-stock (one fourth of which will be duly credited to the State as its interest), and arrangements will be made immediately to lay down one thousand tons of railway iron at the islands for this purpose. For fine goods, the rate will be 30 per ton.

The government of the State will be the owners of outward cargo to the extent of one-fourth. Their cargoes will be purchased by the agents of Alexander Collie & Co, subject to the inspection of the government of the State, who will be debited for one-fourth of the amount, and on the safe arrival in England one-fourth of the proceeds will be duly credited to the

State. The commission chargeable on this business will be the usual one of two and a half per cent on purchases and realizing, and five per cent on ships' disbursements, in addition to the usual brokerage, and such charges as incurred at the islands for transhipment and storing. The government will of course have the option of putting on board their own shares of the cotton; but for many reasons this is hardly desirable. If they do so, however, the buying commission of two and a half per cent will be avoided. In cases when Alexander Collie & Co come under cash advances for account of the State (in place of putting cotton-warrants in the market), Alexander Collie & Co will be entitled to a further commission of two and a half per cent for the amount of such advance; interest at the rate of five per cent to be charged, and the same rate allowed when there is cash in hand. This agreement to be in force till the steamers are sold, captured or destroyed.

With hindsight it seems as though these arrangements were designed to set the scene for the same line of conduct as later gave rise to the losses suffered by, for example, Rainbow and Adamson.

The cotton warrants referred to in the agreement were obligations for the delivery of cotton at the port of Wilmington, or at other ports then in the possession of the Confederate States. It seems that the warrants were not necessarily given in payment to the vendors of the vessels, but were sold generally by Collie and the proceeds of sale used to pay for the ships. Collie made himself responsible to the purchasers of the warrants for their redemption by the State of North Carolina; a responsibility which must have given rise to a considerable loss following the end of the Civil War, when the cotton in the warehouses was either set on fire by the Confederate forces to prevent its capture by the Federals, or, if captured by the Federals, taken by them as war booty. Collie himself took some of the warrants in payment for the goods which he shipped to the State.

Collie's agreement with White seems to have run its course, although the *Hansa* was the only one of the four steamers to see out the war as a blockade runner; the *Don* having been captured off Beaufort, North Carolina, in March 1864, and the *Elsie* at sea in September, whilst the *Edith* had been sold in October to the government of the Confederate States for use as a cruiser.

However, in July 1864, Colin J McRae, the Confederacy's financial agent in Europe, took steps to cancel the contract with

Crenshaw & Co, which he felt was not achieving the hoped-for results. Instead, he entered into arrangements for the building of fourteen steamers to be wholly owned by the Confederacy. However, to cover the period until these steamers would become available, he had entered into a contract with Alexander Collie & Co on 13 June 1864 for the provision of £150,000 worth of clothing and quartermaster's supplies to be purchased by Major J B Ferguson, and for £50,000 worth of medical supplies to be purchased by Major C Huse, to be shipped by Collie.[8] Ferguson and Huse were then in England as purchasing agents for the Confederacy. Collie agreed to provide four large steamers for the purpose. These were the *Falcon*, the *Flamingo*, the *Ptarmigan* and the *Condor*. Collie had ordered them at the beginning of 1864, together with a fifth steamer, the *Evelyn*, from Randolph, Elder & Co of Glasgow at a price of £18,500 [*about £870,000*] each. The vessels were specially adapted for running the blockade of the Confederate States and were built on entirely new principles suggested to the builders by Collie. The first four were delivered on 15 June, 7 July, 19 July and 10 August 1864 respectively.[9] They had all four been sold by Collie early in 1864 to joint ventures formed for the purpose of blockade running, at the price for each ship of £25,000 [*nearly £1,200,000*] in cash and one half of the profits over 100% realised by the joint ventures. In most cases it is not recorded who were the members of these joint ventures, but that they were not only greedy, but gullible as well, seems beyond doubt. Management of the vessels remained in the hands of Collie.

Collie said that his share in his various joint ventures with private interests was small.

But he undertook the management of, and controlled, the ventures and the profits he derived from these activities, consisting principally of the commissions to which he was entitled as manager, were of course earned whether the other venturers made any profits or not.[10]

Thus, Collie could not lose. But what of the other venturers, did they make profits? It was difficult to establish. As late as April 1868 a large number of those people with interests in Collie's various joint ventures were still unable to obtain any accounts from him, and were contemplating legal action to compel him to produce figures.[11]

Collie meanwhile had the cotton stored in Savannah for his own account, the value of which Young was later to try to recover through the United States Courts, without success as we have seen.

But in the light of what was to emerge in 1875, was it really his, or did it properly belong to his joint ventures? The opportunities for fraudulent dealing by Collie were limitless and the evidence which had emerged in the Bankruptcy Court showed how he was prepared to take advantage of them.

Tait becomes involved in the supply of uniforms

But to return now to Peter Tait. While all of this was going on, Tait had despatched his brother, James Tait, who was sometimes known as James Linklater Tait, to be his agent in the Confederate States.

Once there, James Tait had evidently based himself in Richmond and on 15 December 1863 wrote the following remarkable letter to James A Seddon, the Confederacy's Secretary of War - [12]

Sir,

I had the honor to submit to you on the 9th inst an offer to supply Army Cloths and other necessaries for Confederate Military Service.

In doing so I stated my position in the British Service as Captn and Subinspector of Stores and the peculiar facilities I had from my position for supplying cheaply and of superior quality any stores of that description.

As directed by you I waited upon the Quartermaster-General with whom and one of his subordinate officers I had a personal interview on the subject. I failed however to discover any means within the reach of this department to test the prices and qualities of Military stores supplied nor did I ascertain that there was any gentleman sufficiently conversant with the business whose knowledge and experience would be of value to the Government in this respect.

The advantages that from my position I can offer in contracting for supplies are fourfold.

1st The careful inspection and testing of all articles supplied as to <u>durability</u> and <u>color</u> by the tests in use in the Military store department of Great Britain

2nd The purchase of Stores from the most eminent contractors in their respective branches (to whom I am personally known) at the same prices as are paid by the British Government.

3d A knowledge of the lowest contract prices and a thorough familiarity with every trick and detail of the trade by which I can be guided in the purchase of supplies.

4th A rate of remuneration which will be found lower than is paid to any other contractor or agent.

It has been a matter of notoriety in contracting circles in England that the Confederate Government have been in second or third rate hands in the matter of supplies. Goods rejected as unfit for other services have been purchased on Confederate Government account and prices have been charged for these inferior articles vastly in excess of the value of sound and serviceable stores.

There can be no question that apart from the actual loss sustained by such transactions a further and severer loss is experienced in the want of confidence produced in the minds of the respectable mercantile and monied classes.

Seeing the trade in doubtful hands and apparently carried on with an utter disregard of prices or qualities they are disposed to regard its transactions in the category of Gambling ventures and fight shy of it accordingly and nothing would more effectually end this state of things than the restoration of the business to safe honorable and legitimate channels. The ability to deal with manufacturers of the first standing would react beneficially upon the Bonds and other securities of this Government in England and thus the purchasing and selling Departments would find their facilities for both largely increased.

Since my arrival in this country I have been with your armies in the field and have been shocked to perceive the disgraceful cloth which has been palmed off upon your English Agents and which is served out to your soldiers who are called upon to face in the field the inclemencies of a Virginia winter. I think it is doubtful whether one tenth of the cloth that reaches the Confederate States is genuine Broadcloth by far the larger portion consisting of shoddy cloth an article worth about one fifth of the price your Agents pay for it in England and not more than one tenth of the price it costs the Confederate Government when paid for here.[13]

And I may be permitted to mention here that there is no trade in England so beset with snares and pitfalls as the Cloth trade. It is well known that there are agents of these unprincipled shoddy houses lying in wait at Liverpool and elsewhere for the employees of foreign governments who are usually utterly without experience as to the qualities of cloth and who are obnoxious to all the private influences which these agents know so well how to apply.

From a sincere desire to assist the Confederate people in their mighty struggle and in the conviction that to an extent probably beyond your own conception the Confederate Government is injured and robbed and the efficiency of its soldiers imparred I offer to place at their disposal the same facilities for undertaking contracts and the same checks upon agents and contractors with which long experience has armed the British Government.

In conclusion I can truly say that this offer is volunteered solely because I am aware to what extent your government and people stand in need of protection. It is my hope that I can be of material assistance to them in this matter and that it may lead to future transactions in regard to the permanent supply of clothing and other stores for the Confederate Standing Army which will be advantageous to your Government.

I do not wish to leave the Confederate States without at least making available for their Government the experience which my official position has placed in my power and without bringing to the notice of the Government the fiends to which I am concious they are at present a prey.

It is for them to decide whether to avail themselves of an opportunity which accident enables me to offer and which I believe will prove of eminent service to them.

It would not require more than three months from 1st January 1864 (If my departure takes place hence immediately) to have any amount of Army Clothing, Blankets, Boots & Shoes etc etc Shipped from British ports to the Islands.

I have the honor to be Sir
your obedt servt James L Tait

[Enclosure]

To be ready for shipment in 3 months from 1st January 1864

50,000 Caps ready cut (Grey Cloth) with peak	1/6 ea
50,000 Great Coats of Stout Grey Cloth cut ready for sewing (fast dye)	12/- ea
50,000 Suits of Stout Grey Cloth consisting of Jackets and trowsers cut ready for sewing (fast dye)	16/- pr suit
50,000 Strong Grey Flannel Shirts cut ready for sewing	4/- ea
50,000 pairs Army Blankets	5/6 ea
100,000 pairs Army Boots (Ancle Blucher)	10/6 ea
100,000 pairs Strong Woolen Stockings	1/- ea
50,000 Haversacks	1/6 ea
Total Amount	£158,475 Sterlg

The clothing to be cut according to the Size Rolls in use in the British Service to fit men from 5 feet 6 inches to 6 feet.

The quality of all the supplies would be those in use in the British Army and subjected to the same rigid inspection.

James Seddon approved James Tait's proposal to supply the quartermaster's stores listed on the enclosure to his letter and this was confirmed to James Tait in a letter dated 19 December from General A R Lawton, the Confederacy's Quartermaster General. James Tait was told to submit Lawton's letter to McRae in London, who would ratify the proposition for a portion only of the supplies 'should he not find it expedient to accept it in full'.[14]

Nothing seems to have come of this arrangement until, in a letter to Seddon of 4 July 1864, McRae said, inter alia, that he was making a contract with Collie to carry out that made with James Tait at Richmond and that James Tait had arranged with Collie and Major J B Ferguson to furnish '£50,000 of ready made clothing at prices somewhat lower than those in the contract drawn up at Richmond'. It is likely that this £50,000 of ready made clothing was intended to form part of the £150,000 worth of clothing referred to in McRae's contract with Collie of 13 June.

In the event the first, and as it turned out the only, instalment of the clothing in respect of James Tait's contract with Seddon were eventually shipped by Tait & Co partly in August on the *Condor*, one of the four steamers provided by Collie under his contract with McRae, and partly in October on the *Evelyn*.

A contract with the State of Alabama

In addition to the arrangement made with Seddon, James Tait had obtained for Tait & Co a contract with the State of Alabama, for the supply of clothing to that State, upon terms which Tait considered very favourable and he asked Collie to join him in purchasing a steamer for running this clothing in through the blockade and taking out cotton in exchange. Collie said that he did not think well of the contract with Alabama and cautioned Tait not to proceed with it. However, Tait persisted, and this gave rise to Tait's involvement in the purchase of a share in the steamer *Evelyn*, a transaction to which I refer in more detail in Chapter 9 below.[15] According to the *Daily Enquirer* of Columbus, Georgia, on

22 October 1864, at least three States, of which Alabama was one, resorted to blockade running enterprises with England to augment local uniform production. The paper said that the State of Alabama 'on the part of the Quartermaster-General' had entered into such a contract with Tait & Co.

The goods destined for Alabama, consisting of uniforms and boots, were also shipped partly on the *Condor*, and partly on the *Evelyn*.

Then, on 14 October, Major J F Minter, who had been despatched to England by General Edmund Kirby-Smith of the Trans-Mississippi Department, arranged with McRae for Ferguson to let him have fifteen or twenty thousand suits of clothing for shipment to Havana in the first half of November. In the event, just over 15,000 suits were shipped by Minter, to Havana from Liverpool on board the *SS Adelaide*, on 14 November.

Of these suits, 10,000 were supplied by Tait & Co and just over 5,000 by Hebbert & Co.[16] Meanwhile, on 13 October, Tait himself had entered into a separate agreement direct with McRae to supply 40,000 uniforms, viz jackets and trousers, at 18s 6d per suit in cash; to be supplied in accordance with samples deposited with Ferguson. A copy of this contract appears at Appendix D.[17] I have not seen any evidence to suggest that these uniforms, even if they were made before the end of the War, were ever delivered.

An estimate of the number of Tait uniforms shipped to the Confederacy

Bearing in mind James Tait's relationship to Tait, and having regard to what he had said in his letter to Seddon about the quality of the army clothing hitherto supplied to the Confederacy, it seems to me that the Limerick factory cannot have supplied any uniforms to the Confederacy before James Tait wrote his letter to Seddon. If that was the case, then the only uniforms made by Tait & Co which were shipped to the Confederacy were those shipped on the *Condor*, the *Evelyn*, and the *Adelaide*.

Based on the assumption that each bale of clothing contained 150 uniforms, it is possible to arrive at an approximate total number of uniforms delivered by those vessels; 52,500 by the *Condor*, 23,700 by the *Evelyn* (after allowing for those left in

Bermuda - see chapter 9), and 10,000 by the *Adelaide* - a grand total of 86,200 uniforms.

These figures assume that Tait did not supply any uniforms under his contract with McRae of 13 October 1864.

However, so far as the uniforms shipped by Collie are concerned, there is some collateral evidence. The total amount invoiced by Tait & Co to Collie for goods supplied, which covers the period from 25 August 1864 to 10 November 1864, appears to have been about £42,000. I estimate that a total of about 48,500 uniforms were shipped by Collie on the *Condor* and the *Evelyn*. Whether or not these figures tally depends upon the prices charged by Tait & Co, but they do not look too far apart.

It is not possible to say how many of the uniforms made by Tait & Co which were sent to the Confederacy reached their eventual destinations, although it is recorded that 4,000 suits, tunics and trousers, were received into the Richmond Depot at the end of 1864. These were probably some of the uniforms in respect of James Tait's contract with Seddon. Whether the uniforms destined for Alabama ever reached that State I do not know.

It seems likely that the suits sent by Minter on the *Adelaide,* or at least some of them, reached their destination, since buttons with Tait and Hebbert backmarks have been discovered in Texas.

Identifying a Tait uniform

Tait's uniforms which did reach the Confederacy can be identified by their distinctive cut, the materials of which they were made, their machine stitching, and their buttons, which are fitted with a loose eye, or free-floating shank, and are backmarked 'P. TAIT & Co', with or without the addition of 'LIMERICK'. A uniform, although having the same cut and being of the same materials as one made by Tait & Co, should not, in my view, be attributed to that firm with any certainty unless it also bears buttons, which appear to be original to the uniform and which are backmarked 'P. TAIT & Co', with or without the addition of 'LIMERICK'; a combination of the cut, the materials, the stitching, and the buttons must be the only certain way of distinguishing between a uniform made by Tait & Co and one made by another manufacturer.

On the other hand, Confederate officers' buttons with the same free-floating shank as most Tait & Co buttons, but backmarked 'R. T. TAIT & Co/ESSEX STREET STRAND/LONDON', have been found in the former Confederate States.

The establishment in London

It may be helpful at this point to explain the connection between Tait & Co in Limerick and Tait Bros & Co and Robt Thos Tait & Co in London.

A firm called Tait Bros & Co had been established in London early in 1861 by Tait's brothers, James and Robert, as an off-shoot of the business in Limerick. It occupied the old Union Hall in Union Street, Southwark, until June 1861, when it moved to Essex Street, Strand.

Then, in 1863, following the departure to the Confederacy of James, as Tait's agent, the name of the firm was changed to Robt Thos Tait & Co.

It is not clear what part was played in Tait's affairs by the London establishment, but correspondence between Tait Bros & Co and the War Office in 1861 suggests that it made up small orders for uniforms independently of the factory in Limerick. For example, in June 1861 Tait Bros & Co received an order from the Government for Zouaves undress jackets and breeches. This was presumably a small trial order, because although Queen Victoria had in 1858 authorised the use of the Zouave uniform for troops occupying Barbados, these uniforms were not, in the event, brought into official use until nearly a century later.

It is likely that, apart from making up small numbers of uniforms, the London establishment also dealt with the purchase of incidentals, such as buttons and leather goods, required by the factory in Limerick and it may also have been used as a warehouse for uniforms made in Limerick.

Although I have seen no direct evidence to explain the separate existence of buttons backmarked 'R T TAIT & Co', it is probable that they were attached to uniforms either made by that firm in London or made for that firm by subcontractors. Tait's expertise was in mass production and perhaps officers' uniforms destined for the Confederate States, when they formed only a small part of a larger order, were supplied by Robert, who used his own buttons. I do not know whether, before the change of name in 1863, the London establishment used buttons backmarked 'Tait Bros & Co'. Later, on 7 May 1866, when, as we shall see, Tait took his brother Robert, and others, into partnership, the London establishment was merged with the Limerick factory under the name of Tait & Co; at the same time moving from Essex Street to 95 Southwark Street, Southwark.

Tait gives a Shetland pony in support of the Confederacy's war effort

On a lighter note, while these events were unfolding, an event in support of the Confederate States took place in England. In October 1864, a Bazaar was held in St George's Hall, Liverpool in aid of the Southern Prisoners' Relief Fund. Raffles were held each day and, among a number of unusual prizes, was a Shetland pony given by Tait. It was won by a businessman from Mobile, who gave it back to the Bazaar and it was sold by auction on the last day. What then became of it is not recorded.

This Bazaar was but one manifestation of the considerable support afforded to the Confederacy by certain people in Britain. This support was probably based almost entirely on material, and not much affected by moral, considerations.

Britain's cotton industry depended to a great extent on the availability of American cotton. Once the stocks in hand at the start of the Civil War became exhausted the price of imported cotton increased rapidly, from an average of 6¼ pence a pound before the war, to an average of 27½ pence a pound in 1864; imports falling from over 2,000,000 bales in 1860 to less than 200,000 bales in 1864. It was no doubt felt that unless the Confederacy won the war, slavery would be abolished and the cost of cotton would not return to anything like its pre-war level.

Tait is sued by the United States

Tait's involvement in the Civil War was not to end with the end of hostilities. Early in 1869 the United States brought an action against him in the Court of Queen's Bench in London. It was alleged that in April 1865 Maj Ferguson had entered into an agreement with Tait to exchange uniforms for thirty bales of cloth, valued at £4,000, belonging to the Confederacy. It was stated that the cloth had been delivered to Tait and a delivery order for a number of uniforms had been given in exchange. Meanwhile, the news arrived of the collapse of the Confederacy and Tait thereupon refused to deliver the uniforms, on the ground that he had claims against the Government of the Confederate States arising out of prior transactions.

For the United States to sustain this action against Tait, it was necessary for them to show that the Confederacy was a *de facto* State to whose property the United States had succeeded. On the other hand the United States was at the same time engaged in a dispute with the British Government in which a considerable amount was at stake; but to succeed in which it was necessary for them to establish that the Confederacy was <u>not</u> a *de facto* State. This inconsistency was highlighted in a leading article in *The Times* on 11 May 1869. However, for whatever reason, the case against Tait was not pursued by the United States. Perhaps, if it had been, we should know more about the transaction which gave rise to it. Probably the uniforms to be supplied by Tait were part of the £150,000 worth of uniforms Ferguson was to acquire under McRae's contract with Collie. As to what amount, and for what goods, Tait was owed money by the Confederacy there is now no record; perhaps the goods were those supplied to the State of Alabama.

8

The Ill-fated Voyage of the 'SS Condor'

1864

Like her sister vessels the *SS Falcon,* the *SS Flamingo,* the *SS Ptarmigan* and the *SS Evelyn,* built for Alexander Collie in 1864, the *SS Condor* was a paddle steamer. She had three stacks and two masts. Propulsion was provided by a two cylinder simple oscillating steam engine with 48 inch diameter cylinders and a four-foot stroke. She had three boilers with four furnaces in each. Her gross tonnage was 446, her length 220 feet and her breadth 28 feet.[1] She had a draft of only seven feet and was capable of 18 knots.

The 'SS Condor' leaves the Clyde

The *Condor* left Greenock on the Clyde in Scotland on 10 August 1864 under the command of Capt William Nathan Wrighte Hewett VC, who was using the assumed name of Samuel S Ridge.[2] He was an officer in the British navy on half pay, which meant that he had no command at the time. After all, there was nothing much for the British navy to do in 1864 and he, and other officers like him, took to blockade running for adventure; the money probably coming in useful as well.

Hewett was particularly well suited to command a blockade runner; having commanded *HMS Rinaldo* on the North America and West India Station before the Civil War. He was to return to full pay in September 1865; taking command of *HMS Basilisk* at Sheerness for service on the China station.

He was remarkable in that he had twice won the Victoria Cross during the Crimean War; once before Sebastopol on 26 October 1854 and once at Inkerman on 5 November. He was a member of the French Order of the Légion d'Honneur and a Grand Officer of the Ottoman Order of the Medjidie.[3]

The 'Condor' calls at Limerick

The *Condor* reached Limerick on 12 August where, in addition to cargo taken on at Greenock, she took on board 350 bales of uniforms and 28 cases of boots, partly for the account of Collie, presumably some of the £50,000 of uniforms to be supplied by Tait & Co under James Tait's contract with Seddon, and partly a portion of the uniforms and boots in respect of Tait's contract with Alabama.[4]

Collie had intended that the *Condor* should go to Mobile, in Alabama, and this may have been why part of Tait's contract with that State was sent on her, but at the last moment Collie changed her course and sent her to Wilmington instead. He believed that the Federal forces were more likely to try and take Mobile, where there was a large quantity of cotton, than Wilmington, 'as there is no plunder to be got there'.[5]

Lloyd's List in London reported that the *Condor* left Limerick on 13 August for Bermuda, that it reached Halifax from Bermuda on 4 September and was reported to have left there for Nassau on the 24th.

Whether the *Condor* actually called at Nassau after leaving Halifax is not recorded. In any case the US Consul at Halifax reported to his Government that the ship had cleared that port on 24 September with a valuable cargo, including clothing for the Confederacy, destined for Wilmington.

Drama was added to the events that followed by the fact that Mrs Rose O'Neal Greenhow, who had been staying with Col Faris at 34 Sackville Street in London, had boarded the *Condor* at Greenock, with two companions, bound for the Confederacy.

Mrs Greenhow was one of the most important Confederate agents of the war; at the very centre of a web of espionage. It is believed that she was taking to Richmond, not only important Confederate despatches from England, but also a quantity of gold coin destined for the Confederate Treasury.

The loss of the 'Condor'

When the *Condor* approached the entrance to the Cape Fear River just before first light on the morning of 7 October she had been seen, and was closely pursued by, the *USS Niphon* under Acting Master Edmund Kemple. There was mist and spray and the *Condor*'s pilot saw too late a ship aground in the channel ahead of him. In attempting to avoid it, the *Condor* herself went hard aground on the beach off New Inlet, below Fort Fisher. The *Niphon* did not press her advantage as she was dangerously exposed to the guns of Fort Fisher; instead she decided to wait until darkness fell the following night. Although the *Condor* was close to shore there was heavy surf and Hewett decided that it was too dangerous for his passengers or the crew to attempt to leave the vessel until calmer conditions prevailed. However, Mrs Greenhow wanted to be rowed ashore at once; she was too fearful of capture to permit of reason, and Hewett eventually allowed her and her two companions to set out. But their boat was almost at once overwhelmed by the surf and, although Rose's companions and the boat's crew reached the shore in safety, Rose herself was drowned. Her body was washed ashore later and sent to Wilmington for burial. She lay in state in the chapel of Hospital No 4 on a bier draped with the Confederate flag until the funeral at the Catholic Church of St Thomas. Mrs Greenhow was buried in Oakdale Cemetery in the presence of a large crowd of mourners; the arrangements being supervised by the Wilmington Soldier's Aid Society.

Hewett and the remainder of the crew of the *Condor* were able to get ashore later and arrangements were made for the ship's cargo to be transhipped to the *SS Annie* and delivered into Wilmington; a portion of the *Condor*'s machinery was also saved before the vessel was abandoned and, eventually, broke up.[6]

The *Annie* herself suffered misfortune afterwards, in that after leaving Wilmington she went aground at New Inlet and was later taken to New York as a prize by the US Navy.

9

The 'SS Evelyn'
1864-1866

In the autumn of 1864 Tait approached Collie to ask whether he would join with him in purchasing a blockade runner, to take into the Confederacy the uniforms which Tait had contracted to supply to the State of Alabama, and to bring cotton out; Tait having tried without success to obtain a suitable vessel elsewhere.

Apparently either Tait, or his brother Robert, had inspected the four steamers which Collie was providing under his contract with McRae and wanted to purchase one of those. But, Collie having already sold them, Tait agreed to take a two-thirds share in the fifth steamer, the *Evelyn*; Collie retaining a one-third share and having sole management and control of the vessel.

Collie told Tait that the vessel would cost their joint venture £30,000, which Tait assumed was the cost price from the builders, Randolph Elder & Co. After all, since the keel had only been laid on 26 April 1864, it was perhaps natural that he should have thought this; what other meaning could cost have in the circumstances. It was only much later that Tait discovered the cost of the vessel from the builders had been £18,500, and even that was subject to a discount. Collie later explained the difference by saying that he had already bought the vessel from the builders when he agreed to the joint venture with Tait, that its market value was £30,000 at the time, and that it was therefore right that this should be the price charged by him to the joint venture.

Collie justified his estimation of the market value by reference to the *Evelyn*'s ability to carry 1,000 bales of cotton with ease; the value of which was about £12,000 at Wilmington and £60,000 at Liverpool, so that the result of one successful run by the Evelyn would have been a large profit, even after the payment of the cost to the joint venture of the vessel, as well as all the expenses of the voyage. Collie's estimate of the value of the cotton at Liverpool equates to 30 pence a pound, which was in July 1864 about the average price there of American cotton.[1]

The *Evelyn* was completed, and left the Clyde for Limerick, on 25 October 1864, by which time, it may be noted, the average price of American cotton in Liverpool had fallen to about 20 pence a pound.[2] She was under the command of Capt Hugh Talbot Burgoyne VC, using the assumed name of Capt Peters. He had won the Victoria Cross in action on the Black Sea on 29 May 1855, during the Crimean War. Like Capt Hewitt, he was also a member of the Order of the Légion d'Honneur. He was a Knight of the Order of the Medjidie.

The 'SS Evelyn' calls at Limerick

In Limerick, the *Evelyn* took on board 199 bales of uniforms and 25 cases of boots, partly for the account of Collie and partly for the account of Tait. She left Limerick for Bermuda on 27 October.[3]

No word of the *Evelyn*'s arrival at, or departure from, Limerick leaked out there. Tait was uncharacteristically quiet.

Collie told Tait that on the *Evelyn*'s arrival in Bermuda on 14 November, a portion of her cargo, part Collie's, part Tait's, was landed there; it being considered, in Collie's words, 'that in view of the risk of capture too large a quantity of material should not be shipped for the Confederate States on one steamer'.[4] This seems a most unlikely eventuality; the Confederacy was very short of supplies, which is why financial incentives were in place to make it worthwhile for blockade runners to take in as much as they could on each voyage. Much more likely is that Collie replaced some of Tait's goods with some of his own already at Bermuda waiting for a vessel to take them into Wilmington. The goods belonging to Tait which were landed in Bermuda, consisting of 27 bales of clothing and 5 cases of boots, were, in the event, later returned to England; those belonging to Collie, consisting of 14 bales of clothing, were later sent by him to Buenos Aires.

Although the surviving evidence is difficult to interpret, it is probable that Capt Burgoyne left the *Evelyn* at Bermuda and was replaced by a Capt Barrow. Burgoyne was, of course, working for

Collie generally, as opposed to being attached to a particular vessel, and no doubt took command of another of Collie's vessels at Bermuda.

The 'SS Evelyn' runs the blockade into Wilmington

From Bermuda, the *Evelyn* attempted to run the blockade into Wilmington, without success, and put back to Nassau on 28 November. She made a further unsuccessful attempt to run the blockade before returning again to Nassau. She left there again on 19 December and on this occasion, although she succeeded in running the blockade on Christmas Eve, she ran hard aground in the Cape Fear River, but was got off and ran into Wilmington on Christmas Day. She unloaded her cargo there, and by virtue of Collie's contract with McRae she was able to take cotton out of Wilmington at 6d a pound when she left on 12 January 1865. According to Collie she took out 701 bales, although an invoice for a purchase in Wilmington, which Collie eventually produced to Tait, was for only 687 bales.

The *Evelyn* was the last steamer to run the blockade at Wilmington, as a very few days after her departure Fort Fisher fell to the Federal forces. This being so, it is difficult to believe that she would not have taken with her as much cotton as possible, which was at least 1,000 bales. With the benefit of hindsight, it is probably fair to assume that she did, whatever Collie may have told Tait.

Inconsistencies in Collie's account of what followed

Thereafter, it was necessary for blockade runners to change their base of operations from Nassau to Havana and to operate between there and Galveston in Texas. According to Collie, the *Evelyn* reached Nassau from Wilmington on 16 January. This is not recorded in *Lloyd's List,* but that journal did not record all the comings and goings of blockade runners, although it can be useful evidence on those occasions when it did. It was while the *Evelyn* was at Nassau that a Capt Murray took over her command from Capt Barrow. But as to what actually happened next, it is difficult to say. Collie and *Lloyd's List* agree that the *Evelyn* reached Havana on 25 January. But Collie certainly implied to Tait that the vessel operated exclusively out of Havana thereafter. This does not accord with two reports which did appear in *Lloyd's List*. First, a blockade runner which had left Nassau on 5 February, reported that the *Evelyn* had been there then. Second, and perhaps more significant, *Lloyd's List* reported on 9 February that the *Evelyn* 'which was supposed to have been captured in Cape Fear River by the Federals, has arrived at Nassau with cotton; she reports that the *SS North Heath* was the only steamer in Wilmington when she left'. Collie told Tait that the cotton brought out of Wilmington was shipped from Nassau to Liverpool on the *SS Harkaway* on 11 March and sold there on 11 June. By this time the average price was about 18 pence a pound, and so the cotton presumably realised only about £25,000; somewhat less than the £60,000 for a successful run that Tait had looked forward to when he had embarked upon the joint venture in the previous year.

In fact the *Harkaway* had sailed from Nassau on 20 February; reaching Liverpool on 6 April. If the cotton which the *Evelyn* brought out of Wilmington was unloaded in Nassau following her arrival there on 16 January, it is scarcely credible that it could not have been, indeed was not, shipped to Liverpool before 20 February. On the other hand, where did the cotton come from that the *Evelyn* took into Nassau at the beginning of February? Presumably from Havana, in which case it is unlikely to have been the same cotton that she took out of Wilmington on 12 January. Which is perhaps why the amount shipped on the *Harkaway* was, if it was, 701 bales and the invoice produced by Collie in respect of the cotton bought in Wilmington was for a slightly different number of bales.

Without doubt, the *Evelyn* first reached Havana on 25 January. Again, it was Collie's account that, once there, she was docked and thoroughly overhauled. This seems unlikely for such a new vessel, but Collie might have thought that some explanation was needed to cover the time when she was at Nassau at the beginning of February 'with cotton', which Tait had been told nothing about.

Following her return to Havana from Nassau, the *Evelyn* made three abortive attempts to get into Galveston before succeeding at the fourth attempt on 10 March; but not without having run aground while passing the bar off Galveston, when a large portion of her cargo had to be thrown overboard and was lost.[5] In any case, Collie's account of these events was that the goods taken into Galveston by the *Evelyn* did not include any supplies from England, although, again on Collie's evidence, the *Evelyn* brought 508 bales of cotton out of Galveston for the account of the joint venture. Collie accepted a further 231 bales of cotton, from the Confederate agent in Havana in lieu of freight and other costs in relation to the cotton belonging to the Confederacy which had been shipped on the *Evelyn* to Havana, but these further bales were sold there, so Collie said, 'to repay the heavy expenses that had been incurred during the stay of the *Evelyn* at Havana. Of the 508 bales, 483 bales were sent to England on the *SS Aurora* on 18 May, leaving 25 bales in Havana.

The *Aurora* reached Liverpool on 27 June and the cotton was sold in Manchester on 9 August. There is nothing to explain why it took so long, again, for the cotton to be sold after its arrival in England. By August the price had fallen further to 17 pence a pound, which would indicate sales proceeds of some £16,000. The 25 bales left in Havana were eventually sold there on 11 July 1865.

The *Evelyn* had returned to Havana from Galveston on 22 April and on 8 June she left Havana for the Clyde, calling at Halifax on the way; her blockade running days over.

Tait buys the Evelyn from the joint venture

By the time the *Evelyn* reached England in July, war had broken out in South America between Argentina, Uruguay and Brazil on the one hand and Paraguay on the other. Since the *Evelyn* would be well suited to the carriage of troops and light cargoes by one or other of the combatants, Collie suggested that she be sent to South America for sale; he said that he had already sold the *Falcon* and the *Flamingo* there for £18,000 each.

But Tait wanted to purchase the vessel from the joint venture to give himself full ownership, and this he did, in July 1865, for £12,000. Although Collie had not at that stage given Tait any account of the profit or loss of the joint venture, he required Tait to pay the sum of £12,000 into the joint venture account (kept of course by Collie). To do this Tait borrowed £10,000 of the price from Collie, telling Collie that he had suffered losses on his contract with Alabama as well as other losses in his business, although he did not tell Collie what these other losses were.[6]

Following Tait's purchase of the *Evelyn*, the vessel was registered in his name and the Port of Registry was changed, in August 1865, from Glasgow to Limerick.

Collie's statement of account of the joint venture

Eventually, in October 1865, Collie produced a statement of account of the joint venture, which purported to show, after taking account of Tait's purchase of the *Evelyn*, a loss of some £44,000 [*almost £2,000,000*], of which Tait was, of course, responsible for two thirds. Examination of this statement of account by Tait showed, apart from other discrepancies, that it included the whole of the expenses of operating the vessel, from her leaving the Clyde in 1864 to her returning there in 1865.

It was perfectly proper for the expenses of the voyage of the *Evelyn* to Bermuda, and for those incurred in her attempts to run the blockade into Wilmington, and in her return from there to Nassau, to be charged to the joint venture, and Collie explained why these expenses were so high. He said that, during the unsuccessful attempts to reach Wilmington, the *Evelyn* was repeatedly chased by the fastest steamers in the Navy of the Federal States and that, had she not possessed exceptional speed, would certainly have been captured. These attempts, he said, had involved very heavy expenditure.

The vessel was continually obliged to put back for supplies of coal and in each fresh attempt to run the blockade large bounties had to be paid to all the officers and crew and in most instances before, and irrespectively of the success of, the voyages in respect of which they were given. He also said that it was necessary to obtain at a high rate the assistance of extra captains and pilots of experience; the blockade of Wilmington being at this time very stringent.

But instead of the *Evelyn* being used thereafter to ship any more Tait uniforms, those left in Bermuda for example, she was used between Havana and Galveston entirely for the shipment into the Confederacy of goods for the account of Collie and although she brought cotton out it seemed that not all of that had been accounted for. Nevertheless, Collie had charged the joint venture with all the costs.

An assessment of Tait's involvement in the joint venture

In attempting to assess Tait's adventure into blockade running, its scale should be put into the context of the whole, if only because viewed from Limerick he was seen to have played a significant part. During the whole of the Civil War the blockade was successfully run, by a wide variety of vessels, almost one thousand times. But, taking only steamers, which were the larger vessels; in 1864, 98 ran the blockade over 300 times, and, in the following year, 24 ran the blockade 25 times. The *Evelyn* ran the blockade only twice; once in each of those two years.

Tait seems to have become aware by 1864 that some others, like Collie, were making very large profits by engaging in the business of taking cargoes into, and bringing cotton out of, the Confederate States. And he presumably wanted some of the action. But he came to it too late, and, when he did, he had put himself entirely in the hands of Collie. This was perhaps inevitable because, by the time his joint venture with Collie was undertaken, severe restrictions had been placed by the Confederacy on the export of certain commodities, including cotton; only Collie, so he said, being free of these restrictions, by virtue of his contract with McRae. Indeed, Tait, or rather James Tait as his agent, could not obtain a cargo of cotton in exchange for the uniforms shipped to Wilmington by Tait on board the *Evelyn*; this had to be obtained for him by Collie.

Collie had produced his statement of account showing a loss on the joint venture of £44,000. But Tait had no way of checking either how much cotton had actually been brought out of Wilmington and Galveston for the account of the joint venture, or when it was sent back to England, or when it was sold, or what it fetched when it was. He only knew what Collie told him and it would have been quite easy for Collie to intermingle the various shipments of cotton to his own benefit. And in 1865, when the price of cotton was falling following the end of the War, he had every incentive to do so. And, indeed, as we have seen, when the end came for Collie in 1875, his warehouses in England, which were supposed to be full of cotton held on behalf of his customers and others, were found to be almost empty, although in Savannah, at the end of the Civil War, there had been a huge amount of cotton purportedly owned by him personally.

The arrival of the 'SS Evelyn' in Limerick and her subsequent sale

Following the arrival of the *Evelyn* in the Clyde from Havana, Tait sent Patrick Lynch to Glasgow to supervise the work necessary to put her in order to be sent to the Brazils, where Tait intended that she should be chartered to the belligerents in the war against Paraguay, before being sold.

Tait had become attracted to the possibilities offered by ship-owning and he had engaged Lynch to work for him in what Lynch referred to as the 'shipping department'.

Lynch was then about thirty-nine years old. He had married his wife, Fanny, in 1848 and they had eight children. On leaving school he had started work with Ryan Brothers, shipbrokers in Limerick, and remained with them until 1861. Shortly before that, he and his wife had taken the George Hotel in Georges Street and after leaving Ryan Brothers and until taking up employment with Tait, Lynch had devoted the whole of his time to the management of the hotel.

When the work on the *Evelyn* had been completed, she left the Clyde for Limerick; on this occasion under the command of Hewett.

However, on 24 August 1865, in dense fog, she ran ashore on Rathlin Island, off Ballycastle Bay in Antrim. Although she got off by throwing cargo overboard from her forehold, she had to put into Londonderry for repair.[7] The damage must have been more than superficial because Tait himself went immediately to Londonderry to inspect it.

On 3 September 1865 the *Evelyn* arrived at Limerick, no longer painted blockade running grey but with dull yellow funnels, a red bottom and her sides to the bulwarks green.

She was greeted with extraordinary excitement in scenes more appropriate to a carnival than to a serious business endeavour, which were graphically described in the *Limerick Chronicle* of the following day -

> On Sunday morning this beautiful vessel, ... which was so long expected by the citizens of Limerick, arrived in the Shannon, and anchored at Seigh Castle, where she remained until yesterday evening, when she steamed up the river, greeted by the cheers of thousands who went down to meet her. One of the grandest sights we ever enjoyed was presented when the *Evelyn* came in sight of those standing on the dock pier. She was covered with bunting, the river was crowded with boats heavily freighted with men and women; the pier and the quays were literally crowded, while the ships in the harbour were gaily decorated to greet the first visit of the *Evelyn*.
>
> The sun shone delightfully from an unclouded sky, so that the day was all that one could wish for so grand a spectacle, and, when the welcome visitor came in view, cheer after cheer burst forth, filling the air, and mingling with the booming of cannon, reverberated among the distant hills. It would indeed be difficult to describe this animated scene, which was heightened to the utmost intensity when the owner of the *Evelyn*, Alderman Tait, was greeted as he stood on the paddle box, viewing the dense multitude who assembled to pay him all the respect upon the occasion that lay in their power. Before entering the dock, the band of the County [of] Limerick Militia proceeded on board from their boat, and they added to the delightful character of the display, by the performance of several pieces of music.

The following Saturday, 9 September, Tait entertained nearly one hundred guests to an excursion down the Shannon, followed by a cold dinner, on board the *Evelyn*. It must have been an extraordinary occasion; Col Monsell was unable to be there, but a salute was fired from the *Evelyn*'s deck as she passed Tervoe, his residence; others being fired as the vessel passed the residences of the Knight of Glin and Lord Mounteagle. If all this junketting had a serious purpose it was to foster the idea that Limerick could, with sufficient enterprise on the part of its citizens, become the first port in the kingdom for commerce with the New World; this purpose being dear to Tait's heart and emphasised in his after-dinner speech, as well as in those of the Mayor and of Col Vandeleur, one of the Members of Parliament for County Clare. A particular obstacle in the way of the greater use of the port of Limerick was thought to be the excessively high port dues, a problem that Tait was later to address with his practical help in connection with the passage of the Limerick Harbour (Composition of Debt) Act of 1867.

Another speaker proposed the health of Mrs Tait, whom he said he had not met, but from all he had heard he was sure exemplified in her person all that a wife and mother should be. A woman's place ... !

Would the *Evelyn* have received the same welcome from the citizens of Limerick if they had known that she had been put in order, and was sailing to the Brazils, not as the precursor of a line of steamships trading between Limerick and the New World for the benefit of the commerce of Limerick, but for ultimate sale? Probably not.

On 11 September 1865 the *Evelyn* sailed from Foynes for the Brazils, laden, it was reported locally, with a valuable cargo of uniforms.

The following day Tait himself returned to London, in good time for the birth on 5 October of his eighth child, Evelyn Rosina; named presumably after his ship. What fun this must have given to her siblings.

Lynch, representing Tait, sailed with the *Evelyn*, now under the command of a Capt Nutkins, and which, after calling at Madeira and Bahia, reached Rio de Janeiro on 9 October. There, Lynch arranged for the vessel to be chartered by the Brazilian Government for the carriage of troops and cargo to the River Plate. Later in December, while on charter, the vessel ran aground on the English Bank at the mouth of the River Plate and, although undamaged, had to throw about 20 tons of cargo overboard to get off.[8]

Lynch eventually returned to Limerick towards the end of July 1866.

It had been while he was in Limerick waiting for the sailing of the *Evelyn* that Lynch was first introduced to George Cannock; a meeting which was to lead to problems for them both later on.

Robert Tait went out to Montevideo later, and in October 1866 arranged for the sale there of the *Evelyn*, for £20,000.

10

An Eventful Year
1865

In addition to Tait's involvement with the *SS Evelyn* recorded in the previous chapter, 1865 proved to be an eventful year.

In Limerick, in March, Tait had been elected as Alderman for the Castle Ward, in place of Alderman Cullen, who had died in office.

Shortly before this, on 9 February, Tait wrote a letter, from the Grosvenor Hotel, Victoria Station, Pimlico, to the then Mayor of Limerick.

He said -

I have very great pleasure in forwarding to you for distribution amongst the poor of our city £100 in grateful commemoration of the successful trip of the Evelyn, which I despatched from Foynes in October last, laden with Limerick manufactured goods, she being the first steamer which left our noble river for the Western World.

You will be kind enough to give the first £20 to the poor of the Castle Ward, the balance you will, I am sure, distribute impartially in the other parts of the city to those most requiring relief, and in all cases it is my most earnest desire that the distribution be made irrespective of religious distinctions.

With hindsight, this act of generosity seems not to have been wholly disinterested, although perhaps as little as £20 was unlikely to influence many of the voters.

Tait moves to London

But, barely had Tait's election as Alderman taken place than, on 16 March, the *Limerick Chronicle* published the following letter from him, in which he revealed his intention to live in future in London -

Dear Sir,

More than 21 years have elapsed since I first became connected with the trade and commerce of this ancient city, and for a lengthened period my energies have been directed to develop its industrial resources by the establishment of a manufacture which has been heretofore confined to England, and I am confident that the measure of success to which I have attained has been gratifying not only to my personal friends, but to all classes of my fellow citizens.

For some time past an accumulation of business has been pressing on me from all sides; I have but just returned from England, where I have entered into large contracts with our own and foreign governments, the successful carrying out of which has obliged me to open establishments in London and Leeds.[1]

These circumstances have compelled me to take a residence in London, where, in a few weeks, I shall remove, with my family; at the same time, I shall not give up my residence at South Hill, where I hope to spend as many months in the year as my business engagements will permit.

I shall also be obliged to retire from the active management of my establishment in Georges Street, which will, however, be entrusted to gentlemen with whom I have been associated for years in business, and in whom I have the utmost confidence that the policy I have inaugurated will be fully carried out, which has been so well appreciated by the public of all classes.

I take this opportunity of thanking my numerous friends for their liberal patronage of this establishment, which has attained success far surpassing my most sanguine anticipations.

The interests of my friends, the working people of the city of Limerick, has been the object of my earnest solicitude, in all my arrangements, which will not only enable me to provide constant work for those at present employed in my establishment, but to double their number in a short time, on the completion of extensive alterations at present being carried out at my factory.

To the many kind friends who have expressed a strong desire that I should seek for the representation of the City in Parliament at the coming election I beg to return my warmest and most sincere thanks; but feeling deeply the present deplorable state of the trade and commerce of the city, I believe I shall better advance its interests by securing employment for thousands of its working population, which I consider a higher honor than a seat in the first assembly of the world.

In conclusion, I cannot but deeply regret parting from many for whom I entertain feelings of the warmest friendship; and I have only to say that at all times to advance the interests of the citizens of Limerick will be to me a source of the highest pleasure.

I remain, dear Sir,

Yours, very truly,

PETER TAIT.

Before leaving Limerick, Tait put his brother-in-law, Thomas Bruce Hamilton, who had married Rose Tait's sister Margaret in 1851, in charge of his clothing factory, but although this continued to be a significant enterprise throughout the remainder of the 1860s and into the 1870s, it was no longer to be Tait's principal business interest in these years.

It is perhaps not surprising that Tait's increasing business commitments in London should require him to move there. It is easy to forget that these were the days before the perfection of the internal combustion engine, when cabs were horse-drawn, and railways were still in the early days of their development. The railways, in Ireland in particular, left much to be desired at this time; the line between Limerick and Dublin operated by the Great Southern and Western Railway being no exception. An additional irritant for travellers was that the world was not yet neatly divided into time zones; the time in Dublin, for example, being twenty-five minutes later than in London.

On the other hand, a precursor of the modern motorail, passengers were able to take their horses and carriages with them. In 1866 single fares between Limerick and Dublin were - third class 8s 5d, second class 16s 6d, first class 22s, horse 44s 6d, and carriage 67s.

The journey between Limerick and London took, depending upon a morning or evening start and the direction of travel, between about seventeen and nineteen hours. I have included a representative timetable at Appendix E.

The journey to Winchester, for his interview with Col Horne which he described to the Royal Commissioners in 1858, would have taken Tait almost twenty-four hours, if he had done it without a break.

Following his move to London, Tait seems to have stayed briefly at Welbeck House, Sydenham, before moving to Mount Pleasant Lodge in Mount Pleasant Lane, Upper Clapton.

A tribute by the Bard of Thomond

The following tribute, included by Michael Hogan in his *Lays and Legends of Thomond,* published in 1865, was probably written when
Tait moved to London -

A TRIBUTE TO PETER TAIT, ESQ.

If aught in this world could adorn or make bright
The name of a mortal, Philanthropy can -
The God-given feeling that shows, by the light
Of its own noble actions, man's duty to man.

And if ever a heaven-made soul was possess'd
Of that boon, 'mid the ranks of the humble or great,
If it e'er had existence, it lives in the breast
Of the honest, munificent, high-minded Tait.

He who leant on his own mighty efforts, reliant,
Like the eagle that springs to the sun from the shade;
He pursued Enterprise with the stride of a giant,
And gave a new pulse to the genius of trade.

He, whose wealthy position but serves as a hinge
To give action and life to his kindness sincere;
Whose high independence partakes not a tinge
Of the false rampant pride that marks others' career.

He, whose lofty heart never could rest to enjoy
The fruits that Industry and Commerce afford;
Unless that the children of want had employ,
And their labour made sweet with a liberal reward.

Would famine have ravaged our desolate Isle,
Would emigrant ship bear our people away,
Would the angel of Plenty abandon our soil,
Would our cities and villages sink in decay?

Would our harbours be empty - our market-gates closed,
Would the poorhouse brand perishing victims of fate,
Would maidenly virtue, thro' want be exposed,
If Ireland had many true spirits like Tait?

No – there is not a man of reasoning mind,
Save the sordid, the envious, the dull and the base,
But must say, "He has served, and is serving his kind,
And deserves the esteem of our country and race!"

Yes, he who employs the young maids of our town,
And protects heaven's jewel, which else may be lost,
Has won a far brighter and loftier crown,
Than the world-lauded victor who conquers a host.

Fame, fortune, position, rank, country or creed,
Are no measures true virtue or merit to scan;
Tis the kind heart and hand, and the generous deed,
That ennoble, elate and adorn the man.

Whatever great star, in the order of fate,
Future evil or good to our country portends,
Yet Limerick shall honor the dear name of Tait,
The pride of her sons and the best of her friends.

A curious offer to William Monsell

At the Parliamentary election in 1865 the same three candidates put their names forward for the representation of the County of Limerick as had contested the election in 1859; Col William Monsell, who had no political allegiance, Lieut-Col S A Dickson, in the Conservative interest, and Mr E J Synan, a Liberal. In 1859 Monsell and Dickson had been elected, with 4020 and 2626 votes respectively, Synan having come a close third with 2369 votes.

On 7 July 1865, in what seems to be the only letter from Tait preserved in the Emly papers at the National Library of Ireland, he said to William Monsell - [2]

Dear Mr Monsell,

I regret I had not the pleasure of again seeing you before you left town as I had to go to Leeds on important business and have only just returned. I have no Limerick news since I saw you and hope Synan will not put you to the expense of a contested election when he has no chance of success. Should he however determine to do so and should you require for immediate use a thousand or two for expenses I need not say it will give me very great pleasure to lend you any amount you may require free of any interest or any charge whatever and my only regret is that you should be put to any expense. With the greatest regard.

Yours very sincerely

Peter Tait

In the event, during the weeks preceding the election, a considerable opposition to the re-election of Dickson built up and, on Nomination Day, he withdrew his candidacy; Monsell and Synan being elected unopposed.

But could Tait really have been so unaware of local opinion as to believe that the contest would be between Monsell and Synan, rather than between Synan and Dickson, or was that simply the excuse for making the offer to Monsell?

It is hard to believe that anyone could need to spend, on an election, today's equivalent of between £40,000 and £80,000. On the other hand William Monsell was useful to Tait.

Perhaps there was more in Tait's offer than meets the eye, although I have seen no evidence of it; nor do I know whether the offer was taken up by Monsell. In any case, it is interesting that Monsell should have troubled to keep Tait's letter.

Municipal elections in Limerick

The municipal elections due to take place in Limerick on 25 November 1865 were preceded by unusual interest. Tait, in spite of his having moved to London, had been asked by a number of members of the Town Council to allow his name to go forward for election as Mayor for the coming year; a request to which he had acceded. There seems also to have been something of a groundswell of support for Tait not only among the electors, and the franchise was very limited, but also among the townspeople. Unusually, however, since the position was usually uncontested, one of the other councillors, John M'Donnell, put himself forward for Mayor and a sometimes bitter debate ensued between the supporters of Tait and those of M'Donnell. Although in the normal course M'Donnell might have been expected to be unopposed for election as councillor for the Irishtown Ward, Richard Gamble, a supporter of Tait, put up against him. In the event M'Donnell was defeated and Gamble was elected, by 52 votes to 42; M'Donnell thereupon becoming ineligible for office as Mayor.

Tait becomes Mayor of Limerick

Thus, on 2 December 1865, at a special meeting of the Town Council, Tait was unanimously elected Mayor for 1866. The motion on which he was elected had been proposed by John MacSheehy the High Sheriff. He eulogised Tait at some length but it is worth repeating what he said about Tait's generosity, as it is something otherwise hidden from view. He said, inter alia, -

> I shall refer briefly to another matter, the employment procured by Mr Tait for the unemployed females at the Convent of St Mary's. Sir, he went to London at a great sacrifice to himself, he procured the necessary linen for making the shirts, he became responsible for the due execution of the work, and he handed over the profits to the Sisters of Mercy to enable them to support those noble institutions which are in our city. I shall not here in his presence refer to his many, many charities, the good heart and open purse of Peter Tait are known to every man in Limerick. When did the man against whom fortune became adverse ever apply to him in vain? When did the broken down widow or the orphan ever apply to Peter Tait for relief that she did not receive it willingly and cheerfully at his hands? When did the application ever come for the procuring of a home for the orphan, or to enable the good Sisters of Mercy to dispense more freely their charities among our starving poor in the cellars and garrets of the city, when did anyone ever apply to him, who sought for an asylum or reformatory for the outcast daughter of sin - when I ask did they ever apply to Peter Tait in vain? No, sir, no man ever applied to him in vain; he is known to those who ever went to him as the most cheerful of givers, one of the most unostentatious of contributors to our charities, one of those who does good in private, and "blushes to find it fame".

Appropriately, on 21 December, Tait sent to the outgoing Mayor a further donation of £100, for distribution to local charities.

A burglary at South Hill House

Between Tait's election on 2 December and his installation in the New Year, an unfortunate incident occurred. A daring burglary took place at South Hill House, when a quantity of plate was taken, which was never recovered. This was the second burglary from the house, although on the former occasion the property was discovered shortly afterwards, hidden in an adjoining cornfield.

Tait's ill-health

A meeting of the Town Council on 2 January 1866 saw Tait's formal installation as Mayor; his investment with the chain and wand of office.

Tait referred to his state of health in his address to the meeting –

I shall not occupy your time very long, for my health is not in that position that I can occupy your time very much ... Well, gentlemen, you have elected me as Chief Magistrate of your ancient city, and I trust that if a kind Providence spare my life, and I go through my year of office ... I need only say that if I am spared and permitted to live through my year of office'.

The nature of Tait's illness is unknown. Whatever it was, it must have been serious for him to mention it publicly in this way, although there does not seem to be any record of his mentioning it again and so he presumably made a full recovery.

Tait also referred again in his address to his vision that Limerick would one day become a great commercial port.

Tait entertains on a grand scale

Following Tait's installation as Mayor, there came two of those ostentatious displays which were becoming his trade mark. On Thursday 18 January he gave a banquet in the New Hall which he had recently added to the clothing factory. M Lenehan, in his *History of Limerick,* says that the banquet was attended by nearly four hundred persons, comprising the members of the Corporation, Dr Butler the Catholic Bishop of the Diocese, the head of the Presbyterian congregation in Limerick, the County and City Members of Parliament, a large number of gentry, professional and mercantile classes of county and city, the officers of HM's Engineers, of the 73rd Highland Regiment, of *HMS Prince Consort* which was moored in the River, of the Artillery etc. The Hall was a scene of dazzling splendour; the decorations being in excellent taste.

The bill of fare, provided by Mrs Lynch, the wife of Patrick Lynch, of the George Hotel, was nothing if not ambitious; where, in Limerick, did she obtain all the ingredients in January?

Potages:	Tortue, aux Huîtres, Julienne
Poissons:	Turbot sauce Homard, Filets de Sole, Morue Sauce Huîtres
Entrées:	Vol-au-Vents aux Huîtres, Côtelettes de Mouton aux Petit Pois, Kari d'Asperge, Grenadins de Veau Sauce Tomate
Relevés:	Dindons Braisé, Langues de Bœuf, Poulardes à la Béchamel, Selle de Mouton, Périgord Pâté, Hanche de Venaison, Jambons, Bœuf Rôti, Agneau, Bécassines, Canard Sauvage
Entremets:	Gelées au Vin, Crème de Vanille, Pâtisserie, Prince of Wales Pudding
Dessert:	Apples, pears, apricots, plums, cherries, crystallised fruits, grapes, pineapples and other fruits
Wines:	Hock, Madeira, Champagne, Port, Sherry, Frontignac, etc

The band of the 73rd Regiment performed a selection of airs during the evening.

The Times reported the occasion on 22 January and, in doing so, remarked upon the fact that Tait 'is not a Catholic; on the contrary, he is a deacon in the Independent Church, belonging to one of the smallest of the Protestant sects in this country. Yet he had at his banquet not only the Protestant gentry and merchants, but the Roman Catholic Bishop of the diocese, Mr Monsell MP, Mr Synan MP and a large number of the Catholic gentry of the city and county. This union shows the respect in which Mr Tait is held, and which he has earned as a public spirited citizen, ... '.

In proposing the toast of "The Lord-Lieutenant and Prosperity to Ireland", Tait said that they were on the eve of a new session of Parliament, and he trusted that the deliberations of that Parliament would be such as to do for Ireland what ought to be done for her. If Parliament granted proper concessions, he believed they would never hear in Ireland of such a thing as Fenianism. The country had resources within herself which, if properly developed, would make her one of the most prosperous. The building in which they were then assembled was not erected for the mere purposes of entertainment, but as a hive of industry where people would receive employment - a noble, a generous, and a fine-hearted people. It was built to keep them at home and provide for them.

In responding, William Monsell said -

that he bore testimony from personal observation to the deep interest which Lord Wodehouse, the Lord-Lieutenant, takes in the affairs of Ireland, and the great benefit he has already conferred on the country. When that terrible calamity the rinderpest, or cattle-plague, was hanging over them like a cloud, and threatening the agricultural interests of the country, the Lord-Lieutenant came forward and forced the Government to take those steps which, under God, had been the means of preserving the country from a great calamity. They could not but feel deeply grateful to his Excellency, for a more terrible calamity could not have befallen the nation, and never was greater energy used by any man than by his Excellency to avert it. He wished his Excellency were present that evening to witness this demonstration in favour of prosperity to Ireland. He would have seen gentlemen representing every class of a great community. The agricultural, commercial, and other interests assembled to do honour to the Mayor of Limerick, who had raised that noble temple to industry. He would have seen men of every class and shade of political opinions uniting together in the interests of their common country - indicating that there is something higher and holier than party conflicts, and that there was one common ground on which they could meet in the interests of their country. If he were present he might discover what was the real source of Ireland's prosperity. He would find presiding at that banquet a man who by his own individual energy and exertion amassed vast capital, which he devoted to industrial enterprise in Limerick. That was the true cure and remedy for Ireland's misfortunes. He had given vast employment to the people of Limerick, and he had done so with profit to himself. He had shown that by industry and intelligence manufactures might be made to prosper in Ireland. He would state himself that if he had not proper help in the people he could have done nothing. He found in the first instance that the Irish people were capable of becoming in the highest degree skilful artisans. He never had to deal with combinations or strikes. He had never had a difficulty with any of his workpeople, but with their assistance carried on a flourishing trade, and put English competitors out of the field. He had acquired capital and riches, which they all desired to see him further accumulate. He did not transfer his operations to England or Scotland as others might have done; but he had shown by the erection of that splendid building that he nailed his colours to the mast.

Limerick he found was a place where money might be made and where industry could be created. And how had he done so? He had no secret but that of perseverance, intelligence, and industry. What he had done every man could do. He had solved the Irish problem. He had sworn that industry could succeed in Ireland, and that it could be profitably carried on. By doing so he had conferred great benefit on the country, and made Ireland the medium of supplying foreign markets. He had shown that Ireland had great capacity which only required to be developed.

On the following night the Mayor and Mrs Tait gave a grand ball in the New Hall, attended by about 1,300 of the nobility, gentry and citizens of the county and city. The ball was opened at half past ten by the Earl of Dunraven and Mrs Tait leading off in a quadrille; the Queen's representative in the County and the nurseryman's daughter. There was a break for supper at one, and after supper the dancing resumed and continued until a late period of the morning.

What was it that enabled Tait, who had come to Limerick only twenty years before, from humble origins, a boy of only sixteen years old, to carry off these spectacular social occasions? And why was he regarded with such affection and respect by so many of all classes? He undoubtedly said what people wanted to hear, but was it what he believed, or was it what he thought would best serve his own interests?

And what should we make of the letter to the *Limerick Chronicle* in which Tait announced his imminent removal to London?

It has been suggested that, contrary to what he said in his letter, Tait did have political ambitions; as was borne out by his later attempts to become a Member of Parliament. But Members of the House of Commons were specifically forbidden to have any share in, or to profit from, any Government contract, not only by an Act passed in the reign of George III, but also by the terms of Tait's contracts for the supply of army clothing to the Government. Was he, by his move to London, taking the first steps to distance himself from the clothing factory, and, at the same time, beginning to foster in peoples' minds the idea that he could be persuaded to stand for election to Parliament? Was it a case of the Mayor doth protest too much?

On the other hand, was Tait wrong to have political ambitions; or did he rightly see that membership of the House of Commons, far from being inimical to his efforts to advance the interests of the city of Limerick and of Ireland, which he referred to as his adopted country, would give him even greater opportunities for the advancement of those interests?

11

The Hinchy Affair
1859-1869

I have referred in Chapter 1 to the birth of Robert Tait's child by Ellen Hinchy in January 1859. Remarkably, Peter Tait did not learn of the birth until nearly eight months later, when Ellen Hinchy used violent language towards him, for which she was committed to the City Goal. She was sentenced on 14 September to one month's imprisonment or a fine of 20s with 1s 6d costs but was released two days later having paid the fine and the costs.[1] But the result was that the birth became public knowledge. Two things had then happened.

First, Peter Tait had made enquiries of Mr Beauchamp at the City Goal about the child and was told that it had been taken away from Hinchy for safety as she had held it by the legs and threatened to dash its brains against the wall. When giving it up to Mr Beauchamp she had thrown it to him, but fortunately he had caught it in his arms, and saved it from injury.

In the light of this, Tait had suggested, and he was later to say that Hinchy had agreed, that the child should be placed in an institution in London, where she would have occasional access to it. Tait therefore found a place for the child in the Convent of St Vincent de Paul there, and arranged for Hinchy to travel to London, where he provided her with comfortable lodgings and allowed her £1 a week. But, if this was intended to spare Tait any further embarrassment in Limerick, in the event it was eventually to have the opposite effect.

Second, shortly afterwards, Robert had gone, or perhaps had been sent by Peter Tait, to London, where, as already mentioned, he had joined with his brother James in the establishment of Tait Bros & Co.

These two steps appeared to have served their immediate purpose, for nothing more seems to have been heard of the matter in Limerick while Hinchy was in London. However, this was not because she had ceased to be a cause of considerable trouble to the Taits while she was there. She frequently met Robert Tait outside his office, assaulting him, tearing his clothes and watch chain. She became so dangerous to him that he had to have a policeman guarding his office. Eventually he had Hinchy committed to goal, where she remained from April 1863 to April 1864, again from May 1864 to 10 November 1864 and again from 17 November 1864 to November 1865. Following her release on this last occasion, she returned to Limerick.

Then on 25 January 1866 Hinchy came before the City Magistrates, on a charge of 'assault on Mr Abraham [Tait's brother-in-law] and Head Constable Mooder, and threatening to injure Mr Tait'. She was sentenced to twelve months' imprisonment or, alternatively, to give security herself in £50 and two sureties of £25 each 'to keep the peace to all Her Majesty's subjects, especially to Peter Tait and Mr Abraham'. She was discharged on 24 July on entering into her own recognisance in the sum of £50 to keep the peace.

Later that year Hinchy was persuaded by Tait to return to London. He took a cabin passage for her and gave the captain a sovereign so that she should not be without money on her arrival. But, as the steamer was passing through the dock gates, Hinchy got her trunk on shore and left the ship. Shortly after, Tait, who was at home at South Hill House, heard a dreadful ring at the door and sent his man to see what was the matter. It was Hinchy, who, when questioned by Tait, said that she had not done with him yet and threatened to break the windows. It took two of Tait's servants to remove her. After that, Tait had to shut every gate leading to the house and so much did they fear Hinchy's conduct that none of his family could go out.

Then, following discussions with Dr Butler, the Catholic Bishop of Limerick, Hinchy was induced to go to America to be with her brother; £30 being placed in the hands of the Archbishop of New York, for her use on arrival. But before her departure for New York, Hinchy was up before the Magistrates again, on 9 October, for threatening to take the life of Peter Tait. The sentence was the same as on 25 January, but she was discharged on 7 November, having been bailed by John MacSheehy, the High Sheriff of the city, to enable her to sail from Queenstown (the present-day Cobh) for New York. Nothing was achieved, however, because Hinchy's conduct in New York was so scandalously outrageous that the Archbishop sent her back to Limerick.

On 7 May 1867 she was again in Court, for attacking Alderman Peter Tait and endeavouring to assault him and using threatening language towards him. This time the sentence was only six months imprisonment, or the same recognisance as before. This was possibly the occasion, referred to later by Tait, when he was attending a meeting at the Town Hall and Hinchy tried to get into the Council Chamber, kicked up a row, threatened his life and he could not leave while she was there. However, the governor of the goal gave formal notice to the visiting physician, Dr Robert Gelston, that Hinchy was a lunatic, and Dr Gelston went to see her. He later said that when he saw her the first time he was not quite satisfied of her insanity, but on his third or fourth interview he was satisfied that she was suffering from mono-mania, or derangement of the mind in regard to a single subject only, and he signed the necessary certificate of insanity, but not before he had asked Dr Robert Fitzgerald, the resident superintendent of the Lunatic Asylum, to examine her, and he also signed the certificate, which was dated 13 May 1867; the signatures of two physicians being required for a certificate of insanity. The certificate was then submitted to the Lord-Lieutenant through Sir Thomas Larcom the Under-Secretary for Ireland.

Meanwhile Ellen Hinchy wrote to the Lord- Lieutenant - [2]

Sity Goal May 14th 1867
Limerick
To His Excelencey
The Lord Leiutenant of Ireland
been here as a prisoner, I beg of you to see me justified. I am the mother of two children the father of them, is the Mayors Brother of this sity. He wishes to have me put into a madhouse. I am not insain, if such things can take place, why the may make laws themselves, Mr Tait the Mayor, has shipt me to London, They put me in the hands of a Doctor My child

died in the Doctors hands. My health since then has been very bad. They then took away my Child 8 years and a halfe now old, and it is for asking to see him that I have been imprisoned, it is only by trying to baffel justice that they are trying to put me to a madhouse. May it please your Excelency, to see me justified you will have

The prayers of your Humble
Servant Ellen Hinchey

This moving epistle was endorsed 'Mem. Warrant issued for removal of writer to Limk. D. L. Asylum. 17.5.67'. In it, the reference to her second child is to an event discussed later in this chapter.

Of course, by today's standards a Victorian lunatic asylum was probably a pretty awful place in which to be confined. On the other hand, the contemporary reports do speak of care, and not just incarceration. Indeed, the Limerick asylum was one of relatively few to have in use one of the latest innovations, a Turkish bath; Dr Gelston and Dr Fitzgerald both speaking highly of its curative powers.

The following January, the Rev Mr Leahy CC of St Mary's, the assistant Chaplain at the City Goal, wrote to the governors of the Lunatic Asylum - [3]

Gentlemen - I brought under your notice in June last the case of Ellen Hinchy, who had been removed from the City Goal to the Lunatic Asylum. I knew this woman well. She had been several times committed to the City Goal, of which I am assistant Chaplain, on the charge of assault upon Alderman Tait. Before her last committal she was induced to go to America, and a sum of money was placed in the hands of the Archbishop of New York, for her use on her arrival. After a short stay in America she returned home, overcome by her desire to make further efforts to see and to get her only child. On her return, instead of proceeding, in a legal way, from which she was debarred by her poverty, she again had recourse to violence and she became once more an inmate of the City Goal on a charge of an assault on Alderman Tait. I saw her several times after her committal, and I believe, however reprehensible her conduct may be in other respects, that she was no more a subject for the Lunatic Asylum than any other prisoner under my charge, and when I brought her case under the notice of your board, it was the opinion of all present that their own wives or daughters could not acquit themselves more rationally, if suddenly brought before a body of gentlemen. The unfortunate woman is still in the Lunatic Asylum. Under these circumstances, I trust it is not necessary to apologise for bringing the matter under your notice again.

I remain, Gentlemen,

Yours very truly

M Leahy, C.C.

St Mary's,
Jan. 20th, 1868

Leahy was a political opponent of Tait and, like other of Tait's opponents, implied that Hinchy's committal to the Lunatic Asylum had been engineered by Tait as a means of getting her out of the way; sending her first to London and then to New York having failed to do so. In the absence of direct evidence it is impossible to say whether or not there was any justification for this implication.

In any event, the governors of the Lunatic Asylum held an enquiry into the case on 20 January 1868, in private, at which Leahy's letter was considered and at which Hinchy was examined. At this examination Hinchy alleged that in January 1864, while in London, she had been delivered of a further child, of which Robert Tait was again the father, but that the child had been weakly and had died. Questioned about this event by the governors, Hinchy said that she had been attended at the birth by a doctor who lived at Gibson Street, Waterloo Road. The governors therefore sent a letter to the doctor referred to by Hinchy to try to obtain confirmation, or otherwise, of her story, but it was returned undelivered. This was perhaps not surprising if Hinchy had been telling the truth when Dr Gelston saw her the day after the governors' meeting and she told him that the doctor 'had been many years out of the country'.

Worse still for Peter Tait, Hinchy said that she had received money from Peter Tait through this doctor, who she said was a cousin of Peter Tait, and that through him Peter Tait had encompassed the destruction of her child. Earlier, in her letter to the Lord-Lieutenant, Hinchy had of course said 'They put me in the hands of a Doctor my child died in the Doctors hands'.

At this distance of time, one can only speculate as to whether the child was born prematurely, or at the full term, or what else might have occurred. However, what does not seem to be in doubt is that Hinchy's demeanour underwent a change following the birth. Whatever the cause, she became irrational, and at times violent in her hatred of Peter Tait: she took her child away from the Convent and returned to Limerick, where she became a cause of political embarrassment, and at times physical danger, to Tait, as evidenced by her Court appearances referred to above.

At their regular monthly meeting on 3 February 1868, which was open to the public, the governors discussed the report of their enquiry into the case of Hinchy which they had held in private on 20 January. Unfortunately, the governors' minute books, including a copy of the report, have been lost; for evidence of what happened, reliance has therefore to be placed, to a great extent, on reports in the *Limerick Chronicle* and the *Limerick Reporter*, which themselves differ in important respects.

Tait, who was chairman of the governors, had not attended the meeting on 20 January, being absent in London, but he attended the meeting on 3 February, saying that he had come purposely to Limerick to do so. He was particularly disturbed by the fact that, although the governors' enquiry had been held in private, Leahy's letter of 20 January, but no other report of their proceedings, had been published by the *Limerick Reporter* the following day. Tait took the view that it was a cleverly written letter and that, read by itself, it would lead anyone to the conclusion that he, Tait, was the father of the child; a view of the letter shared by several of the other governors. Tait went on to say that, if read in any coffee-house in England, it would give people that impression and he said that he was sure that, having regard to the position he occupied, as a merchant and the chief magistrate of the city, they would excuse him when he asked them to give their most serious attention to the matter.

Tait was obviously concerned for his own reputation; stressing that the Hinchy affair was not in any way his concern, but entirely that of his brother Robert, who had been living in London since at least 1861. But, of course, the fact of the matter was that Tait was the one who was involved in the arrangements for sending Hinchy to London, and for sending her to New York. But, beyond reiterating their belief that Robert Tait was the father of both of

Hinchy's children, there was really nothing more that the other governors could do; particularly bearing in mind that it was while Robert Tait was living with his brother at 4 Bedford Row that the first child had been born.

Tait then went on to refer to the allegations which had been made by Hinchy at the enquiry held on 20 January in connection with the birth of a second child (and which have been referred to above). Referring to Hinchy's allegation that the child had been delivered by a doctor (whose name was variously reported in the newspapers as Robert Brice, Robert Pryce, Bryce, Boyce or Bowyer) who lived at Gibson Street, Waterloo Road, Tait said that he had made the fullest enquiry before he left London, and no such person was to be found there.

He also referred to Hinchy's stay in prison between April 1863 and April 1864 as making it impossible for her to have had a child when she alleged.

However, when Hinchy was called into the meeting later, and asked again by the governors about the birth of the second child, she said that it had been born in the month after the death of Prince Albert, which fixed the date in her mind. Prince Albert died on 14 December 1861, which means that the child would have been born in January 1862 and not in 1864.

And, at the time of the 1861 census, there was living at 37 Gibson Street a Dr Robert Byers, described as a Member of the Royal College of Surgeons and a general practitioner, born in Scotland in 1830.[4] If he was still there the following year, could he perhaps have been the doctor Hinchy was referring to? Byers had been admitted as a Member of the Royal College of Surgeons in 1860,[5] although he did not register as a medical practitioner until March 1863 when his address was given as the Queensland Emigration Commission in London. Then, in that same month, presumably under the auspices of the Commission, he sailed for Australia in the *SS Cairngorm.* The vessel left Liverpool on 23 March and Greenock on the 31st, reaching Brisbane on 30 June 1863.

The Ship Master's Declaration made in Brisbane by the commander, James M Banks, on 3 July indicates that Byers had travelled as the ship's surgeon.[6] Records in Australia show that he did not register there until 5 July 1865 and that by 1868 he was in Sydney.[7]

If Byers was indeed the doctor referred to by Hinchy, and it seems hard to believe otherwise, it is no surprise that Tait failed to find him in Gibson Street in 1868.

And it is easier to see why Tait might have wanted to deny the whole story, if it were true, than to see why Hinchy should have made it up, if it were not.

The governors then considered a further letter from Leahy. In it he said that he had recently held a further meeting with Hinchy, through the courtesy of Dr Fitzgerald, and was quite convinced that she was now as little a subject for a lunatic asylum as she was at the date of the committal. He also said that, some years before, and being on friendly terms with Alderman Tait, he had undertaken to negotiate an arrangement with Hinchy, in exchange for any reasonable demand for money, but that she would be satisfied with nothing less than her child. So nothing came of it. Now, however, Hinchy would be satisfied if the child were to be placed in some institution or with some individual in Limerick where she might be allowed access to see him occasionally. If this were done, she would promise to give Alderman Tait no further annoyance and Leahy thought she would be likely to keep this engagement.

The revelation that Tait had asked Leahy to try and come to some financial arrangement with Hinchy was hardly likely to do Tait's reputation much good, nor, probably, was it intended by Leahy that it should.

The governors concluded their discussion of the Hinchy affair by remitting her to the City Goal to serve out the expiration of the term of six months' imprisonment imposed on 7 May 1867; surprisingly, the time spent by her in the Lunatic Asylum not counting towards this. The governors thought that this would give an opportunity of testing her mental capacity; Dr Gelston undertaking that she would be well cared for. She was eventually discharged from the Goal on 23 July 1868.

On 15 January 1869 she was again imprisoned, for seven days, on a charge of assault, though on whom is not recorded, and on 6 March she was again sent to prison for seven days for endeavouring to commit a breach of the peace on Sir Peter Tait and Patrick Lynch.

After that there is no further record of Hinchy or of what eventually became of her.

But of the destiny of her child, James, there is information, and the implication is that he was brought up by his father, Robert Tait.

Early in 1875, when James was sixteen, he was in Paris, whether as part of his education, or otherwise, is not known. In July he returned to England and worked for Rylands Sons & Co Limited, clothing manufacturers, in London. In the autumn of 1875 he became ill, although he continued working. By 1877 he was staying with a Dr Abraham Toulmin, in Kensington, one of whose specialities was the treatment of tubercular consumption, though whether that is what James was suffering from is not recorded.[8] Then, later in 1877, he emigrated to Australia, settling in Port Adelaide in South Australia. While there, he taught in two of the Adelaide colleges; at Whinham College, North Adelaide, in 1885/86 and at Prince Alfred College, Kent Town, from 1886 to 1888. A letter of reference written on 22 April 1886 by the principals of Whinham College survives -

> Mr J R Tait was with us as a Senior Mathematical Master, for one Session. We have great pleasure in stating that he gave us every satisfaction, and merely left to take a position in another College. His attainments are of a high order, and he was particularly successful in preparing boys for the University Examinations; he maintains good discipline without sacrificing the sympathy of the boys and we wish him every success in his future career.

From 1883 to 1889 James was a Freemason in the Prince of Wales Lodge, South Australia.

On 12 April 1886 his first child, Emily Rose, was born and in the following month he married her mother, Emily Bichan. Soon after, the family moved to Broken Hill in New South Wales and, in about 1892, from there to the small town of Cue in the Murchison goldfields in Western Australia, where James acquired interests in various mining companies. He died at the early age of thirty-nine in 1898. He was survived by Emily, his daughter Emily Rose, another daughter Jean, who had been born not long after James's death, and two sons, Peter and James Alexander Murchison. A third son, the eldest, Robert Thomas, had died in infancy. Interestingly, the boys were given the names of James's father and his two uncles; as if, although he had cut himself off from his past, family was still important. Only his two daughters had children, and their descendants still live in Australia.

12

Caught up in a Mining Speculation
1864-1868

This is an episode in the story of Peter Tait which Tait himself was later to refer to as 'one of the partners' in Cannock Tait & Co 'becoming involved in a mining speculation'.[1] It was George Cannock who became involved, The Glamorgan Iron and Coal Company Limited that was the subject of the speculation, and it was Tait & Co's money that was used. It may be helpful to start at the beginning.

The Windsor-Clive family owned extensive lands in the vicinity of Cardiff in South Wales. In July 1864 they granted to one Charles Brownlow Marshall a lease of the Van Colliery, which extended to 428 acres in the parishes of Eglwysilan and Rudry and the hamlet of Van, in Glamorganshire. The lease was for sixty years from 1 March 1864. It was said that it cost Marshall £820 [*over £38,000*].

In October 1864 Marshall was introduced to an agent, Filton, and agreed to pay him £5,000 if he brought out a joint stock company for the purpose of buying the Van Colliery from Marshall for £30,000 [*over £1,400,000*]. Filton saw Crosley Brothers, stock and share brokers, who introduced him to Moore and Delatorre, company promoters, and Filton arranged for the latter to meet Marshall to discuss the matter further.[2]

Following this meeting, Moore and Delatorre, without further reference to Filton, arranged with Marshall for the formation and flotation of The Glamorgan Iron and Coal Company Limited (GICC) to acquire the colliery.[3] GICC was to have a share capital of £100,000, divided into 5,000 shares of £20 each. Marshall was to receive £48,976 [*about £2,300,000*] for the colliery, payable as to £10,000 in cash on or before 15 August 1865, £24,500 in fully paid up shares in GICC, £7,000 in debentures at three and five years to be issued by GICC, at 5% interest, and £7,476 in bills payable at three months, due on or before 16 November 1865. In exchange Marshall was to grant GICC an underlease of the colliery, for the unexpired term of his own lease from the Windsor-Clive family, less the last two days thereof. This he was to do on 5 August 1865.[4]

The seven subscribers to the Memorandum and Articles of Association of GICC were found by, and were to be described later in a Court case as puppets of, Moore and Delatorre. The original directors were similarly found by Moore and Delatorre.

Cannock becomes a director

In June 1865 a prospectus was issued.[5] By this time, all of the original directors, with the exception of Richard W MacArthur, had been replaced by seven others, who were no doubt intended to inspire confidence in prospective investors. They were, as Chairman, George Scamell a director of the Submarine Telegraph Company, William P Bayliss the former Manager and Engineer to the Madeley Wood Coal and Iron Co, Thomas Miers a director of both the General Iron Screw Colliery Co and of the Metropolitan and Provincial Bank, John Romanes a director of the General Iron Foundry Co, Miles Seton of Wheal Seton in Cornwall and Randolph House in London, George P White a director of the Tividale Iron Co, and George Cannock of Cannock Tait & Co, Limerick. As consulting engineer the company had G H Bond, mineral engineer to Lord and Lady Palmerston, and its brokers were Crosley Brothers. Its offices were the offices of Moore and Delatorre at 15 King Street in the City of London. It all looked very respectable.

The prospectus

The prospectus said nothing about MacArthur, beyond giving his address as Kemp Town, Brighton. Perhaps understandably, as he was the Secretary of the National Provincial Aerated Bread Company Limited and the Oxfordshire and Berkshire Aerated Bread Company Limited at 14 Buckingham Street, Strand; hardly likely to have provided him with much experience of coal mining.

However, he was a close neighbour of Robert Tait at 10 Buckingham Street. Was it perhaps MacArthur who first drew the attention of Robert Tait and, through him, Cannock, to the GICC?

And of course it could hardly have been foreseen that both Bayliss and Seton would shortly become bankrupt; the former in July 1867, the latter in January 1868.

The prospectus referred to a number of expert reports, which were available for inspection. These stated that in the earlier stages the mine was expected to produce a net profit of nearly £28,000 per annum or 33% of the capital necessary to be called up at long intervals. In addition to the cost of the mine payable to Marshall, of £48,976, the directors stated that a sum not exceeding £25,000, extending over two years, would be ample to bring the works into full operation.

The directors called for applications on the basis that £1 per share would be payable on application, and an additional £2 on allotment; further calls not to exceed £3 per share on each occasion and to be made at intervals of not less than two months.

The fraud engineered by Moore and Delatorre

The scene was set for a market-rigging fraud, of a kind all too common at that time.

It is interesting to look at the arithmetic, because, if investors had thought about it, they must surely have seen what was about to happen.

As noted, the capital of the company was £100,000 divided into 5,000 shares of £20 each, with only £1 payable on application and only a further £2 on allotment. Of the 5,000 shares, 1225 were to be issued to Marshall, credited as fully paid up, as part of the purchase price of the colliery. That left 3775 shares available for issue to investors. Assuming all of those shares were applied for and allotted, as was the case, that produced £11,325. But £10,000 in cash was due to be paid immediately to Marshall as a further part of the purchase price, although in the event he agreed to accept only £6000 in cash; the balance being paid in the form of bills of exchange. That left £5,325 towards the £25,000 known to be required for capital expenditure, and nothing at all for working capital: the first call of £3 per share would have to be made at the end of the first two months and probably a second call of £3 per share two months after that.

Worse than that, before they resigned, the original Directors had resolved that the sum of £10,000 [*about £470,000*] should be paid to Moore and Delatorre by way of preliminary expenses. This resolution was subsequently confirmed at a meeting of the new Directors held on 24 July and chaired by MacArthur; the only one of the original Directors left on the Board. Cannock was not present at this latter meeting. There had been no mention in the prospectus of the intention to pay this enormous sum to Moore and Delatorre.

Allowing for the sums eventually payable to Marshall amounting to £24,476, the projected capital expenditure of £25,000, the unquantified need for working capital and now the payment to Moore and Delatorre of £10,000, it became inevitable that there would be a shortage of cash, at least in the short term, and that, with the amount payable on application only £1 per share, a sum very much greater than £2 per share should have been called for on allotment. But that would not have suited what Moore and Delatorre had in mind.

The allotment of the shares

The shares were allotted by a Committee appointed by the Directors, on 22 July 1865. On the face of it, there was nothing in the list of allotments to arouse suspicion, but in fact the applicants for at least 1500 of the shares allotted were undisclosed nominees of Moore and Delatorre; persons either of no worth or even, in some cases, fictitious.

Even at the very low level of £3 per share, Moore and Delatorre had to find £4,500 to pay the sums due on application and allotment of these shares. Among the *bona fide* applications and allotments were Cannock for 70 shares, Romanes for 50 shares and Robert Tait for 20 shares. A market was then created in the shares, £3 paid, and the price worked up to £12, a figure vastly in excess of their true worth, at which figure Moore and Delatorre sold the shares allotted to their nominees for settlement following the expected admission of the shares to the Stock Exchange Daily Official List.

However, by the time an application was made to the Stock Exchange on 22 August 1865, for the appointment of a settling day, suspicions of fraud had been aroused in the market, and the application was opposed. The General Purposes Committee of the Stock Exchange therefore held an enquiry: the circumstances of the allotments were exposed and the payment of £10,000 to Moore and Delatorre was revealed.[6] As to the circumstances of the allotments, three examples found by the Committee will serve to give an idea of the kind of people, who were not *bona fide*, but whose applications had been accepted and to whom allotments had been made -[7]

J H Gibson, 7 Dacre Street, SW Gentleman 50 shares

Dacre Street is situate in the lowest part of Westminster, the houses are let out to people in single rooms, this house has 6 rooms in it, each occupied by separate families. Gibson his mother and aunt have only one room between them for all purposes, he is a clerk to Mr Walmsley, he is probably without means, his mother takes in needlework and she and the aunt have not sufficient clothing to be decent, they are paupers of the lowest description, the premises are filthy in the extreme and the rent of the room 2/6 a week only, the woman quite ridiculed the idea of Gibson being able to pay £150 or even as many shillings.

W O Pratt, 34 Portland Villas, Notting Hill Agent & Merchant 100 shares

Mrs Cobbett the occupant of the house. Does not know where he is. Referred to him as 'a regular swindler' and laughed at the idea of his being able to find £300.

H W Wright, 110 Cheapside, EC Gentleman 100 shares

Gone away. Landlady thought it perfectly ridiculous to suppose he could pay £300, the deposit on 100 shares.

The Stock Exchange refuses to list the shares

Following the Committee's enquiry, the application for a settling day and inclusion in the Daily Official List was refused in the middle of September; the Committee having found 'serious discrepancies between the prospectus and Articles of Association ... , and also that there were many objectionable practices in the promotion of the company and in the allotment of shares'. This meant that settlement of the sales of shares effected by Moore and

Delatorre, as well as by *bona fide* shareholders, could not take place.

The unfortunate, not to say disastrous, consequence of this for GICC was that the original allottees, including of course Moore and Delatorre's nominees, remained shareholders. Thus, there were left only some 2,000 shares, at most, in the hands of *bona fide* shareholders in a position to meet any calls made on their shares.

Early in 1866 the *bona fide* shareholders appointed a Committee, the members of which were drawn from among themselves, to enquire into the position of GICC and to recommend a way forward.

This Committee reported to an Extraordinary General Meeting of shareholders in July 1866.[8] They recommended that GICC should not be wound up, but that it should be carried on. They based their recommendation on the assumption that there were about 2,000 *bona fide* shareholders and that calls of £3 per share would therefore yield on each occasion about £6,000. The Committee's recommendation was agreed to by the meeting.

Disaffected shareholders take legal action

But a difficulty arose, which was to upset the Committee's calculations. A number of *bona fide* shareholders refused to pay the calls made upon them, on the ground that the allotments and the prospectus were fraudulent. GICC therefore sued one of these shareholders, Mr Alexander Lodwick Irvine, in what was regarded as a test case. The case came before Mr Justice Willes and a Special Jury at the Summer Assizes at Guildford in August 1866.[9] Mr Prentice QC opened the case for the defence and, although what he said was largely a recapitulation of what was already known, he revealed the remarkable fact that Marshall, from whom GICC had acquired the mine, had formerly been a cabinetmaker in Bristol, but had become bankrupt. After a trial lasting two days, the jury found in Irvine's favour, whereupon he and a number of other *bona fide* shareholders applied successfully to the Court during the latter part of 1866 for orders to have their names struck off the register of members of GICC. Some 1,000 shares were removed in this way, although in some cases calls had been paid beforehand. GICC was liable to refund the amount of these calls, but by then there were no funds available to enable it to do so.[10]

Cannock and Romanes make themselves liable to GICC's bankers

Meanwhile, on 4 August 1865, GICC had been forced to borrow £10,000 from the Metropolitan and Provincial Bank; the lease of the colliery being deposited as security. In February 1866 the loan became due for repayment and the Chairman was authorised to negotiate for its renewal on the same security as before. However, he was only able to arrange for a new loan of £11,000 (out of which the existing loan would be repaid) on the terms that certain of the Directors would act as sureties for its repayment. Accordingly, two bills of exchange, each for £5,500, payable on 15 June and 18 September 1866 respectively, were accepted by Scamell, Miers, MacArthur, Cannock and Romanes. The lease was to continue on deposit at the bank as additional security, but to the order of these Directors.

The ink was barely dry on these arrangements when it became necessary for GICC to borrow more money. This time, in March 1866, £6,000 was borrowed from the Bank of London, repayable as to £1,000 on 1 June, £1,000 on 1 September, and £4,000 on 1 December 1866, and secured by bills of exchange endorsed by the Directors, and by a second charge on the lease of the colliery.

GICC's lease and other assets are mortgaged to Cannock and Romanes

Eventually, by a deed dated 11 July 1866, between GICC and Stephen Phillips (who was chief clerk to Tait & Co in London) as trustee for Cannock and Romanes, GICC mortgaged the lease of the colliery and all the company's buildings, fixtures, and fixed machinery, and movable assets, as security in respect of the liability of Cannock and Romanes as sureties for the loan of £11,000 made by the Metropolitan and Provincial Bank. In the event of the failure by GICC to repay the loan on certain fixed dates, the sums payable by Cannock and Romanes as sureties were to bear interest at 10% per annum.[11]

When the bills became due for payment, GICC was unable to meet them in full , as might have been foreseen, and Cannock paid £5,500, and Romanes £1500, in respect of them. Scamell, Miers and

MacArthur paid nothing. In addition, Cannock subsequently paid £5,500, and Romanes £50, in respect of the bills given as security for the £6,000 borrowed from the Bank of London.

One might reasonably ask, at this stage: what was Cannock's motive for funding GICC in this way? He had the colliery as security, but, at the end of the day, would ownership of the colliery enable him to recover his, or rather Tait & Co's, money? It seems doubtful. The conclusion must be that, as a director of a company which had issued a prospectus found by a Court to have been fraudulent, he would be liable if either Marshall or any disaffected shareholder should decide to sue. And he was the director against whom action was most likely to be taken, as he seems to have been the only one with the means to pay - or so it appeared at the time. Against that, he had the consolation that the judge in the Irvine case had said, in his summing up, that 'the fraud that is charged, is charged as a fraud on the persons who were acting ... in the allotment of the shares ... . That charge does not appear at all to touch Mr Cannock who ... certainly appears to have proved his genuineness by putting his name to the guarantee to the bankers for £11,000 ... '.[12]

An agreed solution to GICC's problems

In the light of the problems created for GICC by the outcome in the Irvine case, it looked increasingly likely that GICC would have to be put into liquidation. However, a new solution was agreed in discussions between the Committee of shareholders, which had earlier looked into the company's position, and Cannock and Romanes. This was that a new company should be formed to purchase the colliery from GICC and that, meanwhile, those shareholders whose shares had been taken off the register by Court order but who were still owed refunds by GICC should be given 3-year bonds, bearing interest at 3% per annum, exchangeable at their option for preference shares in the new company if it came into being.

In contemplation of the eventual success of this solution, the *bona fide* shareholders, by and large, accepted the proposed bonds for the sums due to them by GICC. As a condition of accepting the bonds the shareholders were required to sign a memorandum, the emphasis in which was the release of GICC itself and of the directors and others from all liability arising out of the events surrounding the formation of GICC and the issue of the prospectus. This tends to confirm that it was, indeed, the fear of legal action which motivated Cannock.

However, before the latest proposals could be put into effect it was necessary to obtain Marshall's agreement not only to what was proposed, but also to certain changes in the company's lease of 5 August 1865.

Following lengthy discussions, agreement was reached, and its terms were embodied in a document dated 6 December 1866, made between Marshall, Phillips, as trustee for Cannock and Romanes as before, and GICC. The principal terms were as follows - [13]

1st Marshall would be paid £5,000 in two bills drawn by Romanes and accepted by Cannock; one for £2,500 maturing on 1 March 1867, the other for a like amount maturing on 1 June 1867.

2nd The lease of 5 August 1865 would be surrendered by GICC.

3rd A new lease would be granted by Marshall with variations to the previous rents and royalties and, more importantly, without any right to forfeiture by Marshall in the event of the winding up of GICC.

4th Cannock would accept a transfer from Marshall of the latter's fully paid up shares in GICC and of the debentures for £7,000 issued to him by GICC.

On the same day, 6 December 1866, GICC created a further charge in favour of Phillips, as trustee for Cannock and Romanes, on the assets comprised in the mortgage of 11 July 1866.

In pursuance of these arrangements, the two bills totalling £5,000 were accepted by Cannock and, in due course, paid by him, and he accepted a transfer of the shares and the debentures.

The passing of a winding-up order

But the original lease had not been surrendered or the intended new lease entered into, when a resolution for the winding up of GICC was passed at a meeting on 13 February 1867. On an application made to the Court by GICC on 2 March, it was ordered that the winding up should be continued under the supervision of the Court.[14] Michael Louisson Levey, a public accountant, who had been one of the original subscribers to the Memorandum and Articles of Association of GICC, was confirmed as Liquidator.

Notwithstanding the passing of the winding-up resolution, the proposed new company, the Van Colliery Company, Limited, was incorporated on 25 February 1867, with an authorised capital of £55,000, divided into 5,000 shares of £8 each and 3,000 shares of £5 each. Four of the six subscribers to the company's Memorandum of Association were nominated by the *bona fide* shareholders of GICC, and two, Peter Tait and Joseph Fogerty, by Cannock and Romanes. Joseph Fogerty, a civil engineer, was the brother of William Fogerty, the architect responsible for Cannock Tait & Co's new building in Limerick.[15]

Failure of the agreed solution

But it was all too late.

The Liquidator refused to complete the arrangements contemplated by the agreement of 6 December 1866, which were a necessary precondition for the purchase of the colliery by the new company.

The shareholders refused to co-operate further, upon discovering that their bonds would be worthless, because Cannock and Romanes had a charge over the whole of GICC's assets, a fact which seems to have been deliberately withheld from them by Cannock and Romanes during the discussions regarding the formation of the new company.

The cost to Tait & Co of Cannock's involvement

Phillips therefore, on 31 May 1867, appointed Romanes as his agent to take possession of the mine, but the Liquidator would not give up possession. Whereupon Phillips applied to the Court for the enforcement of his security and was eventually let into possession by order of the Court on 30 July.[16] By that time, Cannock was owed by GICC a total of almost £31,000 [*over £1,300,000*]. And that was without taking account of interest.

Cannock continued working the mine unprofitably until late in 1868, when he assigned his interest to a Mr Bridell. It was not until Bridell, and two subsequent owners, had been unable to make the mine pay, that it was acquired in 1874 by a company which, even after it had spent £40,000 on improvements, was not entirely out of the wood.[17]

In the summer of 1868, Robert Tait brought an action against Marshall for false representation in the prospectus, but the judge held that there was no evidence of fraud to put to the jury and the case was dismissed;[18] a view upheld on appeal.[19] Much later, in 1885, by which time Cannock was long since dead, an attempt was made, for the benefit of his estate to extract calls from a selection of the shareholders of GICC. By 1889 this had produced only £24; less even than the costs incurred. The Liquidator was therefore discharged and the GICC was dissolved on 10 May 1889.[20]

The amount of Tait & Co's money lost by Cannock was considerable; it would, for example, have been more than sufficient to pay for a new ocean-going steamer.

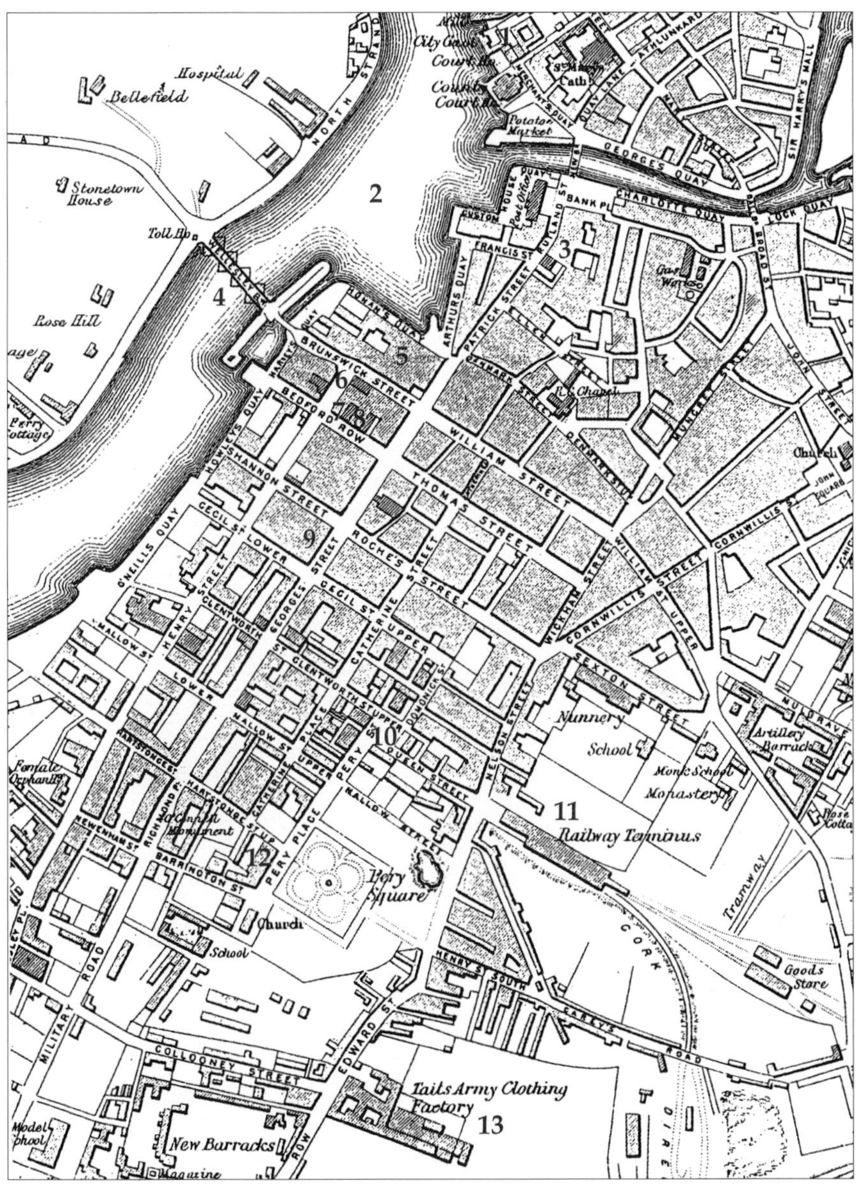

1. Limerick in 1865 showing places referred to in the text: **1** City Goal, **2** River Shannon, **3** Town Hall, **4** Wellesley Bridge, **5** Cannock Tait & Co, **6** 19 Brunswick Street, **7** Independent Chapel, **8** 4 Bedford Row, **9** George Hotel, **10** Baker Place (site of the Tait clock), **11** Railway Terminus, **12** Mechanics' Institute, **13** Tait's Army Clothing Factory.

2. Peter Tait, in about 1860.

3. Early photographs of the sewing and cutting rooms in Tait's army clothing factory in Limerick.

4. South Hill House, Limerick, in about 1990.

5. The greenhouse at South Hill House in about 1990.

6. Cannocks in Georges Street, Limerick; the first eight bays, with the awning, were built by Tait in 1858/59.

7. An 1863 pattern full dress tunic made by Tait for the Volunteer Militia of Canada.

8. Buttons from uniforms supplied by Tait to the Confederate States of America in 1864.

9. A token issued by Tait, possibly in connection with the 1867 Paris Universal Exhibition.

10. A recent photograph of the clock tower erected in Baker Place, Limerick, in 1867 as a testimonial to Tait.

13

Mayor of Limerick
1866-1868

Michael Hogan, the Bard of Thomond, marked Tait's installation as the Mayor of Limerick on 1 January 1866 with a song of congratulation -

Hail to trade's great benefactor! Wreathe for him a laurel crown,
For his bounty like a river has enriched our honor'd town.
Adorn his generous bosom with his chain of shining gold,
But his manly heart is richer than that chain a thousand fold.

Tait, the saviour of the orphan, whom misfortunes grimly press;
Tait, the solace of the widow in the hour of her distress;
Tait, the high and princely hearted, who ne'er spurn'd
the poor man's claim;
Tait, the idol of our homesteads, where a blessing greets his name.

Tait, the sun of our affections, while our gratitude shall live,
Let us thank him with due honor, it is all we have to give.
For he's constantly bestowing bounteous gifts, that none before
Saw such golden-handed kindness held so largely to the poor.

A king may see his glory in the diadem he wears;
But what crown on earth is richer, than a grateful peoples' prayer?
Or what worldly boon is brighter to the mortal that deserves
The true heartfelt affection of the creatures whom he serves?

Another generation shall arise like growing wheat,
But will the coming future bring another Peter Tait?
To promote and cherish labour - to extend a friendly hand,
And scatter daily comforts where black want had made a stand?

Such men are scarce amongst us, and 'tis difficult to know
What blessings or what evils in a future age may flow;
But if Ireland count many such as Peter Tait just now,
The pauper brand of misery might be cancelled from her brow.

Then with every mark of honor, let us greet him while we can
And prove that we are worthy of so great and good a man;
Let us show that we are grateful for the favours he has shown,
To the many toiling poor ones, who depend on him alone.

Meet him - greet him with your blessings like
the flower refreshing dew,
Give the glowing meed of honor where 'tis truly, nobly due;
Toiling maid and strong mechanic, burgess, labourer, artizan,
Show your high appreciation of so great and good a man.

Once installed as Mayor, Tait took remarkably little part in the affairs of the Corporation. Although he attended almost all the Council meetings held in 1866, he was at only eight of the eighteen meetings held in 1867, and attended on only three occasions in 1868. Tait's frequent absences from Council meetings did not reflect a lessening of interest on his part; rather, his business affairs now increasingly required his presence in London. He took few initiatives as Mayor, but, when he did, it was generally to propose matters that would benefit the poor.[1]

The Limerick Harbour Bill

An exception was his interest in the Harbour Bill, and it was probably because of this that, in September 1866, he was appointed a Harbour Commissioner, to serve for two years.[2] The Harbour Bill arose out of the financial difficulties of the Limerick Harbour Commissioners caused by the construction of the Wellesley Bridge, which had been built to carry the road to Ennis across the River Shannon opposite Brunswick Street. The bridge had cost considerably more, and the tolls produced substantially less, than had been estimated. The result was that the Harbour Commissioners owed an increasing amount to the Treasury, which they could not afford to service, in spite of levying very high port dues; the latter being self-defeating, as they militated against the use of Limerick as a port of choice for shipping.

The Harbour Bill, which was passed as the Limerick Harbour (Composition of Debt) Act 1867, reduced the Commissioners indebtedness to the Treasury to £55,000, to be repaid over fifty years at 4% interest. In addition, the Wellesley Bridge was transferred to the Commissioners of Public Works and ceased to be the financial responsibility of the Harbour Commissioners. These changes were regarded as likely to be of great benefit to the sea-borne trade of the city; a matter in which Tait had always taken a close personal interest.

Very shortly after the passing into law of the Harbour Bill, a further Act was passed which, *inter alia,* reconstituted the Harbour Commissioners. Notwithstanding this change, Tait remained a Commissioner, because, as Mayor of Limerick, he became, *ex-officio,* one of the seventeen new Commissioners.

A change in the ownership of Tait's army clothing business

In 1866 there was a significant change in the ownership of Tait's army clothing business. Until then, Tait had been its sole proprietor, but on 7 May 1866 he took into partnership George Cannock, Robert Tait and Balfour Logie. This new partnership, which continued to trade as Tait & Co, took over the army clothing business in Limerick, and the branches in London and Leeds, although Tait himself remained the owner of the lease of the Limerick factory. The London business moved from Essex Street to 95 Southwark Street in Southwark, a very long lease of which was bought by Robert Tait. Very little is known about the branch in Leeds, which was in Alexander Street. It was opened in rented premises in about 1865 and remained there until at least 1870. It was run by a manager, F Goodall. From 1866, Tait used to refer to himself as 'of Limerick, London and Leeds'.

Industrial unrest

Also in 1866, Tait had to contend with a tailors' strike in Limerick, called by the Tailors' Society, a body much like what we should today call a Trade Union. The strike started at the end of March at Cannock Tait & Co, where waistcoats and other light articles of men's clothing, previously sewn by male tailors, had been given to females to sew by machine; there being at the time no other work for the females to do. Although the tailors continued to be fully employed at their usual wages, they demanded that the females should be put out of work; rather than do work normally done by the men.

By the beginning of May the strike had spread to all the other large clothing establishments in the city, with the exception of Tait's army clothing factory, in which about 1500 females were then fully employed, together with nearly 100 journeyman tailors. When representatives of the Society went to the army clothing factory to press the tailors there to join the strike, Tait took a very firm line: he gave notice that any of his tailors who joined the strike would be dismissed. Shortly after that, all the employers, with the exception of Tait, settled with the strikers on the basis that they should be taken back on the same terms as when they had struck; the females continuing to do the light sewing by machine as before. But Tait refused in future to employ any tailors belonging to the Society. He did however, take on any who first left the Society.

If Tait was going to benefit the working classes of Limerick, it was going to be on his terms.

Another shipping venture

Tait was not a committee man; it was in his nature to act alone. And he was very much a 'hands on' manager. Just as he had satisfied himself of the value of Thomas's sewing machine, and gone himself to Winchester to deal with Col Horne's complaint, so he had himself lobbied in London in support of the Harbour Bill.

But an area in which Tait did delegate, was in relation to his shipping interests. In these he seems to have relied very heavily on Patrick Lynch.

After the sale of the *Evelyn*, Tait's next recorded venture into shipping was the sale on commission of the SS *Caroline*; like the *Evelyn*, a former blockade runner.

The *Caroline* had been built by William Denny & Bros at Dumbarton, for James Carlin, the British Agent for the Importing and Exporting Company of South Carolina, at a cost of £22,000. The vessel ran the blockade three times; once in 1864 and twice in 1865.

After the War she was sold by Carlin to his attorney, James Calder. A joint venture between Peter Denny, J N Beach and J S Begbie bought the vessel from Calder, as a speculation, in September 1866, for £10,250.

They calculated that, taking account of the cost of overhaul and alteration, the *Caroline* would stand them in at £17,750, and anticipated selling her in the Brazils for £20,000; this sum, after deducting a selling commission of £250, would give them a profit of 10%.[3]

In July 1866, Tait sent Lynch to Liverpool to look at the *Caroline* and, following that visit, Tait & Co were entrusted with arranging the sale of the vessel. The *Caroline* sailed for the Brazils at the beginning of November 1866 and reached Rio de Janeiro on 20 January 1867.

Lynch, meanwhile, sailed separately for Rio de Janeiro from Southampton on board the *SS Douro* and joined the *Caroline* there. He took her down to Montevideo and sold her for £18,000, before returning home; reaching Southampton early in June. Presumably Tait received the commission of £250. Almost certainly Lynch undertook some other business for Tait while he was away; £250 otherwise seems small recompense for seven months' salary and expenses.

Tait asked to serve as Mayor for a second term

Meanwhile, the Council had asked Tait to serve for a second term as Mayor. The matter came up at a meeting on 11 October 1866, when T C Hastings gave the following notice of motion – [4]

That this being the first meeting of the Council since the munificent acts of the Mayor to the Poor of our City during the threatened visitation of cholera, in acknowledgement of such acts and in accordance with the wishes of the citizens that the only return it is in their power to give to the Mayor be at once expressed by requesting that he will consent to accept the office of Mayor for the ensuing year, I hereby give notice that I will at next meeting of the Council move that Alderman Tait our present worthy and respected Mayor be again elected Mayor of this Borough for the year 1867.

And at the next meeting it was duly resolved -

That as the year of office of our present worthy and respected Mayor is drawing to a close, and in order to testify and acknowledge on behalf of our fellow citizens the dignity, honour and hospitality, and unbounded charity, which he has displayed since he became a Member of this Council, we the Aldermen and Town Councillors of this City hereby request of him to comply with the wishes of his Fellow Citizens and accept the office of Mayor for the ensuing year; which we hereby offer to him as a token of our regard and true appreciation of his great merit.

Tait elected Mayor for a second term

So Tait became Mayor for 1867 and it may be worth repeating here the report which appeared in *The Times* of 4 January -

Alderman Tait's re-election as Mayor of Limerick was celebrated by a brilliant ovation. On the previous night tar-barrels blazed through the streets, and early on New Year's Day the people were busy decorating triumphal arches, and suspending flags and mottoes across the principal thoroughfares. A procession of the trades' and labourers' societies escorted the Mayor from his residence to the Town Hall, which was crowded by the citizens. Having been invested with the insignia of office by the High Sheriff, Tait delivered an address, in the course of which he referred to Fenianism, remarking that:-

"If the people who subscribed immense sums of money on the other side of the Atlantic and placed them at the disposal of James Stephens and other agitators would only show that they really loved their country and devoted such moneys towards the amelioration of its condition, he would be the first to become a 'Head Centre' himself, and in the establishment of manufactures help to regenerate Ireland. Thousands of the bone and sinew of the land were leaving the country, and it was to be deplored. If the right course were taken, they might be profitably employed at home, and the products of their nation and of their industrious hands be shipped, instead of themselves, to the Western hemisphere. Irish labour was skilled labour, and Irishmen were able, if they only got fair play, to compete with the men of any nation in this particular. He could and would maintain that fact."

Let it be recollected that Limerick is a most Catholic city, in the heart of Munster, and that the gentleman whom the inhabitants thus delight to honour above any of their own country and creed is a Briton and a Protestant. Surely the secret by which he is enabled to manage the Irish people can be learnt by others! It is partly revealed in the following sentence of his speech:-

"He had endeavoured to make up for his many shortcomings by striving to become essentially and practically the mayor of the poor, and in relieving and benefiting the poor felt more real pleasure than in all the honours bestowed upon him."

The *Southern Reporter* was later to say -

Sir Peter Tait's career has another and perhaps not less important lesson for our edification and instruction. A few years since he was but an humble apprentice in one of the commercial establishments of Limerick. He is now one of the most extensive manufacturers in Ireland, one of the best known in the markets of Europe; and he is about to extend his commercial relations, for the benefit of his adopted city and country, into the vast field of the great Republic. This is a man whom any country would delight to honour, and Limerick has not been slow to acknowledge and to pay the tribute of public gratitude eminently due to so great a benefactor.

Thus we see what one unaided man, simply by the exercise of his commercial talents, and by putting forth his individual energy can do, in promoting the commercial prosperity and reputation of a city, and giving bread to hundreds of honest hands that only wanted the leave to toil. He has no fear of the Fenians because he is a national benefactor; and while he censures criminal undertakings, he uses language with which no one can find fault, because he abstains from national reproaches, and vituperative calumny on the country at large, and expresses his warmest sympathy with those who are suffering from distress beyond the reach of his benevolence and enterprise.

It gives us much pleasure to see the city of Limerick doing honour to such a man, and with his example before their eyes, we do not see why other towns should not furnish similar instances of individual enterprise and beneficent industry, instead of committing their capital to remote regions from which it is never likely to return to benefit either their country or themselves.

It was perhaps Tait's ambivalence towards the threat posed by the Fenians that Dr Butler, the Roman Catholic Bishop of Limerick, had in mind when writing from Rome to William Monsell in January 1870, by which time William Spillane was Mayor - [5]

It is hoped here that the total failure of the Fenian attempt in Longford will do great good. I should fear very much however, for Limerick, if a vacancy were to occur just now. There seems to be a disposition to revive Taitism, and rig it out once more in Fenian colours, and I am sorry to see the new Mayor apparently lending himself to the scheme.

An ante-mortem memorial

Work had started in 1866 on an ornamental clock tower, first mooted in 1865, to be erected by public subscription in Baker Place in Limerick, as a testimonial to Tait, for his enterprise as an employer and manufacturer.

Among the largest subscriptions to the cost were £100 each from John Arnott and George Cannock, and £60, with a promise of more to come, from John Collie in Manchester.

A competition for the design, of what the *Dublin Builder* referred to as this *ante-mortem* memorial,[6] was won by Mr W E Corbett, the City Surveyor.

On the four sides of the base of the tower are inscribed panels. Starting on the west side and continuing on the south, east and north faces, the inscription reads -

West - Erected by Public subscription in appreciation of the enterprise and usefulness of Alderman Peter Tait
South - As an employer of large numbers of the Working Classes, and of his liberality and benevolence as a Citizen
East - A.D. 1866 and completed in the year 1867
North - During Alderman Tait's Second Mayoralty to Which Office he was unanimously Elected

The tower also bears the motto 'Gratiam dat deus', which was presumably in anticipation of the motto 'God give Grace' shortly to be granted to Tait by Ulster King of Arms.

The clock was handed over to the Corporation at a ceremony held in the afternoon of 21 February 1867.

Later, in September, the Corporation arranged for the erection of an iron railing round the base of the clock tower, with a globe shaped lamp on each corner, at a further cost of more than £200.

The clock tower, recently restored, still stands in Baker Place, although the railings and the lamps were removed in 1967 and the clock is now operated by electricity.

A public banquet to Tait

On the first of January a subscription list for a public banquet to Tait had been opened – [8]

Public Banquet,

To The Mayor of Limerick

We the undersigned Members of the Corporation, Merchants, Bankers, Trades, Citizens of Limerick and friends of the Right Worshipful Peter Tait Mayor of Limerick, hereby propose to invite him, to a public banquet in this City, to be given on such day, as it may be his convenience to name for same, should he accept it, as some acknowledgement of the respect and regard entertained for him, and in recognition of his Exertions as Mayor for the welfare of the City, the many benefits he has conferred on it and the people, his munificent gifts of Charity, and unbounded and graceful hospitality – and for that purpose we subscribe our names for a dinner ticket at one guinea.
Limerick 1st Jany 1867

The first subscriber was Eugene O'Callaghan High Sheriff, followed by Lawrence Quinlivan Alderman and High Sheriff Elect.

A further one hundred and seven subscribers added their names.

The banquet was held in the Theatre Royal in the evening of 21 February, following the handing over of the clock in Baker Place, and was attended by nearly all the leading men not only of the city, but of the county, without distinction of party or religion.[9] Covers for over three hundred were laid in the theatre, which was reported to have been charmingly fitted up; the boxes being occupied by ladies in full dress, whose presence imparted great brilliance to the scene.

Mr Synan, one of the Members of Parliament for the County, was in the chair. *The Times* reported that, in proposing the guest of the evening, he had mentioned Tait's public services in highly eulogistic terms and that he had gone on to refer to Tait's large-handed charity, to the extensive employment he afforded, to the impetus he had given to the trade of the port by his energy, which had started into existence an unrivalled factory, and had projected a line of steamers from the Shannon to the New World.[10]

Tait becomes a Deputy Lieutenant

On 27 February 1867 the Earl of Dunraven, Lord-Lieutenant of the County of Limerick, wrote to Sir Thomas Larcom at Dublin Castle asking for the approval of the Lord-Lieutenant of Ireland, the Marquis of Abercorn, to 'the name of Mr Peter Tait, Mayor of Limerick, for the Deputy Lieutenancy of the City, vacant by the death of Mr Farnell'. There was some discussion following this, as there was evidently no record of Mr Farnell having been a Deputy Lieutenant; the implication being that there was therefore no vacancy. However, Lord Dunraven seems to have become irritated by this quibble and on 5 March he wrote again saying that he had the right to name Tait, whether Farnell was a DL or not as without him there were only three DLs and four were allowed.

At this point William Monsell joined in, with a letter telling Sir Thomas Larcom 'we are anxious to make Mr Peter Tait' a DL 'and I shall be much obliged to you if you will have it done'; which he did, because on 2 April Monsell was able to sign the confirmation appointing Peter Tait.[11] This received the Marquis of Abercorn's approval the same day.[12]

Tait & Co exhibit at the Paris Universal Exhibition

Between April and October of 1867 a Universal Exhibition was held in Paris.[13] The exhibits, covering a wide range of human endeavour, were arranged in ten Groups -

I Works of Art
II Apparatus and Application of the Liberal Arts
III Furniture, etc
IV Clothing
V Raw & Manufactured Products of Mining, Forestry, etc
VI Apparatus etc used in the Common Arts
VII Food, etc
VIII Livestock, etc
IX Live Produce, etc
X Articles for Improving the Physical and Moral Condition of the People

The Groups were themselves sub-divided into a total of ninety-five Classes.

Tait & Co exhibited military and naval uniforms in Group IV, Class 35, Clothing for Both Sexes, which included items as diverse as boots and shoes, bonnets and headdresses, hats, caps and other headgear, artificial flowers, ornamental feathers and fancy work in hair.

The majority of the exhibitors in Class 35 showed boots and shoes of many different kinds including, from a manufacturer in Genoa, 'men's and women's boots and shoes containing firearms', but there were also some other curiosities; from the Viceroy of Egypt, shoes of red kid embroidered with gold, for women of the upper classes, and belts in buffalo skin and brass wire for rich Nubians; from the Bey of Tunis, turbans for Mussulmans, Israelites and Scribes; from Hawaii, a grand royal mantle of oo feathers;[14] from Morocco, women's slippers with and without soles; and from the Cape of Good Hope, a set of muff, boa and cuffs of vultures' down, as well as bonnets exhibiting snake skins and eagles' down as articles of decoration.

In commenting on Class 35, the Exhibition catalogue referred, inter alia, to the use of sewing machines in the French clothing trade, which it said were 'now used to an immense extent; the greater part of seams now being sewn by machine'. But Tait had been using sewing machines for many years for virtually all sewing operations.

Military uniforms were exhibited not only by Tait & Co, but by manufacturers from Barcelona, Madrid, Copenhagen and Stockholm; but, perhaps oddly, not by any French manufacturer, although the catalogue suggested that 'many foreign governments have now recourse to French clothiers for the equipment of their troops'.

Tait & Co received a bronze medal for their exhibit, but this was perhaps not particularly significant since no fewer than five gold, seventy-seven silver and one hundred and twelve bronze medals were awarded in Class 35, together with one hundred and eighty-eight honourable mentions: almost four hundred awards shared between a little less than one thousand exhibitors in the class! Monsieur A Dusantoy of France, himself an army clothier, was President of the jury which judged Class 35.

The jury's report remarked that, although England's external clothing trade was greater than that of France, England hardly exhibited anything, and nothing which merited a mention apart from a few uniforms exhibited by Tait & Co; a display rather too limited to do justice to the importance of the firm's business.

The report noted that Mr Tait 'who is very well known – mainly for the manufacture of uniforms' had set up in Limerick vast workshops, in which the most powerful and comprehensive equipment had been installed. However, the report went on to remark that the wages paid to Tait & Co's workers 'appear to be sufficient for Ireland, but would certainly not be proportionate to the material needs of a worker in France'.

Tait himself was Vice-President of the jury which judged Group VI, Class 57, Apparatus and Processes for Sewing and for Making-up Clothing, which will have afforded him an excellent opportunity to study the methods being used by other clothiers. However, since the catalogue said that 'one of the most important improvements which are now being made in the construction of sewing machines consists in working them by steam', which Tait had been doing since 1856, he may not have found much to learn.

Interestingly, W F Thomas & Co, in an advertisement in the catalogue, said that 'the clothing for nearly the whole of the British Army' was then made by their machines, not only by Tait but also at the Royal Army Clothing Factories at Pimlico and Woolwich. The advertisement also revealed that 'an extensive firm in Paris employs nearly 800' Thomas machines: M. Godillot perhaps?

William Gladstone, in 1867 out of political office, was Vice-President of the jury for Group III, Class 17, Porcelain, Faience and other Luxurious Pottery. It is tempting to speculate that he and Tait may have met during the course of the Exhibition and found common ground in their enthusiasm for the disestablishment of the Irish Church; eventually achieved by Gladstone in 1869.

The Tait token

At about this time, Tait issued a bronze token. It was about four centimetres in diameter and, unusually, had a scalloped edge.

One side bore what was presumably intended as a representation of the castle which forms the Arms of Limerick Corporation, surrounded by the words 'PROSPERITY TO THE TRADE OF LIMERICK'. The other side had in its centre the words 'ARMY CLOTHIERS' surrounded by the words 'PETER TAIT & Co + LIMERICK'.

It is not known how or when Tait used the token, which is of a kind usually issued by a manufacturer for advertisement, but perhaps it was made for the Paris Universal Exhibition.

The tokens are rarely found now, which suggests the possibility that, whatever their purpose, few were ever made.

An order from Prussia

On 6 May, *The Times*, quoting the *Army and Navy Gazette*, reported, with some reservations, that the Prussian Government had ordered 300,000 suits of clothing for their soldiers. Very nice if it were true, but it sounds as though the news had become exaggerated in the telling.

An official visit to the army clothing factory

In June, Chief Justice Monahan and Judge George, accompanied by Alderman Quinlivan, the High Sheriff of the City, paid a visit to the army clothing factory. They were shown over the factory by Thomas Hamilton; first the machine room, where seven or eight hundred women were at work, then the pressing, cutting and other rooms where the different operations were being carried out. They also saw a new button hole machine, which cut and sewed button holes in one operation. Although they were told that there were about 1,500 people employed in the factory altogether, it is difficult to know how many employees there were from time to time; it seems to have depended a good deal upon who was doing the counting.[15]

The Limerick Athenæum

One of the local organisations which Tait supported with contributions over the years was the Limerick Athenæum, which had been opened in 1855 as a place where everyone, irrespective of class, religion or politics, could attend lectures and participate in free debate. In 1867 Tait was elected its President.

It is recorded that, in 1860, he had taken two hundred and fifty of the female operatives from his clothing factory to the Athenæum to see what was advertised as an 'interesting entertainment on mesmeric phenomena' given by a Professor Stone.[16]

Another unusual show was provided by Madame Card, who gave séances at which the audiences 'were highly entertained by her wonderfully clever feats of magic and the singular power she possessed over her subjects in demonstrating the beautiful science of Electro Biology'.[17]

It seems odd that Tait should have had an interest in these disciplines, if such they can be called, in which one person purports to have the ability to exercise control over the mind of another.

Breaking a transport monopoly

In July, Tait provided the *SS Elwy*, a paddle steamer, to ply on the Shannon between Limerick and Kilrush, from where could be reached Kilkee, a favourite resort on the Atlantic coast in Moore Bay. Tait's object was to break the monopoly currently held by Malcomson, the owner of the Limerick to Foynes railway, whose steamers the *SS Vandeleur*, from Foynes, and the *SS Rosa*, from Limerick, already served Kilrush.

On 3 July, the *Munster News* reported that the *Elwy* was about to arrive; saying that Lynch, Tait's 'energetic maritime agent, who left for England some time since, has all but concluded the purchase of a splendid boat. He had a trip to sea in her yesterday, to test her qualities of speed, etc. and if these are approved of, the sale will be completed at once'.

Although Tait himself was careful to say that he had 'provided' the steamer, he did nothing to correct the local and frequently repeated reports that the *Elwy* was new, had been bought by Tait, and was owned by him.

Perhaps Tait had intended to be the owner. It is interesting to note that he had approached the Church of England Life & Fire Assurance Trust & Annuity Institution (the C of E Institution) in June 1867 with a request for a loan of £25,000 to be secured on the freehold of 95 Southwark Street.[18] In the event, this proposed loan was not proceeded with; whether because the C of E Institution was unwilling, or because Tait changed his mind, is not recorded; perhaps the latter. And, if Tait had changed his mind, was the reason George Cannock's mining adventure in Glamorganshire, which had cost more than £31,000?

The *Elwy* had been built by T B Sneath at Rutherglen in 1866 and bought by R W Preston,[19] who had intended to run her between Liverpool and Rhyl in north Wales, which he did during the summer of 1866. Perhaps the route was not as profitable as he had hoped, but, whatever the reason, he evidently chartered the vessel to Tait, at least for the summer of 1867.

However, since Tait referred to his keeping the vessel on the Shannon if she proved popular, he presumably had the option of continuing the charter, or perhaps of buying the vessel, if he wanted to do so.

In the event, the *Elwy* returned to the Liverpool/Rhyl run in the summer of 1868;[20] Preston selling her in July of that year to a merchant in Manchester, who in turn sold her to Turkish owners in Constantinople.[21]

The *Elwy* was probably originally conceived as a blockade runner. She was a paddle steamer with two stacks, unusually standing abreast of each other, 198 feet in length and 19 feet in breadth, very fast - capable of 20 knots - and of very shallow draft. She had a flush deck, running fore and aft, and a hurricane deck between her paddle boxes on which, it was said, 200 persons could easily stand at a time.

Below, there was a grand saloon, a dining saloon, a ladies' cabin, a hold for luggage, and a fore cabin for third class passengers. Her furnaces consumed about a ton of coal an hour when she had full steam up.

The *Elwy* arrived from Liverpool and anchored off Kilrush at midnight on Sunday 7 July. The *Munster News* reported her arrival in the city docks the following morning in enthusiastic terms -

> Her coming was anticipated, and the river edge of the Floating Docks was crowded with citizens of all classes ... Mr Harris's Mill ... was gaily decorated with Union Jacks, the National flag, Trades Banners and other colours, [she] came to anchor abreast of the Docks, ... the crowds on shore cheered, and the *Elwy* received a more enthusiastic reception than any steamer that ever came to the port before.

A letter from Tait on the subject of the *Elwy* appeared in the local papers on 9 July -

Dear Sir,

To provide adequate accommodation for the passenger traffic to Kilrush, and supply a want long felt and expressed by the citizens of Limerick, in not having a fast steamer on the Lower Shannon, I have provided the steamer Elwy, which arrived yesterday from Liverpool.

Before I came to the determination of placing this boat on the Shannon, I, at the request of very many of the citizens of Limerick, in company with a deputation from the Corporation, waited last year on the Directors of the Limerick and Foynes Railway Company, and subsequently on the chairman, Mr Malcomson, with a view to induce them to meet the wishes of the citizens in this matter, but I regret to say, I was unsuccessful in my attempt to prevail on them, either to reduce the fares, or provide the needful accommodation.

While I personally entertain a very high regard for Mr Malcomson, a gentleman of whom Ireland may be justly proud, I very much regret the refusal which has obliged me to start the Elwy, not indeed to create an opposition line, but simply to enable my fellow citizens in a reasonable time, and at moderate charges, to enjoy the beauties of our noble river, and convey their families to our far famed watering place Kilkee.

Having thus given my reason for establishing this line, and provided a steamer, which, I am happy to find, meets with general approbation, I have done my part in the matter, and it now remains for the citizens of Limerick to prove, by their constant steady support of the Elwy, whether the want I have supplied has been real or supposed.

I have the honour, to remain, dear sir,

Yours very truly

PETER TAIT,

Mayor.

The vessel was under the command of a Capt Jevons when she arrived and he remained in command following her return to Rhyl; suggesting that Tait had chartered the vessel with her crew.

And on 11 July, the *Limerick Chronicle* said that Mr Malcomson had to some extent been brought on his knees, for he had reduced the rates between Limerick and Kilrush both by the Foynes railway and the *Vandeleur,* and also by the *Rosa* direct, but that such reduction had come too late, it was not made when requested by Tait; it was because he had started in opposition that Malcomson had reduced the charges. The paper urged the public to support the *Elwy,* suggesting that if she were to be taken off the river tomorrow, the rates on the railway and on the *Vandeleur* and the *Rosa* would at once be raised.

Throwing the Dart

Two days after the arrival of the *Elwy*, Tait invited the Members of the Council, the heads of the public departments in the city, and a few private friends to accompany him on board the vessel for the ceremony of 'Throwing the Dart'. This curious ceremony dates from the establishment of Limerick Corporation in the twelfth century. It is performed by the Mayor in his capacity as Admiral of the Shannon and confirms his suzerainty over the waters up river of the farthest point to which he can throw a dart from a point a little beyond Scattery. Although required to be performed every three years, the ceremony had largely fallen into abeyance. Before 1867, it last took place in 1854, and since then has, I believe, taken place only once, in 1956.

The day appointed by Tait, 10 July, was all that a summer's day should be; the sun shone from an almost cloudless sky, and there was sufficient breeze to prevent the day becoming too hot. The *Elwy* left the Dock at about noon. The band of the County of Limerick Militia was on board and played a selection of mainly Irish and Scottish airs throughout the day. Malcomson's *Rosa* had started for Foynes nearly an hour before the *Elwy* sailed, but, before Foynes was reached, the *Rosa* was overhauled by the *Elwy*; the band playing 'The girl I left behind me' as the vessels passed. The *Elwy* called at Kilrush to take on more guests, before heading for Scattery. The Mayor, when the appointed spot was reached, took a large and handsome bow, made of lancewood, and shot successively three silvered arrows towards the ocean. In accordance with tradition, the shooting of each arrow was accompanied by the discharge of a cannon, so that Neptune should have audible as well as visible evidence of the suzerainty of the Admiral of the Shannon.

This done, there was the inevitable repast, as inevitably provided by Mrs Lynch of the George Hotel; perhaps she was the only caterer in Limerick at that time. Inevitably too, there were toasts and speeches. One of the Councillors proposed the toast of the Lady Mayoress and referred in so doing to her many amiable qualities, her gentle, affectionate disposition, her cordial hospitality to all who visited her, and the general respect in which she was held by every class. Otherwise little new or significant seems to have been said.[22]

However, the report of the proceedings in the *Munster News* of 13 July included an interesting comment. In connection with the halt at Kilrush, it said that the rumour ran that Tait proposed establishing a branch of his business there, where female and other hands were numerous, in extensive premises which, it was said, he proposed to purchase. The paper went on to say that 'Extensive but unoccupied stores were pointed out at the end of the town, and if a fair tender would be accepted for these, little doubt was entertained that the busy hum of manufacturing industry would before long be heard within them'.

Grand visions

Then, on the 16th, only a few days after the ceremony of 'Throwing the Dart' had taken place, Tait was himself entertained to a banquet on board the *Elwy*, by a number of eminent citizens; Justices, Councillors and others. The vessel on this occasion sailed beyond Scattery, where she dropped anchor for dinner to be served by Mrs Lynch again, while the same band played. Eugene O'Callaghan, who had proposed the toast of Mrs Tait earlier in the week, gave the health of Tait on this occasion, to which Tait replied at some length. He said, inter alia – [23]

> I cannot tell you how gratified I feel at the interest already manifested in this ship - I know I have to lose money in sustaining her for your benefit, but that I do not value in the least, if you continue to sustain her, and show you appreciate the accommodation she affords. I trust it will never be said that you failed in encouraging any effort made to improve the trade of your port.
>
> This one may lead to results far greater than you can possibly anticipate - this may open a source of revenue, of which you can have no notion. It may, for instance, direct that fruitful stream of traffic, tourist visitors, more frequently to our neighbourhood; they may be induced to spend a little of their time from the Rhine and other Continental places of attraction, in viewing the beauties of the majestic Shannon - beauties of scenery that extend to its confluence with the sea - that are to be found as well along the banks of its low waters, as on its upper. When Providence

gave us such a river as this, why should we not do all we can to utilize it? Why should we not do all in our power to make it as celebrated as a commercial highway, as Nature has done to make it the Queen of British Rivers?

I ask, ought we not shrink into ourselves with shame if we did not embrace the opportunity, small as it is, which is offered us in this vessel of doing something for our river. This is probably only the infancy of a great project, for if Providence sustains me in life and strength, I hope to be at the head of a Steamship Company which will be second to none in the world, and when the Shannon which has been allowed to remain so long uncultivated, shall bloom forth and blossom like a rose, I shall then indeed feel great pleasure in receiving your congratulations, and shall have an opportunity of entertaining you on board a vessel far different and superior to this. This vessel is the best that can be had for the purposes she is now engaged in, but before many months have passed I hope you will see one of another class and for another purpose floating on the Shannon.

I do not usually indulge in vain hopes, but I believe from what I see going on around me, that a better state of things is rising up, not alone for Limerick, but for the entire country. I believe the dark clouds that have so long obscured our commercial horizon are passing away, and that the dawn of prosperity is not far distant. I refer to Limerick again as a justification of what I assert, and I ask who, ten years ago, would imagine that we could take the lead in any branch of industry, no matter how humble, and that we could compete successfully at the greatest centre of competition in the world.

With hindsight, it might be said that this moment was to mark the end of the beginning, and the beginning of the end, for Tait.

The dangers ahead

As Walter Bagehot was later to observe, many traders, like Tait, supposed that the prosperity they saw about them would last and that it was only the beginning of a greater prosperity. But it was to prove a false dawn, as the increase in business activity which it encouraged increased demand for money, which caused interest rates to rise. And those traders who depended on borrowed money were to find that they had to go on borrowing , in spite of the increased rates of interest, if they were not to permit their acceptances on bills of exchange to be dishonoured. Tait of course had been increasingly committed to borrowing substantial sums on bills of exchange ever since he had bought the Evelyn in 1864.[24]

Another steamer on the Shannon?

Then there appeared in the *Munster News* on 24 July a notice -

> THE TRADE OF THE SHANNON - The commercial public will be gratified to learn that the Mayor is about to place another steamer on the river to supply the passenger and goods traffic of the towns and villages on both sides from Limerick to Kilrush, of course both inclusive. Mr Lynch, by whom the *Elwy* was selected, left for Scotland to effect the purchase. The rates per ton will be reduced below those of the railway company, and the steamer will call at Tarbert, Glin, Caheroon, Foynes etc. No doubt need be entertained of a good fast boat being bought for the purpose. The Mayor would have, and Mr Lynch would choose, no other. The cost will not stand in the way. The *Elwy* will continue to run as usual from port to port without a stoppage.

Was this true, or was the report planted; to bluff Malcomson into reducing his rates to these destinations as well? Or, if it was true, was the intention overtaken by events? I have found no evidence which might answer these questions.

Tait elected Mayor for a third term

Somewhat surprisingly, considering how little Tait was now in Limerick, and how infrequently he had been able to attend Council meetings during 1867, the Council elected Tait as Mayor for a third year; a rare honour. But his installation on this occasion was not marked by the public enthusiasm of previous years, nor by the same demonstrations of support by the Congregated Trades. The High Sheriff, who invested Tait with the chain and robe of office, said all the right things, but it seemed as though the love affair between Tait and the city might be cooling.

The death of Tait's father

Although 1868 started well, with Tait's re-election as Mayor for a third year, only days after his installation his father Thomas Tait died in London of chronic bronchitis. He was 76. In what seems now an extravagant gesture, Tait acquired, at a cost of £22 10s, three adjoining graves, allowing room for twelve burials, in the then fashionable Kensal Green Cemetery in North London. In one of these he buried his father; the fourth and last member of the family later to be buried there being Tait's elder son Peter in 1902. Any dynastic ambitions Tait may have had were never to be realised.

A threat to Tait's pre-eminent position as army clothier

It has already been noted that, since 1855, Government contracts for army clothing were only awarded following competitive tender. However, in February 1868, during a debate in the House of Commons on the subject of Army Clothing Contracts, the Secretary of State for War was asked 'whether it was his intention, with reference to the contracts now about to be made for army clothing, to require that public tenders should be invited for the supply of each article'. In reply Sir J Packington said that 'he had given orders that the War-office should obtain patterns of army clothing, and invitations would shortly be issued for public tenders to supply the articles required'.[25]

The reason for this exchange is, in the circumstances, not clear, unless perhaps it had become the practice for only clothiers known to the War-office to be asked to tender, and the questioner wanted to ensure that a wider public should be given the opportunity to do so. In any case, the outcome of the tenders is not recorded and so it is not known whether, or not, Tait & Co maintained its previous position as the only outside contractor to receive orders.

A curious incident at the clothing factory

Also in that month, a curious but perhaps instructive incident occurred in the clothing factory at Limerick. It had evidently been the practice of the Rev Father Thomas Browne, who was the parish priest of most of Tait's workpeople, for the past five or six years to pay one or two official visits to the factory each year. He would go through all the departments of the factory, visiting and speaking to his parishioners. He said their spiritual interests might require it, and these interests could not be consulted so easily elsewhere.

However, Father Browne had recently gone to the factory for one of these visits, but had been told by Thomas Hamilton, who was of course now in charge, that there was a regulation forbidding visitors to speak to any of the workpeople and that he would not make an exception for Father Browne.

The clergyman thereupon wrote to Tait, who happened to be in Limerick at the time, and who replied that, as the other members of his firm were in London, he would, on his return there from Limerick, submit the matter to them for their consideration.

In the result, Father Browne was sent a letter not by Tait, but by Tait & Co, saying that, while they intended no discourtesy whatever to Father Browne personally, they had given distinct instructions that no persons, lay or clerical of whatever religious persuasion, could be permitted to collect money or give religious instruction in their factory, where any such interruption would, in their opinion, interfere with their business.[26]

This small affair shows a distinct shift in Tait's attitude. On past evidence it is difficult to imagine him avoiding personal responsibility, and sheltering behind the other members of the firm, in this way. Something had upset him.

Mayoral business

In April, Tait and his wife, together with other notables from both the city and the county of Limerick, were present at the grand ball given at the Mansion House in Dublin to HRH The Prince Edward, Prince of Wales and HRH The Princess of Wales, who were visiting Dublin for the Prince's installation as a Knight of St Patrick, which took place in St Patrick's Cathedral the following day.

Although Tait was not present at their meeting, the Members of the Council, later that month, petitioned the House of Commons in support of Gladstone's resolutions for the disestablishment and disendowment of the Protestant Episcopalian Church, which it was hoped would remove a prime sense of discontent among the Catholics of Ireland; the city and county Members being asked to give the petition their support in the House.[27] As already mentioned, Tait was an enthusiastic supporter of disestablishment and will almost certainly have had a hand in the preparation of the resolution.

And in October, at a meeting this time chaired by Tait, the Council resolved that the Fenian political prisoners had expiated their offences and should be released, and the Mayor and five other Members of the Council were chosen to wait on the Lord-Lieutenant to request the resolution's favourable consideration by the Government.[28] The Lord-Lieutenant declined to receive them.

Benjamin Disraeli had become Prime Minister for the first time in February 1868, following the resignation of Lord Derby, but in October 1868 his administration resigned. At the subsequent general election, to be held on 19 November, the main issues were the disestablishment and disendowment of the Protestant Episcopalian Church in Ireland and Irish land reform.

Tait was nominated for election as one of the candidates for the County of the City of Limerick.

Electoral malpractices

Elections in Limerick in the 1860s were very different from those we know today. It was said that they brought 'so much animosity, and such bad feeling between the parties, that even the better classes have really a horror of it when they hear of any probable dissolution of parliament'.[29] This horror was occasioned largely by the treating of non-electors and the hiring of mobs to intimidate electors, which had become the universal practice at parliamentary elections in Limerick.

The qualification for electors was very narrow; the occupation of property having an annual value of at least £4, and of course women did not have the vote. Each elector had two votes. There were about 2,000 eligible electors, of whom about one third to one half lived in the rural parts of the constituency; the remainder living in the city itself. The great majority of the electors were Roman Catholics.

The vote was not secret. The voter had to sign and hand in a written paper giving the name and address of the candidate that he voted for, and an accredited agent of each candidate was entitled to be present in the voting booth while the votes were being cast. Although the term 'booth' was used, this usually consisted of a room in a house with access direct from the street. In addition it was the practice for representatives of the candidates to wait outside the polling booths and accost voters as they left the booths, to find out for whom they had voted. There were only eight polling booths, one in each of the city wards. Electors in the rural areas had to come into the city to vote there. These arrangements together meant that, during the course of polling day, a running tally of the votes cast for each candidate could readily be kept.

Candidates did not put themselves forward, but were nominated by their supporters on 'nomination day', which was always two days before the day of the election.

Treating was done by friends of the candidates. They would provide money to non-electors to spend on the purchase of drink from publicans or small grocers to secure their votes; the latter having previously indicated that they expected to get orders from the friends of whatever candidates they were intending to vote for.

The hiring of mobs was altogether more sinister. Several hundred idlers, drunks and layabouts would be hired by each side, for about 2s 6d a day, on, or just before, nomination day. The hiring would be done by friends of the candidates; the candidates themselves not knowing anything about it, as it was thought objectionable in a candidate to employ the mob, and he never did. The mobs went about the city, frequently armed with bludgeons, and endeavoured to intimidate the voters into voting for the candidate they represented. This they did very often by choosing one house in a street, belonging to a known supporter of the opposing party, and breaking the windows, sometimes actually breaking into the house itself and destroying anything inside, in order to provide an example of what would happen to anyone else opposed to their man. And since it would be known how a voter had cast his vote, he would be subjected to popular indignation later, if he did not vote in a particular way.

Once a mob had been hired by one candidate, it became imperative that an opposing mob should be hired by the other side. The mobs then fought each other and that gave rise to great tumult and disorder in the town.

The mobs were, however, normally only active during nomination day and night and during the following day and night. Polling day itself was almost always quiet, the mobs seeming to understand that the law required that there must be no obstruction on that day.

On top of all that, electors had to contend with the very considerable influence, in favour of the Liberal candidates, wielded on their parishioners by the parish or secular clergy of the Roman Catholic Church, and in the rural areas the pressure exerted by the landlords and their agents on their tenants in favour of the Conservative candidates.

Although it was generally considered that the Catholic voters would not vote against the wishes of their priests, the activities of the mob hired by the Liberal candidates was intended to ensure that they did not do so. As well as encouraging the mob, Roman Catholic priests also engaged in treating.

The position in the rural areas was more complex. The Catholic elector was caught between following the advice of his priest and the wishes of his landlord. Faced with this dilemma, he very often gave one of his votes to each side. Voters in the rural areas also faced the prospect that the mob of one side or the other would try to prevent them from coming into the city to vote on polling day. They were therefore often brought into the town the night before polling day and kept in a safe house overnight.

Tait and Piggott nominated

In the case of the 1868 election, Tuesday 17 November was nomination day and Thursday 19 November was polling day.

Until a very late stage, it had been expected that the two sitting members, Maj George Gavin and Francis W Russell, both Liberals, would be the only nominations and that they would be returned unopposed. After all, Tait had earlier been asked by some of his friends to stand, had said he intended to do so and had engaged Mr J Ellard, the town clerk, as his conducting agent. But three weeks or more before the election he had told Ellard that, because of his business commitments, he had given up altogether his intention of standing and all preparations for his nomination ceased.

However, in the event, both Tait and Richard Piggott, an Irish Catholic Fenian and the proprietor of the Fenian newspaper, *The Irishman*, were nominated to stand against Gavin and Russell; a circumstance which, in Ellard's words 'sprang up in a very peculiar manner'.

Shortly before nomination day, a newspaper published in Cork appeared in Limerick and it contained an article by its Limerick correspondent containing very strong and insulting language about anyone friendly to Tait. This created such strong feeling among Tait's friends, who had previously accepted his refusal to stand and to allow the nomination of Gavin and Russell to go forward unopposed, that they convened a meeting on Friday 13 November to discuss the matter. At this meeting they decided to nominate Tait, without asking him at all, and to nominate Piggott in the same way as his running mate. The chairman of the meeting agreed with Ellard that he, Ellard, would act as conducting agent for both Tait and Piggott, but not until the evening of the 15th were the arrangements finally settled.

On the Monday morning, the day before nomination day, a large canvassing party for Tait and Piggott, composed of respectable electors, went into the streets; followed, out of curiosity, by a large crowd cheering and shouting, and making a general noise. Although the crowd following the canvassers was not an organised or paid mob, Mr J Murphy, Russell's agent thought it was, and at once set about hiring a mob on behalf of the Liberal candidates, alleging that they could not otherwise have gone out to canvass. As it turned out, the crowd following Tait and Piggott's canvassing party might as well have been a hired mob, since, on the appearance of that hired by Murphy, tumult, disorder, and the breaking of windows developed on both sides. The following day, nomination day, one of Tait's employees was killed when the Liberal mob surrounded the Tait Memorial Clock in Baker Place. The commotion continued until by the Wednesday afternoon the party canvassing for Tait and Piggott, and the crowd that was with them, had disappeared altogether; they were afraid to go onto the streets.

It emerged later that those canvassing for Tait and Piggott belonged to the Fenian party and were acting upon their own initiative in opposing Gavin and Russell. Neither Tait nor Piggott had any personal involvement; indeed neither was present in Limerick during the election.

On polling day the town was perfectly quiet during the whole of the morning, until about 1 o'clock, and during the whole of that time Tait headed the poll, if only by a small margin. But then a very remarkable change took place and there was a good deal of excitement. It was the practice for vehicles to be provided by the candidates to convey electors to the polling booths and these would bear election posters to show which candidate they belonged to. After 1 o'clock several of the vehicles bearing electors intending to vote for Tait were driven off the streets and a general system of intimidation went on.

It was thought that without this intimidation Tait would have maintained his lead, whereas Gavin, with 1,026 votes, and Russell, with 796 votes, topped the poll and were elected. Tait obtained 724 votes and Piggott 186.[30] Nationally, the Liberals under William Gladstone were returned with a majority of about 120.

Tait and Piggott had been an ill-assorted pair to find themselves fighting an election together. Their committees, canvassing parties, committee rooms, conducting agent, inspectors and poll clerks, in fact the whole of their election machinery, was joint. And yet, neither of them put forward any address to the electors.

Piggott's views were well known; they were those of the Fenians, but Tait's views were not known. Tait was not a Conservative and was not recognised as one by the Conservative party, although this was not made clear to the electors at the time. Murphy said that the great complaint against Tait was that he did not put forward an address. If he had put forward an address his principles would have been known - the people were not going to vote for a man who would not put forward any principles.

Ellard said that when Tait originally agreed to stand it was understood that it would be on Liberal principles, but that he was taken more on personal than on political grounds. He was generally so popular that everyone was speaking about having him as member; he was so energetic and active.

Mr J Spaight, who would have stood in the Conservative interest had the party felt there was any chance of success, said that Tait occupied a very peculiar position. A great many Roman Catholics voted for him under the impression that he would vote in religious matters in accordance with their views, although he never gave any indication himself how he would vote.[31]

That Tait should have allowed himself to be associated with Richard Piggott in the 1868 election shows, not for the first time, and not for the last, that Tait was a very poor judge of men. He repeatedly formed the most unsuitable associations.

And Piggott was undoubtedly an unsuitable associate for a man in Tait's position; even though Tait could not have foreseen that Piggott's chief claim to fame was to be as the forger of the letters, purporting to have been written by Charles Stewart Parnell, a Member of Parliament and the leading exponent of Home Rule, which were published by *The Times* in April 1887, one of which crucially implied Parnell's support for the assassination of the Right Hon Lord Frederick Cavendish, Chief Secretary for Ireland, and Mr T H Burke in Phoenix Park, Dublin, on 6 May 1882. Following his exposure by a Parliamentary Special Commission in 1889, Piggott fled to Madrid, where he shot himself.

Recriminations

Following the election, six of the electors lodged a petition against the return of Gavin and Russell, under the terms of the Parliamentary Elections Act, 1868, on the grounds of bribery, treating and undue influence.

But before that trial came on, an application was made in the Court of Common Pleas for an attachment against Tait's brother-in-law, William Abraham, and three others, for contempt of Court in publishing a placard holding out an inducement to come forward and prove bribery in the forthcoming trial. The application was refused by Judge Keogh, with costs. He was reported as having said, inter alia, that it was not unusual for the Government and others to offer rewards for information in criminal cases, and was bribery to be treated differently? He could not believe that money had been offered to induce persons falsely to say that they had been bribed.[32]

The petition itself was heard by Judge Fitzgerald at the end of January, but he concluded that the petitioners had failed in satisfying him that their case could well and properly be sustained. He said that no corrupt practice was proved to have been committed by, or with the knowledge and consent of, any candidate and that he had no reason to believe that corrupt practices extensively prevailed at the election. He therefore certified to the Speaker of the House of Commons that the sitting Members were elected.[33] Although it had been confidently expected by Tait's friends in Limerick that the trial would have produced the opposite result, the judge seemed to think that both sides had exerted undue influence; making it impossible to say that either was more guilty than the other.

Tait resigns the Mayoralty

Tait's credibility was inevitably damaged by the manner of his involvement in the election, and by its outcome. Whether or not this was the reason, or perhaps the excuse, for his next move one does not know. On 25 November, he penned a letter to the Council, in the following terms - [34]

Gentlemen,

I regret that urgent business in London will not admit of my attending your meeting on 1st December, as I intended to announce to you personally, what I now do in writing; my resignation of the office of Mayor of Our Ancient City; and at the same time to tender my thanks for the honor you have conferred on me by electing me to that office for Three Successive Years.

My time being so much taken up in commercial transactions, renders it impossible for me to devote the time requisite to discharge the duties of a Member of your Council. I have therefore not sought re-election to it, and cease this day to be one of your Number.

To the Burgesses of the Castle Ward which I represented, I beg to return my deep and heartfelt thanks for the kind consideration experienced by me at their hands.

I have also to offer thanks to the Officers of the Corporation and their staff for the efficient aid I always received in the discharge of their duties.

In conclusion, allow me to add, that I shall never cease to take a deep interest in the prosperity of our City and it will always be to me a pride, and pleasure to promote as far as in me lies, the welfare of Limerick and its worthy people.

I have the honor to be, Gentlemen,
Your obedient servant,
Peter Tait

The letter was read to the Council at their meeting on 1 December, and Tait's resignation was accepted. A nominal penalty of one penny was imposed to comply with the relevant Act of Parliament. Perhaps everyone had, by then, had enough of Tait, because there seems to have been no attempt to persuade him to stay, nor any expression of regret at his going.

Although Tait had attended meetings of the Council increasingly infrequently during his Mayoralty, he had been assiduous in presiding, as Chief Magistrate, over the Spring and Summer Assizes in each year. And, as High Sheriff for 1869, he was to attend both the Spring and Summer Assizes in that year also.

Tait receives the honour of knighthood

On 5 December 1868, the Lord-Lieutenant, now the Duke of Abercorn, conferred the honour of knighthood on Tait, in recognition of the services he had rendered to the people of Limerick.[35] It is probably true to say that for Tait this was not the least useful legacy of his connection with Limerick. In the mid-nineteenth century knights were fewer than they have since become, and enjoyed a correspondingly greater status than they do now.

And on the same day, Tait received from Sir Bernard Burke, Ulster King of Arms, a Grant of Arms - [36]

> Argent, a Saltire engrailed Gules [an ordinary in the form of an ornamented red cross of St Patrick], on a Chief of the second a Castle, on each tower an obtuse spire with a weather-cock, and on an arch over the curtain a Cross flory, all of the first. For Crest. Out of a civic Crown an Arm in armour embowed, the hand grasping a red Rose, slipped and leaved, all proper. And for Motto. GOD GIVE GRACE.

A most unseemly row

However, Tait's last act as Mayor was to give rise to a most unseemly, and well publicised, row.

The principal Mayoral chain of office, used on State occasions, and made of gold links, had been purchased in 1820. From 1822 it had been the case that some Mayors had added a gold roundel engraved with their name and year of office and, in later years, a note on the reverse of any particularly memorable event, or events, which occurred during their Mayoralty.

Without consulting the Council, what Tait had done was to remove from the chain the roundels placed in it by the first two Roman Catholic Mayors in order to make room for a larger medallion than usual to commemorate his own three year term as Mayor. This gave rise to a complaint by one of the Members of the Council. An exchange of correspondence did not resolve the matter and so the Council resolved that the roundels removed by Tait should be put back, and that Tait should be asked to replace his medallion by a roundel of the normal size. A copy of this resolution was sent to Tait, who replied as follows -

I have the pleasure to acknowledge the receipt of your letter, enclosing copy of the resolution of the Town Council, declining the acceptance of the memorial of my years in office to the civic chain, and informing me at the same time that their reason for so doing was its want of uniformity.

In reply to that resolution, I most respectfully decline to depart from the decision expressed in my former letter, as I still consider that the circumstances connected with my Mayoralty warranted the change, and that the medallion was an ornament to the chain, and was intended by me to be a compliment to my fellow citizens.

But as I have no personal feelings to gratify, I cheerfully accept the decision of the Council, and am quite content that the memorial of the services I have rendered, and am still rendering to the city, will be found engraved on the grateful hearts of the poor and working classes.

The Bard of Thomond had this to say –

Is Limerick's municipal chain,
Always with Mohawks to remain?
As if it was by fraud or bribe,
The heirloom of a rascal tribe.
Its prestige cannot be restored,
Since good John Mahony was ignored,[37]
A noble son of the old times, when
Limerick could show true gentlemen.
Long have its honours been disgraced
By scoundrels socially debased,
Scarcely three honest men were called
For every dozen rogues installed.

When princely Tait resigned that chain,
After three years' bounteous reign;
He added to its links enrolled,
A grand medallion of massive gold;
'Twas like his own majestic mind,
Noble and rich and purely kind;
But the Pharisees, never at a loss
His acts to controvert and cross;
To gratify their devilish spleen,
Tore the medallion from the chain;
And, with a slanderous attack
Upon his kindness, sent it back.

And so, to this day, the chain does not include any commemoration of Tait's Mayoralty.

A Deacon in his Church, Tait should have known and taken heed of Proverbs XVI 18: 'Pride goeth before destruction, and an haughty spirit before a fall'. The fall was not to be long delayed.

And perhaps anticipating the financial storm that was about to break over his head, it was about now that Tait formed a new partnership, Sir Peter Tait & Co, consisting of himself, Robert Tait and William Abraham, to take over the business of the clothing factory in Limerick from Tait & Co; leaving that firm with only its shipping interests.

Not only was Cannock not a partner in the new firm, but nor was Logie, who, as we shall see later, was to take over the London end of the army clothing business in partnership with Thomas Nicoll.

14

Robert Tait: an Illicit Liaison
1866-1878

Ann Taylor was born at Burford in Oxfordshire in April 1839, the fifth of the six children of Samuel Taylor, a cordwainer, and his wife, Mary.

Nothing is known about Ann until she had a son, Charles, who was born in Chelsea in London on 2 March 1860. Another son, William, was born towards the end of that year, but died early in 1861. The children's father was Benigno Gonzales Vigil, of Lima, who had been Secretary of the Peruvian Legation in London since early in 1859; a posting which ended in 1863, when he returned to Lima. It seems that Vigil was married but that his wife remained at home in Lima during the time he was in London.

It is unlikely that Vigil lived with Annie, as he knew her, but he undoubtedly supported her and Charles, and there is every indication that he was very fond of them both. After he left London in 1863, Vigil maintained a regular correspondence with Annie, who kept his letters. These letters have been passed down to Charles's descendants and they make fascinating reading.[1] Although not strictly part of the Tait story, the letters are germane as they tell us something of the background to Robert Tait's later involvement with Annie.

In 1863 Annie was renting 44 Sussex Street in Pimlico and in one of his earliest letters Vigil said that he was pleased to know that a Miss Ross was no longer in the house. He hoped that Annie would not let any of it 'to people of that sort'. It does not seem to have occurred to him that Annie herself was what he presumably meant by 'of that sort'.

Vigil was also nervous that Annie's existence might become known in Lima. She wanted him to address his letters to Mrs

Vigil, as she now called herself. But he said he could not do that, as the Postmaster in Lima was an uncle of his, who knew there was no such person as Mrs Vigil in London. Then, later, Annie must have told him she had another lodger and he was curious to know more - 'is he an old man, or who is it'. The following February he noticed that the address on the envelope of one of Annie's letter to him was not in her handwriting - 'who wrote it', he asked.

In June 1864 Vigil was posted to Buenos Aires. To get there from Peru, he sailed from Lima to Liverpool and then from Southampton to Buenos Aires. He spent a few days in London while in England and was able to see Annie. However, a letter which he wrote to her from Southampton reveals that he had found that she had been having an affair with a Mr Dine, whom Vigil thought had taught Annie 'to be lazy, careless, and a little more extravagant than is convenient for you. ... in fact the Annie I have found now is like a different person from my dear own Annie that I left when I went to Lima. I do not like the change and I hope that you will do your best to be again what you were before'.

However, in spite of this, Vigil continued to send money to Annie; £30 every three months, more or less regularly. Sometimes he sent a bill of exchange, drawn on a bank in London, together with detailed instructions as to how Annie should obtain payment; on other occasions he sent banknotes. The latter he cut in half to deter theft; sending one half to Annie, the other to her sister who lived nearby.

It was a paradox that Vigil expected Annie to remain faithful to him, notwithstanding that he could not ask her to join him in Lima, but was himself unlikely ever to return permanently to England to be with her. And he remained jealous of any other friendship that Annie might form. It was thus a continual worry to Vigil that Annie did not tell him how she spent her time. It was of course an impossible situation. With a wife in Lima, he could hardly keep his mistress there, nor could he have her living openly with him in his various postings; yet it was unreasonable to expect someone of Annie's age and temperament to be content to stay at home with just Charles for company. Something had to give.

However, in May 1865 Vigil wrote a letter to Annie which seems to indicate that she had told him that she and Dine were to be married. This Vigil appeared to accept with a good grace. Was it also with a sense of relief?

But, Vigil was not to get off so lightly. The marriage did not take place; instead, Annie turned up in Buenos Aires. We do not know what took place between them, but Vigil evidently persuaded her to return home. A letter written by him in December, which followed Annie to England, indicates that she had wanted Vigil to marry her, but he says that he 'cannot and will not' marry her, although without assigning any reason for this continuing refusal. He went on to say that 'After you deceived me (and you have done it twice) you have learned to be a little cunning and deceitful and I feel afraid that you do not love me as much as you say'; also that he had forgiven twice but would not the third time.

In reply to a letter from Annie following her return home, Vigil says, rather archly, 'I doubt very much what you tell me about your being in the way you say'. Was Annie applying yet more pressure, either to persuade him to marry her or in order to extract money from him.

Although it is not always easy to interpret Vigil's letters, it is likely that it was not until much later that he eventually revealed to Annie that he was already married. If Vigil's wife was with him at this time, it would explain why he sent Annie back to England and why he was desperately anxious that she should now remain there.

Annie, on the other hand, was determined to return to South America. Vigil wrote to her on 24 April 1866; not 'My dear Annie' as usual, but 'Dear Miss Taylor'. He said he was 'exceedingly annoyed by your last letter. I cannot understand how is it that you insist upon coming when you know it is so much against my wishes. I hope notwithstanding that you will stop there, as I feel determined to send you back to England immediately should you come'. Two weeks later, on 9 May, he wrote again to say that if she came he would have nothing to do with her.

Nevertheless, Annie did return to South America; to Montevideo where Vigil now had a posting. It is almost certain that it was on this occasion that she met Robert Tait. According to Annie, she was moving in a good position in Montevideo when she met Robert and he induced her to live with him and pass as his wife. She said that they left Montevideo and came to England; staying initially at the Grosvenor Hotel in London.[2]

We do not know Robert's version of the story but what Annie said is in substance quite plausible. Their meeting probably took place at about the time of the sale of the *SS Evelyn* in October 1866.

Unfortunately, there is no letter from Vigil to Annie between his letter of 9 May 1866 referred to above and a letter he wrote to her on 16 March 1867, setting out the terms on which he was prepared to continue to provide for her. He would pay her £10 each month as long as she resided in England and remained single, or under no other protection, and as long as he held a diplomatic appointment.

This of course did not suit Annie; she wanted a single cash payment, which Vigil refused; saying that she never knew him to be worth so much money! But he renewed his offer of £10 per month. Annie then allowed herself to be sent back again to England by the next boat, which sailed from Montevideo on 29 March, although not without Vigil having to pay her fare as well as her hotel expenses in Montevideo. By Annie's account, Robert Tait must have travelled on the same boat.

Annie continued to enjoy Vigil's promised financial support until the middle of 1868, when he wrote to say that he was out of official employment; adding that 'it is long since I believe that you have some other means to depend upon'.

Subsequently, Annie must have heard that Vigil's wife had died in Montevideo early in 1868, because she wrote to him again threatening to visit. She must have mentioned marriage again, because Vigil replied saying 'I do not and never did intend marrying you. I may marry somebody else in my own Country'. It seems very unlikely, in view of her latest liaison with Robert Tait, that Annie any longer wanted to marry Vigil and one is left with the thought that she was just making one last attempt to extract some money from the poor man before it was too late. And indeed it was later than Annie could have known.

Vigil had left Montevideo soon after his wife's death and had been posted to Chile as Minister there. He died in Chile about two years later.

There is nothing, beyond what Annie said, to suggest that, following their return to England, Robert either lived with Annie, or passed her off as his wife. However, he paid for her to rent a house, Oriental Villa, in South Norwood. She took it in the name of Benigno Gonzales Vigil and continued to call herself Mrs Vigil.

It was at Oriental Villa, on Christmas Day 1868, that Annie bore Robert a son; registered by her with the forenames Ernest William Tait. The child already bore its father's surname, but Annie evidently did not intend that there should be any doubt as to who was the father, although, as it happened, Robert never denied that the child was his.

On the other hand, Robert, perhaps wisely, was not a letter writer, unlike Vigil. As a result, we know almost nothing about the time during which Annie was Robert's mistress.

However, we do know that, perhaps because he was richer, Robert was also considerably more generous than Vigil had been. According to Annie, Stephen Phillips, Tait & Co's manager at 95 Southwark Street, paid her £30 each month and £100 when she wanted it, and she was kept in the best style, which included a servant.[3]

A curious survival is an account rendered, at Xmas 1869, to Robert Vigil Esq by Daniel Cornish, of Bagnall House, South Norwood, for Master Charles, totalling £7 19s 3d, made up of Tuition etc £7, Drilling 7s, Stationery 2s 6d, Copy & 4 Books 1s, Geography 3s, History 9d, Poetry 1s, Child's Guide 3s, and Grammar 1s. Whether Robert was expected to pay for this, or whether Annie met it out of her allowance, is not recorded.

Then three apparently unrelated events happened in, or in about, 1872, which one is tempted to think were actually in some way related to each other. These events were as follows.

Annie put in hand, probably in June or July, through a firm of solicitors in Montevideo, an enquiry as to the then whereabouts of Vigil. It was doubtless in reply to this enquiry that she learnt of his death.

Robert Tait had a fourth child, a daughter Blanche Edith, who was born in Burgundy on 2 October 1872. The mother was probably Harriet Young Harwood.

And, also on 2 October 1872, Annie made a Will, in which she appointed her 'friend' Robert Tait the sole Executor. She left her Estate to her son Charles, and in the event of his death, to her son Ernest. In the event of the deaths of both Charles and Ernest, Annie left the whole of her Estate to Robert. She directed that her plate and jewels should not be sold, but kept in safe custody for the benefit of whichever of the three potential beneficiaries should become entitled to inherit her Estate.

Annie was evidently unaware of Robert's liaison with the mother of Blanche Edith, since she made him her Executor, and potentially the beneficiary, of her Will; after all there were her siblings, and her mother was still living. A possible explanation of what happened is that Annie became ill and decided to put her affairs in order. If that was so, it was a false alarm, and there is no indication that she was not soon fully restored to health.

Robert, on the other hand, had a fifth child, Isabel Maud, who was born at 1 Hamlet Villas, Hamlet Road, Penge, in South London, on 23 August 1877. The mother on this occasion was definitely Harriet Harwood.

Meanwhile, on 8 May 1876, Annie had bought a house at 50 Rosaville Road, Fulham, for £350, payable in twenty-four monthly instalments, and on 10 October she attended an auction at Taylor's Depository in Southwark, where she spent £332 15s on furnishings. These, among much else, included an iron crib bedstead and mattress, and a bassinette. Had she perhaps found another protector, whose child was intended to enjoy these amenities?

Annie's last appearance in this story took place at Westminster Police Court in February 1878, when Robert Tait was summoned to show cause why he should not pay for the support of her child, Ernest. Annie gave her name as Annie Vigil and her address as 11 Shalcombe Street, Chelsea. She said that, two years before, Robert had begun to treat her coolly, and had formed the acquaintance of another lady. Annie said that, since then, she had subsisted on her savings and the proceeds of her jewels, and now, being destitute, was left to resorting to the Police Court for the miserable pittance of 2s 6d a week for the support of her child.[4] She made no mention of Charles, now eighteen, and presumably well able to make a useful contribution towards the support of the family. Neither Robert Tait nor Stephen Phillips appeared in Court and the case was adjourned for their attendance. At the adjourned hearing an affiliation order was made against Robert for the maintenance of Ernest.

Annie, Charles and Ernest continued to live at Rosaville Road, at least until after the 1881 census, when there was a Mrs Murry, a thirty-year-old widow, there as well. What eventually became of Annie is not known. On the other hand, both Charles and Ernest grew up and had fourteen children between them. They remained in touch with each other in later life, whereas Robert Tait seems to have faded out of the picture following his break with Annie.

15

The Head of a Steamship Company

1868-1870

On 12 July 1867, the *Limerick Reporter* included an item -

FIRST CLASS MAIL STEAMER FOR THE SHANNON - On the 1st of November next a first class Ocean Mail Steamer will be placed on the Shannon by the enterprising Alderman Tait, D.L.

And on 1 August the *Limerick Chronicle* provided more shipping news -

A new line of first class screw steamers will sail between London and several ports of commercial importance in South America; Rio de Janeiro, Montevideo and Buenos Aires. The manager and principal owner is the Mayor of Limerick, Mr Peter Tait who may now be ranked among the princes of the world.
The commercial relations between Great Britain and the several ports named are of the greatest importance and are increasing daily in magnitude; so this line has a career before it which we trust may be long and prosperous.
It is the intention of our Mayor, Mr Peter Tait, after a few months, to bring his vessels to the Shannon and thus establish a direct communication between our port and the South American continent. To the well being and future prosperity of our city this will prove an impetus, the magnitude of which we can have no conception.

This appeared to be confirmation of what Tait had said at the banquet given to him on board the *SS Elwy*, on 16 July, when he expressed his enthusiasm for the development of the River Shannon as a commercial highway and said that he hoped soon to be the head of a steamship company which would be second to none in the world and which, he implied, would provide the direct link between Limerick and the New World so dear to his heart.

Except that, in the event, the steamship company was to have nothing to do with Limerick or with Ireland.

The influence of Alexander Collie

It is not possible, on the surviving evidence, to say with certainty why this change of plan took place, but it seems to have been the influence of Alexander Collie at work.

In September 1864 Collie had ordered from Randolph Elder & Co a number of steamers. The first of these, the *SS Whitworth,* was completed early in 1867 and Collie approached Tait to see if he would be interested in purchasing the vessel; telling Tait that he, Collie, had originally intended to employ the steamers in the passenger and goods trade between Europe and the West Indies or South America, but that he had now abandoned the intention of working them himself.[1]

At the same time he arranged for William Every to furnish Robert Tait with plans of the *Whitworth.*

The purchase of the first two steamers

The result was that on 8 July 1867 Tait & Co entered into an agreement with Collie to purchase the vessel, by then renamed the *SS City of Limerick.* The purchase price was £30,500, which was to be settled by a series of bills of exchange maturing over the following two years. The bills were drawn on Tait & Co by Collie and discounted by him to enable him to pay Randolph Elder & Co. The vessel was registered in the name of Thomas Hamilton and the amounts due to Collie by Tait & Co on the bills of exchange were secured by a legal lien in favour of O Blair Graham and Every.[2]

The vessel was of 1,135 tons, 238 feet long and 32 feet in breadth and burnt about 600 tons of coal on each return voyage to the River Plate. She was fitted with accommodation for nearly one hundred first class passengers and carried a surgeon and a stewardess on each voyage.[3] It seems amazing that one hundred passengers, the crew, and the cargo, the propelling machinery and the coal, could all be fitted into such a small vessel.

Single fares were £30 per person to Rio de Janeiro, and £35 to Montevideo or Buenos Aires; children under 12, half price, under 12 months, free.

Few details survive of the comforts, or perhaps by today's standards the discomforts, provided for the passengers. Their cabins were equipped with iron berths 'of an unusual pattern', apparently made to the order of Robert Tait. The mattresses, bolsters and pillows were stuffed with hair, but in the dining saloon they used silver plated King's pattern cutlery.[4]

There was a good selection of liquor; hock, champagne, claret, sherry, port, brandy, whiskey, Hollands, gin, ale and porter. There were tobacco and cigars. Rum, in gallons, was presumably for the crew. Two kinds of bread were available on board, cabin bread for the passengers and crew's bread; oatmeal was similarly distinguished.[5]

On a typical voyage from Buenos Aires, one of the *City of Limerick*'s sister ships, acquired later, brought back, as well as thirty passengers, 600 bales of wool, 50 bales of hair, 2,500 dry hides, 3,400 salted hides, 35 casks of glue, 63 casks of extract of meat, and 3,000 bags of coffee.[6]

The *City of Limerick* sailed for South America on 31 August 1867, carrying more than fifty passengers, thus inaugurating Tait's new line. She reached Rio de Janeiro on 25 September, before going on to Montevideo and Buenos Aires. On her return she left Buenos Aires on 20 October, Montevideo on the 22nd and Rio de Janeiro on the 31st; arriving back at the Victoria Docks in London on 28 November.

Meanwhile, on 8 November Tait & Co had bought the *SS City of Buenos Ayres,* a new vessel built by Richardson Duck & Co at Stockton on Tees.[7] As in the case of the *City of Limerick,* the purchase price of the vessel was raised by the discounting of bills of exchange drawn on Tait & Co by Collie. The *City of Buenos Ayres* left London on her maiden voyage on 14 November; not returning to London until nearly the middle of March 1868.[8]

Postal contracts

Tait & Co had already concluded a contract with the Postmaster General for the carriage of mails from Falmouth to Rio de Janeiro and the River Plate, which required the provision of four steamers for its operation, and he was intending to conclude a further contract with the Belgian Government for the carriage of mails from Ostend by the same service. One of the advantages of this would be that the vessels could bring cargoes of wool back from the Argentine, a major producer, to Belgium, one of the principal European markets.

Nevertheless, in the light of what Tait had said in July, the following report in *The Times* of 20 December 1867 must have caused some raised eyebrows in Limerick -

Mail Steamers to the River Plate. Messrs Tait, of London and Limerick, have just completed a contract for ten years with the Belgian Government for a monthly mail service between Ostend and the Brazils. The line will consist of four powerful steamships, fitted for first class passengers only, and sailing from London on the 14th, Ostend on the 16th, and Falmouth on the 18th of each month. The *City of Limerick*, the pioneer ship, sailed from Falmouth yesterday, at 4pm, upon her second voyage and she will be followed in succession by the *City of Buenos Ayres*, the *City of Brussels*, and the *City of Rio de Janeiro*. On the return voyage all the ships will call at Falmouth to land mails and passengers, and then go on to discharge cargo at Antwerp and in London.

The Ambassador in Brussels, Lord Howard de Walden, gave the news to Lord Stanley at the Foreign Office in London - [9]

My Lord,

The Belgian Government have made arrangements with Messrs Tait of Limerick for the conveyance of mails monthly to & from Rio de Janeiro & La Plata. The mails are to be taken up and delivered at Ostend.

Alderman Peter Tait who came over to negotiate the terms of the Contract preferred the port of Ostend to that of Antwerp.

I fear that this is a mistake, at least for the homeward bound vessels, as the postal service is combined with the carriage of wools, wh. it may often be difficult to land at Ostend - the access to the port being frequently very difficult and dangerous for large vessels. The Government gives no actual subsidy to the Company; but they allow the whole of the sea portage dues & also a portion of the rates for land transport, whether on letters originating in Belgium or in transit from other countries. The service is intended to come into operation next month.

The mails are to be taken up & delivered in combination with the La Plata service already established by H M's Post Office with Messrs Tait.

The periods as at present indicated are the 16th of the month from Ostend & the 1st from Monte Video, and the vessels are to touch at Falmouth on both the outward and homeward voyage.

The Ambassador's advice about the use of Ostend was followed by Tait, and the vessels used Antwerp instead. But Antwerp was further from London than Ostend.

Notwithstanding this latest development, it must surely have been Tait's original intention that his steamers should also call at Limerick on their voyages to and from the River Plate; he had allowed plenty of extra time for this in the schedules agreed with the Post Office. But some of that extra time would now be taken up by the inclusion of Antwerp in the schedules. Was that why Limerick was not included, or was it perhaps because Collie, who was after all putting up the money in the form of discounted bills of exchange, was more realistic than Tait and foresaw that there would not be a sufficient number of passengers, or a sufficient amount of cargo, to make the call at Limerick worth while? And whereas the inclusion of Antwerp still allowed direct passenger sailings from Falmouth to the River Plate, the inclusion of Limerick would have meant the vessels having to call there between those two places. This would have extended the length of the voyages considerably and been less attractive for passengers.

The purchase of a third steamer

Apart from his new contract with Belgium, Tait still needed two more steamers to maintain the schedule called for by his contract with the Post Office.

Another of the steamers which Collie had ordered from Randolph Elder & Co in 1864, but which he said he no longer wanted to employ himself, was the *City of Brussels.* This was nearing completion in November 1867 and Collie entered into negotiations with Tait & Co for her sale to them. The outcome was that, in December, Tait & Co agreed to purchase the vessel for a price which was eventually settled at £34,000, although Collie was to 'take £10,000 interest in the steamer or an approximation to that amount in 64ths of the steamer'.[10] But on this occasion management and control of the vessel was to be with Tait & Co. and not with Collie.

Payment by Tait & Co for their share was to be made in amounts of not less than £3,000 quarterly, dating from the first sailing of the vessel; but the whole amount was to be repaid, in any event, by 1 January 1870. Yet again, these amounts were found by the discounting of bills of exchange drawn on Tait & Co by Collie.

Provision was made in the contract for what was to happen if Tait put the shipping line into a newly formed company.

The *City of Brussels* was completed by Randolph Elder on 5 March 1868 and on the 14th she sailed for Antwerp from London.[11]

A gala in Antwerp

Tait then put on the last great show of his career, a lunch on board the *City of Brussels* at Antwerp, on St Patrick's Day, Monday 17 March 1868, to mark the formal inauguration of the new mail service between that port and South America. And Tait really excelled himself.[12]

The vessels in the port were gaily decked out in honour of the occasion and at noon a salute of nineteen guns announced the arrival of the guests, while the band played the national anthems of Britain and Belgium.

Tait had been presented to the King of the Belgians when he was negotiating the mail contract, and had hoped that he would be present at the inauguration ceremonies. Instead he was represented by Lieut-Gen Baron Goethals, who attended with his staff.

The other principal guests were -

General Pletinckx, Military Commander of the Province of Antwerp
Baron Lambermont, Secretary for Foreign Affairs
M.Kissel, Chief of Division of Marine in the Foreign Office
M. Bidant, Secretary General for Public Works
M. Fassaux, Director General of Railways
M. Bronne, Director of Postal Service
M. Andre and M. Gife, Inspectors of Postal Service
M. Adam, Director General of Customs

M. Fisca, Inspector General, and M. Van Roost, Director, of Customs
His Excellency Marquis Lisbon, Brazilian Minister and the Secretaries of Legation
M. Moriero, Brazilian Consul General
Mr Percy Ffrench and Mr Egerton, Secretaries of British Legation
Mr Grattan, British Consul General at Antwerp
M. Emile Pecher, Brazilian Consul at Antwerp
M. Eduard Pecher, Belgian Consul General at Rio de Janeiro
M. Van den Eyndt, Argentine Consul, and M. Jean Mants, Vice-Consul
M. Coppenrath, Montevidean Consul
M. Victor Lynen, Chilean Consul General
Baron Ferwangue, Portuguese Consul General
M. Bruynseraide, Vice President of Chamber of Commerce
M. Cateaux Wattel, President of Tribunal of Commerce
Mr Mulhall, Editor of the Buenos Ayres Standard

It is clear that Tait's new shipping line was being taken very seriously indeed.

Lunch was laid out in the saloon for eighty persons. The menu, as ambitious as the guest list, was -

Huîtres d'Ostend
Potage à la Printanière Royale
Bouchée à la Reine
Saumon à la Chambord
Sole Matelote à la Normande
Filet de Bœuf aux Pommes Duchesse
Jambon d'York aux Épinards
Dindonneaux Truffes sauce Périgueux
Côtelettes d'Agneau aux Pointes d'Asperges
Aspic de Foie Gras
Topinambour à la Hollandaise et Petit Pois à la Française
Galettes d'Amérique
Bécasses et Bécassines
Salade de Laitue

Unfortunately there is nothing in the record to say what was drunk with all this food. However, after lunch no less than fifteen toasts were drunk, and as many speeches made, before the company retired to the quarter deck for coffee and cigars.

And at 5pm the *City of Brussels* weighed anchor; those of the guests not sailing with the vessel following in the Government steamer for about three miles down river before taking leave of the vessel with three hearty cheers.

The purchase of the fourth and last steamer

For the monthly sailings in April and May 1868, Tait chartered vessels; the *SS Meander* and the *SS Union* respectively. Then in September he bought, at a cost of £33,500, a fourth steamer, the *City of Rio de Janeiro,* a sister ship of, though slightly larger than, the *City of Limerick* and the *City of Brussels,* also built by Randolph Elder & Co.[13] Yet again, the purchase price of the vessel was found by the discounting of bills of exchange drawn on Tait & Co by Collie. These bills of exchange, as also those drawn for the purchase of the three other vessels, were never met, but repeatedly renewed. Thus the cost of the vessels to Tait & Co remained as an outstanding debt, greatly added to by the cost of discounting the bills.

The formation of a company to take over the shipping line

Even before Tait bought the *City of Limerick,* it had been his intention that a new joint stock company should be formed and floated on the Stock Exchange, to purchase his projected shipping line from him and to enable him to pay for the steamships, which, by the time they were all bought and fitted out, were to cost him about £151,000 [*about £6,650,000*].

To this end, in June 1868, Tait & Co entered into an agreement with a company promoter, Gendall Wilmot, for the formation of a company with a nominal capital of £200,000 in 10,000 shares of £20 each.

The agreement provided that the company would buy the four '*City*' steamers, together with all the furnishings and stores on board, at their original cost to Tait & Co; also that the company would purchase a transfer of the Belgian postal contract for £10,000, with the proviso that if, within two years, the profits payable to the shareholders should amount to 9%, Tait & Co would be paid a further £5,000.

£50,000 of the total purchase price of £161,000 was to be satisfied by the issue to Tait & Co of 2,500 shares credited as fully paid up; the balance of £111,000 to be paid in cash in four equal instalments, the first following the allotment of the shares and then at intervals of four, eight and twelve months thereafter.[14]

But there was a sting in the tail; the company's ability to pay the cash of £111,000 was dependent upon at least 5,550 shares, over and above the 2,500 shares to be issued to Tait & Co, being taken up by the public. Although Wilmot no doubt assured Tait that there was ample margin for error, had Tait learned nothing from Cannock's mining adventure in Glamorganshire?

For good measure, Robert Tait was to be the Manager of the company for five years at a salary of £1,000 per annum and the company was to use 95 Southwark Street as its office, at a rent of £500 per annum.

Even if all had gone well, which was not to be the case, these arrangements left Tait & Co with a substantial debt, as the four steamers had been bought with borrowed money, which still had to be repaid and for which Tait needed cash, not shares.

And although Tait was to become chairman of the proposed company, control would effectively rest not with Tait & Co, as holders of only 25% of the shares, but with the holders of the remaining 75%; not quite the same thing as Tait's dream of being the head of a steamship company. Collie, to whom Tait owed the money raised on the bills of exchange, was the one who would in reality be the head of the steamship company.

However, on 1 July 1868 The London, Belgium, Brazil and River Plate Royal Mail Steam Ship Company, Limited (the Steamship Company) was duly incorporated and adopted the agreement between Wilmot and Tait.

Tait became the chairman, and William Every became a director on 10 February 1869 in recognition of Collie's financial interest in the company's steamships. Alexander Howden, a respected ship and insurance broker, was a director from the outset until February 1869 when he resigned because he could not agree with Tait as to the management of the company, then in the hands of Tait and his brother Robert. Howden was re-elected by the Board in the following July, but at a General Meeting of shareholders his re-election was defeated by what Every was to refer to as Tait's 'fictitious' majority. Howden eventually rejoined the Board in March 1870.[15]

Patrick Lynch ceased to be employed by Tait & Co and was instead employed by the new company as Superintendent at a salary of £400 per annum.

The Steamship Company encounters problems

However, the new company did not get off to a good start. By November, only 3,390 shares in total had been issued, and that included 850 shares issued to Tait & Co for the property by then transferred to the company; out of the 7,500 shares available to the public, only 2,540 had been taken up.[16]

After that, although a further 900 shares were issued to Tait & Co under the agreement of June 1868, no more shares were taken up by the public. But, in order to give himself practical control at shareholders' meetings, the 'fictitious' majority, Tait had distributed 300 of the further 900 shares, in lots of 10 shares, among thirty friends and relations; an arrangement which gave him an extra 240 votes, because each shareholder had one vote for each of his first ten shares, but only one vote for every five shares held in excess of ten. This tactic was looked on with some disfavour by those members of the Board who were anxious to wrest control from Tait. However, they did succeed by January 1870 in taking control out of his hands and he was followed as chairman by Robert Fowler, a partner in the City banking firm of Dimsdale, Fowler & Barnard, and the holder of 125 shares in the company.[17]

Of course, the result of the poor response from the public was that the Steamship Company, and even more so Tait, were acutely short of cash.

Not only that, but, although Tait had agreed to sell the Belgian mail concession to the new company, and had agreed to do whatever was necessary to give effect to that, it was found there was no provision in the concession for its sale or transfer. When approached, the Belgian Government initially refused to consider any transfer at all, and, indeed, threatened to cancel the concession altogether. However, after protracted and difficult negotiations, which involved Every, Howden and others in visits to, and lengthy stays in, Brussels, agreement was reached and the concession was transferred to the Steamship Company.[18]

But an indication of Tait's own problems was the passing of a Special Resolution of the shareholders of the Steamship Company in June 1869 varying the agreement of June 1868 to empower the company to accept each of the steamships from Tait & Co, subject to a mortgage of £15,000; the purchase consideration being reduced by £60,000.[19] Not that this really altered anything; the company could not afford to buy the vessels at the originally agreed price as it had not raised anything like enough money.

Notwithstanding its financial problems, the company entered into a contract with the Postmaster General on 9 July for the carriage of mails to Brazil and the River Plate. This replaced the contract previously being operated by Tait & Co. Both Tait and Every guaranteed the due performance of this new contract.[20]

A crisis erupts

Then, only a week later, Tait & Co collapsed into bankruptcy and, following this development, William Emmens, one of the Inspectors appointed to represent Tait & Co's estate, was appointed a director of the Steamship Company.

But, apart from this, to outward appearances at least, things went on much as before.

Distractions

However, while the Steamship Company continued to lurch from financial crisis to financial crisis, there were times when the directors were beset by the more mundane day-to-day problems of running a shipping line.

In August 1868 the *City of Brussels,* approaching Montevideo, had been in collision with a small German ship, the *SS Teutonia.* The latter, which had lost her main mast and was leaking badly, was towed into Montevideo by the *City of Brussels,* which, however, had not suffered any damage herself.[21] The owner of the *Teutonia* eventually claimed £1,750 for the damage to his ship, but a compromise satisfactory to both parties was agreed.

On another occasion the *City of Buenos Ayres* ran down the *SS Bismarck,* another German vessel. The *City of Buenos Ayres* was arrested at the instigation of the *Bismarck*'s owners, as security for the damage sustained by their vessel, and was only released following an application to the Court of Admiralty in June 1869.[22] The owners' claim was eventually settled for just over £800, fortunately covered by insurance.

And cargo was sometimes a problem.

In January 1870 a London merchant shipped 300 packages of codfish, by the *City of Rio de Janeiro,* to Montevideo, for delivery there on or about 20 February, which was before the start of Lent. Although the vessel arrived at Montevideo by the due date, it could not unload there because the port was in quarantine. The codfish was therefore carried on to Buenos Aires, but not of course unloaded there.

When the vessel called at Montevideo on her return voyage, the Master did not supply enough lighterage to unload more than three of the packages of codfish; the remainder being taken on to Rio de Janeiro, unloaded there and then sent back to Montevideo by the company's next monthly sailing. That it was then past the end of Lent was not the only problem, for, perhaps not surprisingly, the codfish had become 'partly spoilt by keeping and being exposed to a warm climate'. The company agreed the owner's claim for compensation.[23]

Later on, the Northern Railway of Buenos Ayres Company shipped from London to Buenos Aires 26 packages containing all the parts of a complete railway locomotive. The Railway Company undertook to ensure that proper arrangements would be in place at Buenos Aires for the unloading there of the packages; one of which contained the boiler and its frame weighing 17 tons. The Master of the *City of Buenos Ayres* later described the wholly inadequate arrangements provided by the Railway Company for the unloading of the boiler out of the hold of his vessel. Disaster was only avoided by his insistence in putting bales of wool under the boiler, as lifting started, and before the tackle gave way, as the Master had foreseen it would. The boiler fell back into the hold and he reported to London that, if it had not been for the bales of wool, the boiler would have gone through the bottom of the ship. In the event, the boiler had to remain on board and was taken back to London. It was successfully unloaded on the vessel's next voyage, but by the Master and crew, with tackle taken from London for the purpose.[24]

The collapse of the Steamship Company

By the middle of 1870, still beset by financial problems, the directors of the Steamship Company had devised a scheme for the issue of preference stock. They had obtained promises to take a considerable amount of the stock, and, if the scheme had been carried into effect, it was believed it would have given the company a fair chance of success. Emmens, representing the Inspectors in Tait & Co's bankruptcy, supported the idea, which was approved at a meeting of the shareholders in August. However, it was opposed by the other Inspectors of Tait & Co's estate, although, as Every put it, no intelligible or consistent reason was ever assigned for their opposition. Emmens himself thereupon resigned not only as a director of the Steamship Company but also as an Inspector of Tait & Co's estate.[25]

One of the company's principal creditors, who supplied its ships abroad, had been at the meeting when the Inspectors' decision became known and immediately stopped the company's credit; following which the Merchant Banking Company, by now mortgagee of all four of the company's steamers, refused to allow them to put to sea.

There was no choice left for the company but to suspend business and sell the Belgian concession. This it did, to John Ryde, whose firm, Ryde & Co, carried it on until 1878, when they in turn put it into a newly formed company, the Belgian Royal Mail Company, Limited.[26]

Then on 15 September 1870 the Steamship Company was put into liquidation by the Court; William Every and Alexander Howden becoming the Official Liquidators. Although it was not until 1876 that the liquidation was finally completed, it was not particularly complicated, if only because, once the steamships had been sold by the mortgagees, there were hardly any other assets to be realised.

The Merchant Banking Company was first mortgagee of all four vessels, to secure the amounts payable on bills of exchange accepted by the Bank, of £15,000 on each vessel, together with the balance on the company's current account with the bank, and interest accrued. Collie had second and third mortgages on the

City of Rio de Janeiro to secure the balance of various advances he had made to the company.

The steamships were sold by the Merchant Banking Company for a total of only £76,500, compared to the sum of £151,000 which they had cost Tait, and at which figure he had agreed to sell them to the company in 1868.

Nevertheless, the £76,500 was sufficient to cover the sums due to the Merchant Banking Company and Collie; leaving about £12,600 over for the unsecured creditors.

The claims of the unsecured creditors totalled just over £19,000; on which dividends totalling 13s 2½p (or 66%) in the pound were paid. There was nothing for the shareholders.[27]

Tait & Co had received shares with a paid up value of £35,000 [*almost £1,600,000*] in return for assets transferred to the company. The other shareholders had subscribed a total of £50,800 [*nearly £2,300,000*] in cash for their shares. It had all been lost.

It was a double blow for Tait, because many of the people who had subscribed cash for shares were his friends or business associates, and it came on top of the bankruptcy of Tait & Co.

16

Bankruptcy and its Aftermath

1869-1872

The first the world knew of Tait's financial difficulties was the following paragraph in *The Times* of 26 July 1869 -

Money Market - City Intelligence
The acceptances of Messrs Tait & Co, Southwark, army contractors, have been returned. The debts and liabilities are large; but the prospects of assets have yet to be ascertained. A meeting of creditors has been called to deliberate on the state of affairs.

What had happened was that Tait & Co had been unable to meet, on their due date, bills of exchange drawn upon them by Alexander Collie & Co.

The firm's creditors met on 28 July and were given an optimistic report on the position. The total unsecured liabilities were estimated at £133,000 and the assets, over and above those held as security, were represented to be £202,000. This last figure included the value of the partners' private estates. It appeared that the firm was solvent; that there was simply a cash flow problem.

The creditors decided that Tait & Co's affairs should be wound up, but expressed the wish that the unfinished contracts should be undertaken by Sir Peter Tait.[1] Five Inspectors, representing the principal creditors, were appointed; their appointment being formalised by a Deed of Inspectorship executed on 23 December 1869 under the provisions of the Bankruptcy Act 1869.[2] This deed provided that the debtors, Tait, Cannock, Robert Tait and Logie, 'should conduct manage carry on and wind up the ... trade or business of the firm of Tait & Co' and also realise their own real and personal estates, including, in the case of Tait, his interest in the capital and property of Cannock Tait & Co, Lock & Co,[3] and Sir Peter Tait & Co, but under the direction and control of the Inspectors.[4] As already mentioned, Sir Peter Tait & Co had been formed by Tait in June 1869 to take over from Tait & Co the business of the clothing factory; leaving that firm with only its shipping interests. And following the formation of Sir Peter Tait & Co, Tait seems to have regarded himself as no longer a partner in Tait & Co.

Although it is not clear when the new firm actually took over the business of the clothing factory from Tait & Co, there is no reason to think that the changeover did not take place immediately. At the same time, it seems to have been arranged that Tait & Co should not only retain responsibility for the operation of shipping side of the business, but also take over the debts associated with the acquisition of the four vessels which had been sold to the Steamship Company.

Tait's reasons for taking these actions are obscure but he may have intended that by forming the new firm, and ceasing to be a partner in the old, he could avoid personal involvement in the impending bankruptcy.

It would be interesting to know what the remaining partners in Tait & Co thought about the arrangements.

However, for whatever reason, Tait failed in this intention and was treated for the purposes of the Bankruptcy Acts as a partner in Tait & Co and liable for its debts alongside the remaining partners.

Cannock Tait & Co, in which Tait, Cannock and Peter Thom were the partners, was of course caught up in the bankruptcy of Tait & Co because the shares in it of Tait and Cannock were part of their private estates, which had to be realised for the benefit of the creditors of Tait & Co. A meeting of the creditors of Cannock Tait & Co was therefore held on 26 October 1869 to consider the position.

The meeting was told that, even under the most adverse circumstances, the assets of Cannock Tait & Co would realise more than sufficient to pay its creditors in full; in which case there would be something left over for the three partners. Various ways of carrying on the business, as opposed to its liquidation, were considered as affording the most benefit to all concerned. In the event, it was sold as a going concern; the purchasers paying £20,000 in cash on completion of the purchase, the balance being payable in instalments over the following fifteen months. No record survives to show the total consideration paid.[5] Alfred Augustus James, of the firm of James, Edwards, Cash & Stone, was elected by the meeting as Trustee on behalf of the creditors and a deed was entered into on 1 January 1870, by which Tait, Cannock and Thom assigned their interests in the firm to James.[6] This assignment clearly created a conflict with the arrangements envisaged by the Deed of Inspectorship, which already encompassed the interests of Tait and Cannock in Cannock Tait & Co as part of their private estates.

A further deed was then executed on 29 August 1870, by which title to the assets of Tait & Co and of its four partners, which had not by then been realised, was transferred to the Inspectors as Trustees.[7] This deed seems to have had the effect of transferring to the Inspectors direct responsibility for the winding up, which the Deed of Inspectorship had previously given to the debtors themselves.

The Inspectors were Philip Ellis, cloth manufacturer, William Emmens, a director of the National Bank and of the C of E Institution, George Boulton Denham, pin manufacturer, James Harper, cloth manufacturer, and Henry Elworthy, serge manufacturer, but, following the death of Denham and the resignation of Emmens, James Harper's son, William, became an Inspector in their place on 10 December 1870.

It had emerged from the schedules attached to the original Deed of Inspectorship executed in December 1869 that the position of Tait & Co was far more serious than had been envisaged when the firm's creditors had met in July. In December the amount of the unsecured debts was estimated at £196,208 and the assets available for the unsecured creditors were estimated at £76,360; a deficiency of almost £120,000.[8] Unfortunately, no detailed lists of the assets or of the amounts owed to each of the creditors have survived. It is recorded, however, that the Harpers' firm, James Harper & Sons, were creditors for the not inconsiderable sum of over £9,700.

The unsecured creditors were eventually to receive dividends totalling less than six shillings (or 30%) in the pound.[9] Of this sum, about three shillings and six pence was paid out of the assets of Tait & Co, Sir Peter Tait, Robert Tait and Balfour Logie. The balance came mainly from the estate of George Cannock, after protracted negotiations which lasted until March 1872, although the bankruptcy proceedings were not finally concluded, and a final dividend paid, until well into the 1880s. As I have mentioned earlier, as late as 1885 the Inspectors initiated a further, unsuccessful, attempt to collect unpaid calls on the shares of the Glamorgan Iron and Coal Company Limited, for the benefit of Cannock's estate, and therefore of the creditors of Tait & Co.

Warning signs

Although the world at large knew nothing of Tait's financial problems until July 1869, others closer at hand should perhaps have become aware before then that all was not well.

The first straw in the wind came in June 1867, when it looked as though Tait was intending to purchase the *SS Elwy* and had approached the C of E Institution for a loan. Although this proposal did not proceed, it was renewed in September, when the C of E Institution agreed to lend Robert Tait £20,000 at 5% interest, secured on the premises at 95 Southwark Street. This loan was completed in the following March.

In March 1868, the National Bank required Tait & Co to furnish additional security for their overdraft in Limerick, although the amount of the overdraft is not recorded.

In October 1868 Tait borrowed £10,000 from the C of E Institution, secured on the Limerick factory and in January 1869 a further £7,500 was borrowed from the National Bank, secured on the premises of Cannock Tait & Co in Georges Street, Limerick. In the following June a further £2,500 was borrowed from the National Bank, on the collateral security of claims of £5,062 on the Canadian Government for the firm's May shipments of uniforms.[10]

On the other hand, it seems as though Tait had been taking some pains to prevent his bankers, at least, from seeing the whole picture. For example, in 1866 he had separate accounts with at least five banks; the National Bank, the Union Bank, the Munster Bank, the Provincial Bank and with Barclay Bevan & Co.

How had all this come about?

The part played by Alexander Collie

It came about because, like so many others, Tait had fallen under the spell of Alexander Collie.

Tait was undoubtedly ambitious, but until he met Collie, ambitious for his adopted country. Collie, on the other hand, had seen how he could turn Tait's ambition to his own advantage. He had shown Tait how virtually limitless sums of money could be obtained for almost indefinite periods by the use, or more accurately the misuse, of the market in bills of exchange.

Of course, it was inevitable that retribution would follow, as it did for Tait in 1869 and for Collie in 1875; but that was tomorrow's concern, not that of today.

Very intricate financial arrangements

Unfortunately, our knowledge of the dealings between Tait and Collie in the years from 1864 to 1869 is very incomplete. However, a broad outline emerges.

On the face of it, there were relatively few transactions between them which one would expect to find reflected in their books of account.

First, Tait sold uniforms to Collie during the American Civil War, but not until the middle of 1864. Second there was the *SS Evelyn* joint venture, but Collie submitted only one account of that, in October 1865. Thirdly there was the purchase from Collie by Tait of the *SS City of Limerick* and the *SS City of Brussels.*

Amazingly, although Collie had received some accounts from Tait and submitted some accounts to him over the years, no overall settlement had ever been made between them. Collie's solicitor said that the transactions between Collie and Tait exceeded half a million pounds in amount and that it was necessary for their comprehension to investigate very intricate arrangements and accounts. Which may explain why, with most of the evidence now lost, it is difficult for us to understand what went on.

What we do know is that the arrangements were so intricate that between March 1864 and October 1869 Collie wrote 278 letters to, and received 277 letters from, Tait, although none of this considerable correspondence has survived.

However, following Tait's bankruptcy something had to be done and Collie was asked by the Inspectors to submit an account of what he believed was then owed to him. This he did, but the Inspectors disagreed with many of the items included in it. As a result, they filed a Bill of Complaint against Collie in the Court of Chancery in August 1870, in which they asked that the account between Tait and Collie should be settled under the supervision of the Court.[11]

It is from the preliminary proceedings in this Case that almost all our knowledge of the dealings between Tait and Collie is derived, including the volume of the correspondence referred to above. These preliminary proceedings took so long that they were overtaken by Collie's own bankruptcy in 1875; being carried on by Young, his trustee in Bankruptcy. Although it looked as though the Case would finally come to trial early in 1877, it did not do so; nothing further being heard of it. Presumably it was settled out of Court, or perhaps just abandoned.

However, some of the Court records survive; principally the statements by each side setting out their version of events during the five years of their business relationship, together with summaries, but not the details, of the transactions during the period. It is perhaps not surprising that the two sides gave differing versions of events. What is disconcerting is that each side produced largely irreconcilable accounts of the actual cash and other transactions between them.

The records show that Collie's accounts included an item 'Amount at credit of Tait & Co for goods supplied, from 25 August to 10 November 1864, £41,571.7s.6d', which, subject to a small difference, was accepted by the Inspectors. I have referred to this in Chapter 9 in relation to the number of uniforms which I estimate were bought by Collie from Tait & Co.

The accounts also deal with Tait's purchase of his two-thirds share in the *Evelyn*, in payment for which he accepted bills of exchange drawn by Collie. These bills Collie discounted for his own benefit, but, when the due date for payment drew near, it was clear that Tait & Co would not have the money to pay them. So Tait accepted new bills which Collie drew on him and which Collie again discounted; passing the proceeds to Tait to enable the original bills to be met. But the new bills were for more than the original bills to cover the cost of discounting, which Collie of course charged to Tait. This process was indefinite. In 1869 Tait still owed Collie on bills of exchange for the cost of the *Evelyn.*

Unexpected items in Collie's account were charges in 1865 and 1866 totalling £14,646 in respect of the purchase by Tait of North Carolina Warrants. These had, of course, become worthless by then as title to cotton, but their payment had been guaranteed to the original investors by Collie and it was perhaps on this basis that Tait acquired them. Or did Collie make out to Tait that there was still cotton there? Like the *Evelyn,* the cost to Tait was settled by bills of exchange, which, again, were renewed again and again.

Then, in 1867 Tait bought the *City of Limerick* and the *City of Brussels* from Collie; more bills of exchange, more renewals. And because Tait could not pay for the *City of Buenos Ayres* and the *City of Rio de Janeiro,* Collie came to the rescue with more bills of exchange, which he discounted to put Tait in funds.

Fraudulent practices

And whenever bills of exchange were renewed, they were renewed in such a way that the new bills did not match the old. For example six bills, each for a different number of pounds, shillings and pence, but totalling £13,000, were drawn to cover a single maturing bill for £13,000 in June 1866.

This was to disguise from the bill brokers and the banks the fact that the new bills were simply replacements for the old ones. If they had known the truth, it is unlikely that either the brokers, or the banks, would have discounted the bills.

By July 1868 Tait & Co owed Collie over £60,000 [*about £2,640,000*] on current bills of exchange drawn on them by Collie. After that, cash was obtained, not only by further discounting of bills of exchange drawn on Tait & Co by Collie but also through the agency of the Merchant Banking Company, secured by mortgages of £15,000 on each of the four steamships which Tait & Co had agreed to sell to the Steamship Company.

The procedure was for Tait & Co to draw on the bank, in respect of each vessel, bills of exchange for £15,000, usually at four months, and which were guaranteed by Collie and which the Bank accepted. The bills were then discounted by Collie and the proceeds paid to the Bank, which credited Tait & Co's account. On maturity the bills would be paid by the bank, which charged the payments to Tait & Co's account. The bills would then be replaced by new bills for the same amounts, which, like the original bills would be discounted, the proceeds paid again to the bank which again credited Tait & Co's account. This same system obtained without interruption even after the transfer of the vessels to the Steamship Company, except that the bills were then drawn by the Company instead of by Tait & Co.

When the Steamship Company failed, bills for a total of £60,000 were still outstanding and, as already noted, Tait & Co had been left with nothing, once the mortgagees had been satisfied, except some worthless shares in the Company.

By 1869 Collie had charged Tait over £37,600 [*almost £1,700,000*] for discount on bills of exchange. And although the charges by Collie making up this sum referred generally to 'discount', which was payable to the bill brokers or banks who had discounted the bills, they also included a commission charged by Collie for making the arrangements; for example, in the case of each of the loans from the Merchant Banking Company which he had arranged, he charged a commission of 2½%.

No wonder Collie was able to tell William Every in 1869 that he did not need to charge the Steamship Company for guarantees given on its behalf by him in that year, because 'Messrs Collie & Co. had dealings with the firm of Tait & Co in 1869 which Messrs Collie & Co. considered sufficiently remunerated them for the risk and trouble of engaging in the said guarantees'.[12]

Collie's motives

What were Collie's motives?

First, there was the *Evelyn*, which was specially adapted as a blockade runner and of limited use for any other purpose. Collie made out that he was reluctant to sell a share in the vessel to Tait, but was persuaded by Tait to do so. Was this really the truth of it? Collie was committed to the purchase of the vessel from Randolph Elder & Co, the builders. But, by the autumn of 1864 the outcome of the Civil War was increasingly in doubt. Collie knew that, whereas the profits realised whenever a cargo was successfully run through the blockade had, earlier in the War, been very substantial, by 1864 they were little or nothing. It seems likely that Collie seized the opportunity to dispose of the *Evelyn*. He not only did this, but he charged Tait, for his two-thirds share, enough to cover the whole cost of the vessel to Collie.

Then what of Collie's sale to Tait of the *City of Limerick* and the *City of Brussels*? His motives here may have been more complex, even devious.

As in the case of the *Evelyn*, Collie was committed to buying the two vessels from the builders. He told Tait that he had intended to use them in the passenger and goods trade between Europe and the West Indies or South America. By coincidence, this was just the purpose for which Tait was in the market for steamships. But was it coincidence, or had Collie put the idea into Tait's mind in the first place?

Then what happened was that Collie, by his manipulation of the bill market, kept Tait in funds, albeit at great expense to Tait, but great profit to Collie, until Tait's projected shipping line should be established.

There can be little doubt that Tait's objective at the outset was to float the Steamship Company and unwind his commitments; the outstanding bills of exchange and the loans from the Merchant Banking Company.

But, by the time the Steamship Company was floated, even if the flotation had been a success, his commitments were too great to enable this to happen.

It looked very much as though Collie had created a situation in which Tait would have to cede control of the company to Collie. Collie had not only avoided having to pay for the steamships himself, but was on the way to becoming the owner of a shipping line in the passenger and goods trade between Europe and South America.

Did Collie attempt with the Steamship Company what Cannock seems to have attempted with the GICC; to become the mortgagee in possession? Both succeeded in that, but, although for differing reasons, found that possession, which had cost so much, was worthless.

The effect of the bankruptcy

What effect did the bankruptcy have on Tait?

The answer seems to have been, remarkably little; to outward appearances things went on much as before. Tait was not going to let a little local difficulty like a bankruptcy interfere with his public or his private life.

An exception was the firm of Cannock Tait & Co, which had been sold. The amounts due to the firm by Tait & Co had been excluded from that sale. These comprised, on a current account of normal commercial transactions rather more than £22,000, and liabilities on bills of exchange of some £25,000; the latter figure being made up of bills accepted for Tait & Co £11,616, and bills drawn on Tait & Co £13,300.

The bills accepted for Tait & Co were renewals of bills originally drawn on Tait & Co by Collie. But in 1868, when these original bills had to be renewed, Collie had told Tait that 'as the firm of Tait & Co was then losing its mercantile position' he required some better security than that of Tait & Co, if he was to agree to their renewal.[13]

As a result, Tait arranged for Cannock Tait & Co to accept the renewal of some of the acceptances of Tait & Co which were still running. This proved to have been a wise move on the part of Collie, because the bills were, of course, paid in full by Cannock Tait & Co, whereas had they been drawn on Tait & Co they would have had to rank for dividend with the other unsecured creditors. As it was, Cannock Tait & Co ranked as unsecured creditors of Tait & Co for the amount of the bills. This is unlikely to have gone down well with Tait.

New domestic and business arrangements

On the domestic front, in November 1869, the National Bank, which held the leases of Tait's residences, Mount Pleasant Lodge in London and South Hill House in Limerick, as collateral security for Tait & Co's overdraft, caused them to be put up for sale. Mount Pleasant Lodge was sold on the open market; Tait moving from there to Erina House in Lime Green Park, Putney, where the household consisted of Tait, his wife, their nine children and a general servant, Mary Eyan, aged 28, from Limerick. Tait himself redeemed South Hill House, with money borrowed from the banking firm of Brown Janson & Co, but after May 1870 the property was let, until he eventually sold it in October 1873.

Also in about 1873, Tait and his family moved from Erina House to Tingwall House, Poynders Road, Clapham Park, also in South London. Both these houses have long since disappeared.

The business of the clothing factory in Limerick, now carried on by Sir Peter Tait & Co, appears to have been relatively unaffected by the bankruptcy, although ownership of the lease of the factory itself had passed to the Inspectors, as Trustees of the deed of 29 August 1870, subject to the C of E Institution's mortgage. It is not clear, however, whether Tait's share of the business of the clothing factory, since June 1869 owned by Sir Peter Tait & Co, passed to the Inspectors as well.

What happened to the London end of the clothing business is not at all clear. Tait himself became the tenant of 95 Southwark Street, following its re-possession by the C of E Institution, and remained so until 1878.

Following the bankruptcy of Tait & Co, Logie went into partnership with Thomas Nicoll, who had been working at Cannock Tait & Co until 1869, trading as army contractors on their own account, but in 1879 they instituted proceedings under the Bankruptcy Act 1869 for liquidation by arrangement with their creditors. The circumstances which gave rise to this are unclear because the official record shows that they had assets of £6,000 and liabilities of only £4,000.

George Cannock, who said that the Inspectors had sold his bed from under him, was obliged to return to Limerick, where he worked as manager for the new owners of Cannock Tait & Co, until he was forced to retire in 1875 due to ill health. He died the following year, aged 67. His connection with Tait had ended with the bankruptcy in 1869.

Tait dispenses with the services of the Bard

Unfortunately Tait's relationship with Michael Hogan, the Bard of Thomond, was a casualty of the bankruptcy. Tait wrote to the Bard from his office at Southwark Street in London on 11 April 1870 –

Dear Bard,

I duly received your note and if you will call on Mr Abraham at the factory he will give you the list and my subscription, which I deeply regret to say I am unable to make five times as large which I should much have liked to do. Hoping that you may long enjoy health and happiness in your new home and wishing still to be favoured with contributions from your pen,

I am,

Dear Bard,

Yours very truly,

Peter Tait

Litigation over 'pressed leather'

Tait, who was not averse to a little litigation now and then, had successfully sued Laing and Irvine, cloth manufacturers of Hawick and Peebles, a couple of weeks before the bankruptcy, for breach of contract. He was awarded damages of £300 for their failure to deliver 60,000 yards of black tartan cloth, which Tait was under contract to deliver to the War Office.[14] Perhaps emboldened by this success, he became involved in a further dispute in 1870; with the firm of Nicholls & Co, shoe manufacturers of Thrapston in Northamptonshire, then the great seat of shoe manufacture. It appears that, towards the end of the war in France in April 1870, Tait had a contract with the French Government to supply them with 100,000 pairs of shoes, of which Tait had ordered 10,000 pairs from Nicholls & Co. After 7,750 of these pairs had been delivered, Tait discovered that they were not made in accordance with what he believed had been the agreed sample and would therefore not be accepted for use in the French army. What had happened was that the space between the inner sole and the outer sole of the shoes had been filled, not with a piece of solid leather, but with 'pressed leather'. This latter, which consisted either of small pieces of leather, or of paper, pressed together, was quite generally used in the manufacture of shoes, although it had the disadvantage that, if the outer sole became worn and let in water, the pressed leather became pulpy. After lengthy and highly technical argument in Court, a compromise was reached, under which Tait agreed to accept the shoes, but at a reduced price;[15] for sale later to some unsuspecting customer?

Mr H Lloyd QC appeared for Tait in this case, as he had in the earlier one. Linklater & Co had taken the place of Ashurst Morris & Co as Tait's solicitors.

Brown Janson & Co, of Leeds and London, had by now become his principal bankers.

Business as usual

It may have been the case that Tait was not going to let the bankruptcy stand in his way, but it seems remarkable that no-one else seems to have done so either. It was very much business as usual.

Indeed, it was reported that when Tait arrived at Limerick on a June evening in 1870, he was met at the station by a large circle of old acquaintances, who gave him a hearty welcome to the city. Shortly after nine o'clock, a number of rockets, Catherine wheels etc were exploded from the parapet of one of the houses in Georges Street, which was crowded by hundreds of spectators who had assembled to see the fireworks. The greatest enthusiasm prevailed.

It was also reported that the employment of a large number of operatives in Tait's factory, which was in full employment, was an important auxiliary to the trade of Limerick, which was, at the time, in a very depressed condition. Extensive orders had been received, which were estimated to keep a large number of hands in active employment until Christmas.

But, of course, the Steamship Company did not fail, publicly at least, until the September of that year.

By-election in Limerick

Then, in August 1871, Russell, who had so narrowly defeated Tait in the 1868 election in Limerick, died. A by-election was called for 20 September. There was no lack of suitors for the honour of being one of the representatives of the City of Limerick in his place. Isaac Butt , the Home Rule leader, was first in the field, closely followed by Tait, and then by Charles Barry, the Attorney General although without a seat in Parliament, James Spaight and Col C S Vereker. However, by polling day only Isaac Butt remained, to be elected unopposed; the others, although all of them professed support for Home Rule, having melted away when they saw the tremendous popular support accorded to Butt.

By the time Isaac Butt won the Limerick by-election in 1871, the Fenians, who had sought to establish a nationalist movement for an independent republican Ireland, had all but failed due to a lack of popular support for their cause. Butt, on the other hand, was the leader of what became the next phase of Irish nationalism; the Home Rule movement for the establishment of an Irish Parliament under a federal connection with the British Crown. In this aim he had the support of the Fenians, or the Irish Republican Brotherhood as they had become known. For this reason it was not difficult for opponents of Home Rule to suggest that its supporters had Fenian sympathies.

Tait, perhaps more than others, was susceptible to such accusations, because of his earlier involvement with Pigott in the 1868 election. But, more than this, Tait had attended, and spoken at, a banquet to Butt given in Limerick on 10 January 1872, which was portrayed by Butt's opponents as a Fenian event. In fact, the banquet had been given by the Limerick and Clare Tenant Farmers' Club in recognition of the services rendered by Butt to the cause of the tenant farmers in Ireland, by assisting in the passing of Gladstone's Land Act; an Act which gave tenants evicted, other than for non payment of rent, the right to compensation for improvements made by them during their tenancy. While these associations probably did Tait no harm in Limerick, they were to prove an embarrassment elsewhere later on.

Tait regains ownership of the clothing factory

However, Tait had other things on his mind in 1871. Negotiations were taking place, between the C of E Institution, the Inspectors, and Tait, over the future ownership of the clothing factory and the repayment of the Institution's mortgage of £10,000, which was still outstanding. The object was to find a way by which Tait could buy back the 1858 lease, which had been transferred to the Inspectors in August 1870.[16] The outcome was that at the beginning of October 1871 the Inspectors repaid the Institution's mortgage and then immediately sold the lease to Tait for £10,000. To enable Tait to pay for the lease he again mortgaged it to the Institution, this time to secure a loan of £5,000, at 5% interest as before, with repayments to start in October 1873.

As was the custom, the mortgage took the form of a grant to the Institution of an underlease of the clothing factory for a period ten days shorter than the unexpired term of the 1858 lease. The mortgage also included an assignment of the fixed and the movable plant and machinery. Although the Institution did not have to pay any rent to Tait, he remained liable to pay the original rent of £160 a year to John Westropp.

However, the mortgage deed contained two important provisions.

First, that Tait should occupy the clothing factory as the Institution's tenant, paying rent to the Institution equal to the interest on the £5,000 which he had borrowed.

Second, that, in the event of Tait's failure to repay the loan, the Institution could sell their underlease, in which event Tait was to hold the last ten days of the 1858 lease, which were otherwise excluded from the underlease, 'upon trust for the purchaser ... of the premises ... and assign and dispose of the same as such purchaser ... shall direct'.

Where Tait obtained the other £5,000 of the purchase price, which he did not borrow from the Institution, is not known, but it is likely that he borrowed it from Brown Janson & Co.

The annual dinner of the Royal Literary Fund

After his half-hearted attempt to stand again for Parliament in 1871, Tait seems to have maintained a low profile, in public at least, until 1872, when he accepted an invitation to attend the annual dinner of the Royal Literary Fund to be held on 8 May 1872 in St James's Hall in London. The Fund had been founded in 1790 to support aspiring authors. The annual dinner was a fund raising event; the backs of the menus being cheques for completion by the diners! The King of the Belgians was to be in the chair, and Tait had been invited as on the list of persons on the King's Book. The significance of the term 'on the King's Book' is not recorded, but it seems likely that it was a list of persons invited by the King, rather than by the Fund. Although Tait had been presented to the King when he was negotiating Tait & Co's Belgian postal contract, it is perhaps surprising, having regard to the circumstances surrounding the subsequent collapse of the Steamship Company, that he should not only have received, but that he should have accepted, an invitation to the dinner. However, accept he did, and, not only that, sent with his acceptance 11 guineas to become a life member of the Fund.

He also accepted a stewardship at the dinner, to which he also took two guests of his own.[17]

The dinner itself far surpassed even Tait's most ambitious efforts; consisting of the following seven courses –

Potages:	Tortue Claire, Tortue à l'Anglaise, À la Reine Jardinière
Poissons:	Darne de Saumon à la Montpellier, Truites Saumonées Garnies à la Royale, Buisson de Coquillages
Entrées:	Salade de Homard, Bastion d'Anguilles, Filets de Sole à la Mayonaise, Côtelettes de Mouton aux Petit Pois, Ballotine de Volaille à la Périgord, Oeufs de Pluviers à la Gelée, Salade à la Russe
Relevés:	Quartier d'Agneau, Bœuf Rôti, Bœuf Epicé, Poulet à la Printanière Rôti, Galantines de Veau, Langue de Bœuf, Jambon de York, Pâtés de Pigeonnaux, Pâtés de Foie Gras
Hors d'Oeuvres:	Asperges à la Crème, Choux-fleurs au Parmesan, Timbale aux Choux
Entremets:	Gelée Victoria, Crème Vanille, Blanc-manger, Gelée aux Macédoines, Crème aux Fraises, Chartreuse d'Oranges, Gelée Marbrée, Charlotte Russe, Compote d'Abricots, Compote d'Ananas, Chartreuse aux Fraises, Gâteaux Napolitain, Gâteaux Royale, Talmouse au Sucre, Tourte de Groseilles, Meringues Françaises, Petit Gâteaux Génoise, Petites Bouchées aux Confitures, Pouding Diplomate, Pouding St Claire, Pouding Glacé Belgique
Dessert:	Divers

That it was socially acceptable for Tait to attend a function such as this, was perhaps a further sign that no stigma attached to him as a result of his bankruptcy and the failure of the Steamship Company.

President of the Limerick Mechanics Institute

Unfortunately the records of the Mechanics Institute have not survived to show when Tait became its President, but he was certainly President at the time of the Institute's anniversary banquet in October 1872, although not able to be present at it. He had evidently been involved with the Institute in one way or another for several years before 1872.

Mr Forrest, the Vice-President, and Mr Dooley, the Treasurer, both referred to Tait in eulogistic terms in their speeches at the banquet.[18] I quote them here because they show how Tait was still perceived by members of the working class in Limerick.

Mr Forrest said, referring to Tait -

> We have in this city merchants who give large employment - I could name some who are an honour to this city - and foremost amongst them I would place Sir Peter Tait. It is not our province to dispense praise; but the man who gives a stimulus to industry, and occupation to numbers by circulating his capital among the people, enabling it to fructify and them to live, deserves the highest encomium that the citizens and the working classes in general can bestow. I need not remind you of the good he has done, and the gift he has given to this Institution, to which he sends a subscription of £20. He has a large heart, and contributes largely to the welfare of Limerick; and if we had a few more like Sir Peter Tait, we would hear very little about deserted quays, the grass of the Custom-house, or the things which are individually used to depreciate our city in public estimation.

Mr Dooley was no less enthusiastic. He said -

> As an old working man of this city, and from my long experience of the course of trade in Limerick, I must honestly say I never knew a better man as a citizen, a friend and an employer. I need not speak of his donations to the charities of the city; some are known, but there has been an amount of charity given by him in a private way that perhaps the recipients alone will ever know. Sir Peter Tait is a true friend to the poor, and his consideration for them is another link that binds him closer to the people and the people to him. We find his name amongst the contributors to the fuel fund, which is so deserving of every man, irrespective of creed or class. He deserves the highest encomiums we could express in this regard. When our Institute wanted funds he, whilst

Mayor of Limerick, came to our aid, and not alone to ours but every other institution in Limerick that required any. And in the lists his subscriptions were and are amongst the highest and foremost. Gentlemen, he is one who "does good by stealth and cares not to find it fame". He is to visit us next week, and I am happy to tell you it is with the intention of promoting still further the manufacture by which so many of our working people earn good wages. It is not alone his - there is another whose goodness demands an acknowledgement - for, gentlemen, it has been experienced and ought to be extolled - I mean Lady Tait's. She is a benefactress in the truest sense of the word, and the happiness she has afforded to many a poor fireside in her native city, will not be forgotten by those who enjoyed it. She extends her charity to the indigent, no matter what their creed may be, and she would not shrink from the poorest cottage herself in giving comfort, where before only misery and want were found.

As foreshadowed by Dooley, Tait arrived in Limerick on 26 October; but his stay was brief; he left by the 10.45pm train for London on the 28th. The Member of Parliament for Orkney and Shetland had died on the 26th and Tait, still presumably hankering after a seat in the House of Commons, had decided to contest the by-election for his successor. He may have felt that, following his recent failure in Limerick in 1871, no better opportunity than this would present itself and should be seized. He may also have felt that the constituency of Orkney and Shetland was at a safe distance from his recent financial misfortunes but, if so, he was to be proved terribly wrong.

However, before coming to that, it might be well to look at an episode which highlights Tait's lack of judgement in choosing his business associates.

17

An Extraordinary Charge of Seduction

1865-1871

In March 1871 an action was brought against Patrick Lynch by George Cannock, for the seduction of his elder daughter, Mary Hamilton Cannock.

The allegation was that Lynch had seduced Mary Cannock; had had sexual intercourse with her on 15 August 1870, and on three other occasions during that month; and that, as a result, she was now pregnant with his child.

The case was heard at the Cork Spring Assizes in the County Record Court before Lord Chief Baron Pigott, and an all male jury. It started on Saturday 25 March and was not concluded until the following Friday 31 March. The case attracted intense interest; the proceedings being reported almost verbatim in the *Cork Daily Herald* and summarised in other papers, including *The Times* which described it as 'an extraordinary charge of seduction'.[1]

Mr Clarke QC, counsel for the plaintiff, Cannock, stated the case to the Court. This was an action, he said, brought by the plaintiff for the seduction of his daughter, a young lady eighteen years of age. An action for seduction was about the most serious that could be brought before a Court. Clarke went on to outline the circumstances in which Cannock had welcomed Lynch into his home, and had been repaid; by Lynch's acting with the greatest cruelty to Mary Cannock and the greatest ingratitude towards her father.

On the other hand, Mr Heron QC, for Lynch, endeavoured, in his examination of Lynch, to show a hard working, respectable family man; living at home with his family and sharing his wife's bed. Lynch said that he had visited Mary Cannock and walked with her because she did not know many people in Limerick; her illegitimacy making it difficult for her to be accepted in society. He vehemently denied the charge of seduction.

Clarke told the Court that Cannock had been born in about 1809. On coming to Ireland he had gone into business in Cork with John Arnott. In 1845 they had opened an establishment in Dublin and had later acquired the business of Cumine and Mitchell in Limerick.

In 1852, when his daughter Mary was born, Cannock was living in a house near Dublin. Mary's mother, to whom Cannock was not married, was his housekeeper. Cannock said that she could read, but he thought she could not write. Two years later the couple had a second daughter, Fanny, but after her birth Cannock separated from the children's mother, making ample provision for her, and went to live at his place of business in Dublin.

Clarke went on to say that Cannock looked carefully after his daughters; bringing them up as if they had been his legitimate children. He treated them with a greater amount of affection, if that were possible, than could be bestowed on legitimate children by a legitimate father - the fondest parent could not have displayed greater kindness towards his offspring.

The children remained with their mother for some years after their parents' separation. Cannock was in the habit of constantly visiting them and taking them out, and, when they reached a suitable age, he took them from their mother, with her consent, to educate them.

He first placed them with a Mrs Eaves at Rathmines, near Dublin, where they stayed for about two years, and then he sent them to a boarding school at Chepstow in Monmouthshire and, later, to a school in Paris.

Cannock's connection with Sir Peter Tait and Robert Tait

Clarke told the Court of Cannock's connection with Sir Peter Tait and Robert Tait, both in business and socially, the latter more particularly following Cannock's move to 23 Aberdeen Park in London following his retirement in 1865, where the Tait brothers frequently partook of Cannock's hospitality. Cannock's household there consisted of himself, his daughters, Miss Pearse a lady governess, and three servants.

Before his retirement, apart from his interests in the business he owned with Arnott in Dublin, and in Cannock Tait & Co in Limerick, Cannock had been a partner in the firm of Silber & Fleming, warehousemen, of Wood Street in the City of London and Rue de Paradis, Poissonière, Paris. When he retired, he possessed a fortune of about £150,000 and had settled his capital of £44,000 in Silber & Fleming on his two daughters.

Shortly thereafter, Mary had met, fallen in love with, and, with her father's blessing, become engaged to a Mr Sadlier, son of Dr Sadlier, late of Dublin; an assistant in Ellis's drapery business on Ludgate Hill in the City of London.

But, following the bankruptcy of Tait & Co in 1869, Cannock had lost virtually everything; the creditors had even managed to break his daughters' settlement and they were left with only £4,000. In these altered circumstances, he had thought it right to break off Mary's engagement to Sadlier; a move to which both Mary and Sadlier consented, albeit reluctantly. Notwithstanding this, Sadlier continued to visit Mary while she was still in London, but not as a suitor, and they occasionally wrote to each other when Mary later moved to Limerick.

Lynch introduced to Cannock

Although Patrick Lynch had met Cannock in Limerick, while waiting for the sailing of the *SS Evelyn* in September 1865, he had not met Cannock socially until he was introduced to him, in London, by Tait and his brother Robert. Lynch became a close friend of Cannock, who used to invite him both to visit and occasionally to sleep at Aberdeen Park. On one occasion, Lynch's eldest daughter, Josephine, who was at school near London, spent the Christmas holidays with Cannock and his daughters. Lynch was described by Cannock's Counsel as like an uncle or near relative to Cannock's two girls.

In evidence, Mary said that while she was a child in London she used to kiss her papa when she was going to bed, and if Lynch were there she would kiss him too; she used to kiss him in the same way in Limerick.

On his return to Limerick in 1869, Cannock had rented a house in Barrington Street, and once he was settled there, Mrs Silber, the wife of one of Cannock's partners in Silber & Fleming, with whom Mary and Fanny had remained behind in London, brought them to Ireland to join their father.

Cannock's household at Barrington Street thereafter consisted of himself, his daughters Mary and Fanny, a cook, and a parlour-maid.

On their arrival in Limerick, Cannock sent his two children for music lessons to an academy run by Madame de Prins. The girls went on different days; Mary on Mondays and Wednesdays, Fanny on Tuesdays and Fridays, from half-past-two to four. Fanny also went to Mrs Tracy's school in Catharine Street for English lessons on Mondays and Wednesdays from ten till two.

And Cannock, not unnaturally, invited Lynch to visit his home, since Lynch, now nearly forty-four years old, lived at the George Hotel with his wife and their eight children. Lynch thus renewed his friendship with Mary and Fanny.

Lynch's visits to Mary Cannock

Mary Cannock's testimony was that Lynch's visits, which led up to her seduction, started in the April of 1870. Her father always left the house for his business at eleven o'clock; not returning until seven in the evening. Lynch would come when Mary was alone in the house apart from the servants; Fanny being either at Mrs Tracy's or at Madame de Prins's. He used not to come often, or stay long at first, but the visits increased in frequency, as did their length. He used to stop an hour, an hour and a half and sometimes two hours. After a time he used to call nearly every day. Mary received him sometimes in the dining-room and sometimes in the drawing-room. The visits continued from April until October, when they ceased. Lynch also frequently walked out with Mary.

Thomas Price, a boatman, gave evidence that he ferried them on one occasion from the Ferry Slip to Barrington's Quay and they went along the bank towards Tervoe, not returning for an hour and a half. He took them three more times after that: 'he supposed they went to the same place and on the same errand too'.

Michael Riordan, toll-keeper at the Wellesley Bridge, remembered seeing Mr Lynch and Miss Cannock pass over the bridge five or six times and it would be a couple of hours before they would pass back again.

Cannock's servants at Barrington Street, a cook and a parlour-maid, although not very satisfactory as servants, played a part as witnesses to the comings and goings of the principals in the drama. The cook, Margaret Hogan, who said that she 'had not a good head, and half a glass of wine made her drunk', lasted little more than eight months; leaving shortly after August 1870 at her own request, 'because people talked of the house and Lynch'. One parlour-maid, Kate O'Donnell, was dismissed by Cannock in August or September after alleging, quite correctly as it turned out later, that Lynch was taking improper liberties with Miss Cannock; something which Cannock would not believe. Her replacement, thought to be a married woman, gave birth to a child in the house, and was dismissed; ending up 'on the town'.

It would do her no harm

Mary went on to say that after Lynch had been visiting some time, his demeanour began to change; he became more intimate and familiar, but he never took liberties until the cause of the action occurred. This was on 15 August and took place in the drawing-room. Mary described how Lynch used a great deal of persuasion: told her that it would do her no harm. She said that he had pressed her frequently before and often put his arms around her waist; indeed had attempted, unsuccessfully, to seduce her a few days before the 15th.

The criminal intercourse was repeated a few days later with the parties standing up in the dining-room, which was described by Counsel as the most insulting and outrageous way that an insult could be offered to a woman.

In a field and in a sort of ditch

Mary said that the last two occasions on which Lynch had intercourse with her were on their walks; the first time in a field off the Circular Road, the second in a sort of ditch running through the field. Remarkably, Mary said that, when she went with Lynch on that last occasion, she did not suspect him of any improper intention. Strange girl.

Mary had first begun to feel a change in her condition in September. She told Lynch she thought she was pregnant but he laughed and said she was not. It was not until a visit to her doctor at the beginning of January, when she told him what had occurred, that he confirmed her suspicions. After that, the news spread rapidly; not least to Mrs Lynch, who was told by Mary herself, who also told her that it was Lynch who was responsible.

Lynch's defence

Mr Heron's response to Mary Cannock's allegations was to attempt to show that it was not Lynch, but someone else, who had made her pregnant.

In addition to giving music and singing lessons, Madame de Prins let rooms in her house to three young gentlemen, clerks in the Provincial Bank in Limerick. One of these lodgers was John Campbell Macandie, from Scotland, who was twenty-four years old. It was in April or May 1870 that Mary was first introduced to Macandie, when he came into the room during one of her music lessons. She met him several times after that at Madame de Prins's, when she and her sister were invited for tea and dancing. These occasions would start at seven or eight in the evening and finish at ten or eleven. Cannock was of course aware of them and there was no suggestion that anything improper happened at them.

In the following months Macandie began to take the place of Sadlier in Mary's affections, and, as well as meeting two or three times a week, they exchanged letters. In due course Macandie asked Mary to marry him and she promised to do so, if her father would consent, although she did not tell her father of this until the evening before the Court case started.

Mary admitted in Court that she had, on occasion, been alone with Macandie at Barrington Street, apart from the servants, and that they had also walked out together alone. She said that he had often kissed her, but swore on oath that criminal intercourse had never taken place between them. Counsel for Lynch produced a witness, John J Blake, an officer in the custom-house in Limerick, who had seen the couple, one evening in August at about six o'clock, sitting alongside one another by a haycock in a field by the

Corkanree embankment below Limerick docks. He believed they were sitting there as sweethearts. In reply to the judge, Blake said that he did not form any opinion that anything improper was going on between them.

Heron suggested to the jury that it was Macandie who was responsible for Mary's pregnancy.

Clarke, on the other hand, tried to demonstrate another side to Lynch. In certain quarters he certainly had a bad reputation. For example, it emerged in evidence that Kate O'Donnell, the parlour-maid at Barrington Street, had been told by the cook that Lynch was a very bad man, that he had left his wife for two years, and that he had gone away with another woman to South America. His association with Robert Tait also counted against him. From his first employment by Tait in March 1865, whenever business took him to London, he lived with Robert Tait in Buckingham Street; he and Robert often going about in the evenings together. Clarke, in his cross examination of Lynch, suggested that Robert was a dissolute and very dissipated young man and that he and Lynch went after girls together in London; a line of questioning evidently intended to show that Lynch was not the respectable family man portrayed by Heron. But, since Clarke's instructions can only have come from Cannock, what it did show was what Cannock thought of Robert Tait. The bankruptcy had evidently left Cannock with bitter feelings.

The verdict of the jury

But, at the end, it was Mary's testimony that the members of the jury believed. They found for Cannock; awarding him damages of £100 and 6d costs.

Lynch was, of course, ruined by the verdict. He had already lost his job with the Steamship Company, when it went into liquidation, and, in addition, it still owed him about £800.

Then, presumably in an effort to salvage something from the wreckage, in 1872 Lynch himself, and in 1873 Mrs Lynch, who it will be remembered provided most of the meals, sued Tait in the Court of Bankruptcy for a total of over £2,000.[2] This, they alleged, was the unpaid cost of 'déjeuners, dinners, banquets and other entertainment' given by Tait to the Judges, the Members of the

Corporation, Tait's employees and others, during his time in Limerick in the years 1866, 1867 and 1868, when he was Mayor, and in 1869, when he was High Sheriff; years characterised by his frequently lavish entertainment of sometimes large numbers of people.

The claims were resisted mainly on the grounds that they had been satisfied by payment, that they had been unduly delayed and that the charges were exorbitant: also, in the case of Mrs Lynch, because she had kept no books and had made out her account from memory! These claims, which surely cannot have been entirely without merit, seem to illuminate an unexpected side to Tait's character during the years of his greatest affluence, when he liked to give the impression that money hardly mattered. Even if his relationship with Patrick Lynch was to a certain extent complicated by his being an employee, Tait should surely at least have paid Mrs Lynch for all her much praised culinary efforts.

It had been a very unusual feature of a Court case alleging seduction; that it had been brought before the birth of the child. On Lynch's behalf it was argued that there was no corroboration of Mary Cannock's allegation that intercourse had taken place, as she said, in the previous August. It would have been usual to await the birth of the child; that being the only corroboration there could be. However, in the event, the child was born as predicted. Mary gave birth to a daughter, Josephine Frances, on 6 May 1871. It is not recorded what became of the child, but it would have been usual, in the circumstances, for her to be put into the care of one of the local convents.

A new start

Following the birth of Josephine, Mary herself moved to England and, on 12 September 1874, at Tidenham in Gloucestershire, she and John Macandie were married and started a family; the first of several children, Christina Mary, being born at Tigworth, a small village near Gloucester, on 13 July 1875. On the marriage certificate John's occupation was shown as 'Gentleman', which, if not perhaps accurate in relation to his position on the social scale, seems a fair description of his conduct towards Mary Cannock.

18

The Orkney and Shetland By-Election

1872-1873

On 26 October 1872, Frederick Dundas, the Member of Parliament for the constituency of Orkney and Shetland, died at his home in London. He was a staunch Liberal and had held the seat since 1837, apart from a short break between 1847 and 1851.[1]

On 2 November, Samuel Laing, who had been without a seat in Parliament since his rejection by the electors of Wick in 1868, published an address offering himself as a candidate to fill the vacancy. He said -

A vacancy having occurred by the death of your old and respected Member, Mr F DUNDAS, I beg to offer myself as a Candidate for the honor of representing my native County in Parliament.

There is none which I should value more highly, both from early associations and from the long and intimate connection with it, of my Father and Family. Whether I deserve this honor is for you to judge.

I have now been before the public for the last 30 years, as Secretary to the late Lord Dalhousie at the Board of Trade; as a Member of Lord Palmerston's Government; as Finance Minister of India; and as an independent Member of Parliament, and Chairman of important Commercial Companies.

It is for you, and not for me, to say whether this career has been, on the whole, such as to merit your confidence, and make me a useful and creditable representative of my native County.

As regards politics, my opinions are unchanged since I served under Lord Palmerston.

I am a decided but Moderate Liberal, sincerely attached to the Monarchy and leading Institutions of the country, though always ready by timely reforms, not inconsistent with their spirit, to keep them in harmony with the progress of the age, and thus avert the danger of revolutionary changes.

So long as the Liberal party remains united, and men like Lord Granville, the Marquis of Hartington, and Sir Roundel Palmer continue in the Cabinet, I shall give them a general support; but if the time came when the Liberal party was broken up, by the exigencies of its Radical or Ultramontane Sections, I should go with the Moderates.

In looking at the future, it seems probable that religious differences will enter more than they have done into general politics, and that a contest is everywhere impending between Ultramontanism and the principles of modern, and specially, of Protestant society.

In this contest, I have no doubt of the part we should take. The honor and interests of Great Britain alike require that we should pursue a firm Protestant policy; cultivate a cordial alliance with the great Protestant German Empire and offer a decided resistance to Ultramontane aggressions in Ireland.

As regards local affairs, and specially as regards local taxation, if returned as your Member, every tie both of gratitude and common interest, would induce me to give them every attention in my power.

Being now among you, I shall be happy to give you any further explanations that may be desired, with a view to which I propose to take the earliest opportunity of meeting the Electors in the principal districts of Orkney and Shetland.

In the meantime I commit my cause to your hands, in the confident belief that the support which has on all occasions been so freely and generously given me by my native Burgh, Kirkwall, will not be withdrawn from me by my native County.

The principal of the commercial companies referred to by Laing was the London, Brighton and South Coast Railway, of which Laing was the full time chairman; a position he had held from 1848 to 1855 and again since 1868.

What Laing did not mention was the subject matter of a paragraph which had appeared in the *Scotsman* -

The *Economist* notices a curious action raised by Mr Erlanger, banker, Paris; Mr Laing MP; Sir Drummond Wolff, and three other English capitalists, to get a Mr Merton to account for £880,000 [*about £40,000,000*] put into his hands for the *purpose of securing the assistance of influential persons* in Turkey to certain arrangements [in connection with the Turkish Government Loans, which arrangements would be advantageous to Mr Erlanger and the others]. Mr Merton's position is stated to have been that it was specially fixed that he was to dispose of the money according to his own discretion, *and was not to account.* The Tribunal of Commerce [in Paris] dismissed the action on the ground that the *original pactio* [made by Mr Laing and his friends] was IMMORAL and ILLEGAL, and COULD NOT *therefore be taken cognisance of by a Court of Law.*

Backsheesh on the grandest scale! Though the electors of Orkney and Shetland did not seem to mind; after all, that was how business was done in the East, as Tait was later to discover to his cost.

Tait enters the contest

It was not until 14 November that Tait entered the contest with the publication of an address which was initially circulated in Shetland, but not in Orkney -

The death of your old and esteemed Member, Mr F Dundas, having caused a vacancy in the Representation of my native County, I beg to offer myself as a Candidate for the honor of representing you in Parliament.

My Political Opinions are Liberal. I am for progress, and am an earnest worker to promote the material prosperity of our country; and I am sincerely attached to the Crown and Constitution of the Empire.

From my experience of the Public Expenditure in the Army and Navy, I believe there can, and ought to be, considerable reduction and retrenchment without impairing the efficiency of these important services.

One of the most urgent questions of the day, and which commands special attention, is Local Taxation; at present pressing so unequally on the different communities.

I feel that much could be done to promote the Commercial and Agricultural prosperity of Orkney and Shetland, by union, aided by an energetic and enterprising Representative.

I consider that the integrity of the Empire as handed down to us by our Ancestors should be maintained, and that the ties which connect us with our brethren in the colonies should not be lightly severed.

My Family have long supported, and ardently laboured to maintain the Liberal Cause in the County; should I have the honor of being returned as your Representative, you may rely upon my constant efforts to promote and further the best interests of the Constituency.

I hope to have the pleasure of waiting upon you in a few days.

The *Zetland Times* commented that this address, though breathing the true spirit of Liberalism, seemed too concise: the subjects treated on being few. However, the paper believed that once Tait was among them, he would enlighten them as to his opinions on many of the most important topics of the day; as also on local subjects, such as a public pier for Lerwick, the better recognition of Shetland's fishing by Government, and the insertion of some provisions in the Scottish Poor Law with reference to Shetland, where the taxes pressed so heavily on the rate-paying community.

On 20 November, the same address was circulated in Orkney, but with the inclusion of an additional paragraph, between the third and fourth paragraphs of the original, as follows-

> Being fully convinced that true religion would be advanced and promoted by being released from all state control, resting alone on its own divine merits and the exertions and zeal of its members, I am an earnest supporter of Disestablishment, and an advocate of perfect religious equality.

What Tait did not mention was the failure either of Tait & Co or, more significantly, of the Steamship Company. And, although details of the former were to become an issue in the election, the failure of the Steamship Company, Tait's first and only business enterprise based outside Limerick, was not mentioned at all.

And something happened which suggests that he may perhaps have been over-confident of success.

On 18 November, The Army and Navy and General Outfitting Company Limited had been formed. Its objects were to undertake contracts for the supply of army and navy and police equipment of all kinds. The eight subscribers to its Memorandum of Association were Tait, William Abraham, Thomas B Hamilton, Stephen Phillips, Laurence Nicoll (a rare appearance), Robert Linklater jnr (one of Tait's nephews) and a clerk in Tait's office; each subscribing for one share. The authorised share capital of the company was £50,000, in 5,000 shares of £10 each.[2]

Perhaps Tait had remembered in good time on this occasion that, as a Member of the House of Commons, he would not be able to remain a Government contractor and had formed this new company so that it could take over his Government contracts if he won the election.

The Orkney and Shetland by-election held in January 1873 was one of the first Parliamentary elections to be held following the passing of the Ballot Act of 1872, which introduced secret voting at local and general elections for the first time. The Act put a stop to the abuses which had been so conspicuously evident in the 1868 election in Limerick. However, the franchise itself was still very limited; being confined to men having real property with an annual value of £10 or more. Of the total of 1537 electors in the Islands, a substantial majority lived in Orkney; although the total population of Orkney was approaching 30,000, and of Shetland 28,000.

The campaign itself was not only carried on by the candidates and their agents, who canvassed individuals and held public meetings, but also, to a great extent, in the press; the various local journals supporting one or other candidate in a most partisan manner.

Laing had the support of the *Orcadian* in Orkney, the *Northern Ensign* in Wick, and the *Edinburgh Courant.* Tait was supported in Orkney by the *Orkney Herald* and in Shetland by the *Zetland Times.*

Laing had been born in 1812 and, although he had made his career on the national, rather than the local, stage, was from an Orkney family and was well known there. Indeed his grandfather Malcolm Laing had been Liberal MP for Orkney and Shetland from 1807 to 1812.

Tait, on the other hand, although from a Shetland family, had made his career and reputation in Limerick, often referring to Ireland as his adopted country. He was virtually unknown in the Islands, although he was helped by receiving support in the form of testimonials from friends in Ireland. Which is not to say that, particularly in Shetland, Tait was not greeted with enthusiasm as the candidate to oppose Laing; he was.

Since both candidates fought the election as Liberals, although Laing acknowledged that he was a 'moderate' Liberal, whereas Tait professed to be a 'staunch' Liberal, there was not much of real political substance to separate the two of them.

Tait's Protestantism questioned

Tait was for, Laing against, the disestablishment of the Church of Scotland; this issue giving rise to accusations by Tait's supporters that Laing was a High Church Puseyite, and by Laing's supporters that Tait was not a good Protestant and had Popish leanings. The accusation about Tait's Protestantism was made very early on. It may well have touched a raw nerve, because although his Protestantism was well known in Limerick, Tait had always managed to maintain good relations, not only with the Roman Catholic Church there, but with the leading Roman Catholic laity as well.

But Alexander Smith, a dissenting Minister in Orkney, came to Tait's aid. He wrote to the *Orkney Herald*, not only enclosing a letter which he had received from William Tarbotton, the Secretary of the Irish Evengelical Society, but also attesting to the fact that Tait's parents had regularly attended Smith's church at Rendall, and that both Tait's sister, Barbara, and her husband, Balfour Logie, had been members of the Congrgational Church in Kirkwall, while they were all living in Orkney in the 1850s. Mr Tarbotton's letter speaks for itself -

LONDON, November 30, 1872

REV. AND DEAR SIR, - I have just heard, with the utmost astonishment, that my old and valued friend, Sir Peter Tait, who is now appealing to the constituency of Orkney and Shetland, has been charged by his opponents with not being a thorough Protestant! Most happy am I to assure you that such a charge is *absolutely false.* I have had the privilege of personally and most intimately knowing Sir Peter for only one month short of twenty-five years, and I can testify that a sounder or more scriptural Protestant than he is cannot be found throughout the Empire.

From the year 1848 to 1858, I was Pastor of the Congregational Church in Limerick; and during all that time he was one of the most active members of the Church, devoting himself with a zeal very rarely surpassed to the diffusion of the gospel around. I have since been Secretary, for the last ten years or more, to the Irish Evangelical Society, which - as you are aware - is the organ of the English Independents, for the spread of pure Protestant truth in Ireland; and I am able to state that Sir Peter has been one of our most liberal supporters, having on several occasions contributed as much as one hundred pounds per annum. The aid he rendered to the Congregational Church, in Limerick itself, for many years, far exceeded that amount.

To all who know Sir Peter Tait, any insinuation impeaching the sincerity of his attachment to simple Evangelical, Protestant truth, is so utterly and preposterously absurd as to be worthy only of their laughter, unless, indeed, it should provoke their indignation. All his life long, since the days of his youth, in his love for the gospel, for entire spiritual freedom, for Protestant progress and triumph, Sir Peter Tait has been *true and sound to the very core.*

Having heard this outrageous report, I cannot refrain - owing to my high personal regard for him as a man, a Protestant, and a Christian - from troubling you with this letter.

In the other relations of life, I will merely add that Sir Peter Tait's name is only a synonym for benevolence, energy, uprightness, honour, and devoted loyalty.

You are at liberty to make any use of this which you think may best contribute to his success.

Believe me to remain,

Rev. and dear Sir,

Yours with much esteem,
WM. TARBOTTON,
Independt. Minister, and
Secy. of the "Irish Evangelical Society".

It was not only in relation to his Protestantism that Tait found himself on the defensive.

His Liberalism was questioned; it being alleged that he had stood as a Conservative in the 1868 election in Limerick. In response to this he said that he had never stood as a Tory, or any other candidate, for any constituency; but at the general election of 1868 he was put forward by the Liberal and working portion of the constituency of Limerick, without his sanction, and contrary to his express wish.

He was not in Ireland at the time; he did not issue any address to the electors, and never attended any meeting; but repeatedly telegraphed to his friends not to proceed in the matter; yet, notwithstanding this, he came within about thirty votes of being returned as member for the third city of Ireland, and but for the strenuous opposition of the Roman Catholic priesthood would have been returned by a large majority.

He emphatically denied that any change had taken place in his opinions, either political or religious, and asserted that he had always been a consistent Liberal and a Dissenter, and if his opponent had been equally consistent he need not on the present occasion have been obliged so thoroughly to cast in his lot with the Tory party.

It was also alleged that Tait had been a supporter of Fenianism and that he had supported Isaac Butt in the 1871 election in Limerick. Both of these allegations he refuted at one of his public meetings; stressing his loyalty to the Crown and Constitution. However, he was a supporter of Home Rule for Ireland, holding, he said, the same view as that held by the leading members of the Liberal Party.

Contagious diseases and intoxicating liquor

There were two issues in the election which came to the fore because they had become causes of public concern.

One was the Contagious Diseases Acts of 1864, 1866 and 1869, the administration and operation of which had been examined by a Royal Commission which reported in 1871.[3] The first of the Acts, passed in 1864, was described as 'An Act for the Prevention of Contagious Diseases at certain Naval and Military Stations'. The Report of the Royal Commission explained its purpose - [4]

The attention of the Government had for some years previously been directed to the injury caused to the health of the seamen and soldiers by the prevalence of venereal disease; but the difficulties of dealing with the evil by extraordinary and exceptional measures were very great. It was considered, however, that without recognising incontinence as an avoidable evil, or prostitution as a consequent necessity, the peculiar conditions of the naval and military services, and the temptations to which the men were exposed, justified special precautions for the protection of their health, and their maintenance in a state of physical efficiency. Accordingly by the Act of 1864, the operation of which was limited to 11 military stations, garrisons, and seaport towns, provision was made for the surgical examination of prostitutes supposed to be infected, for their detention in certified hospitals during a limited period, and for the punishment of brothel keepers who knowingly harboured diseased prostitutes. This Act passed without much notice either in or out of Parliament. It was carried out in England under the exclusive direction of officers carefully selected from the Metropolitan Police, and in Ireland by the constabulary; and hospital accommodation was gradually provided in the several districts.

The Contagious Diseases Act of 1866 repealed the 1864 Act, but the provisions of the latter were largely re-enacted, although with two important changes; first, provision was made for the periodic examination, by a medical officer, of every common prostitute within the eleven prescribed districts, upon a magistrate's order, or by voluntary submission, and, second, provision was made for the detention in a certified hospital of every prostitute found to be affected with contagious disease, for up to three, or exceptionally six, months.

The Act of 1869 amended, and extended, the Act of 1866. The main change it introduced was that all the prostitutes in the prescribed districts were required to appear, and the medical inspections which had taken place at periods varying from three weeks to three months were enforced, every two weeks. It also extended the number of districts to which the Acts applied, from eleven to eighteen.

A great many of the prostitutes to whom the law applied were what, today, we should regard as mere children; albeit the Royal Commission recommended that the age of consent should be increased from twelve to fourteen years old, which would have been some improvement, if not much.

Following the passing of the Act of 1869 an association comprising many eminent authorities was organised to press for the extension of the Acts beyond the then existing limits, with branch associations in many large towns promoting such extension.

However, before the end of 1869 a formidable public opposition to the Acts had arisen; a movement 'supported by many persons of station and intelligence, and among others by several ladies who resented this legislation as insulting to their sex, and tending to the depravation of public morals'.[5]

The result was the appointment of the Royal Commission, which found that among the principal objections urged by the opponents of the Acts were; that they were designed to provide sound prostitutes for soldiers and sailors; that rendering vicious indulgence less hazardous tended to promote immorality; that married men and youths were induced to visit the registered women by the security they were supposed to offer from contagion; that registering prostitutes and subjecting them to medical examination was an outrage on public decency and morality; that the system was virtually a recognition of the trade of prostitution by the State, and that it was unfair to exempt men from the restraints and regulations to which women were subjected.

On a more practical level, occasions had arisen on which wholly innocent and respectable women had been taken in by the police for examination. In addition, the fact that the police sometimes operated in plain clothes, caused some misgivings.

However, the Royal Commission found evidence that in Devonport, one of the two districts in which the Acts had been fully administered from the outset, the number of prostitutes had been reduced from 2000 to 600 and involved the total disappearance from the brothels of some 200 to 300 children of from 13 to 15 years of age.

The Commission took the view that 'if such results have been attained either wholly or partially through the operation of the Acts, those who demand their absolute repeal are bound to show that they have produced evils to counterbalance the good, which, after all reasonable deductions have been made, may be fairly attributed to them'.

The conclusion reached by the Royal Commission was that the existing legislation should not be repealed, but should be amended, principally by the discontinuance of the periodical examination of the prostitutes. But this did nothing to allay the public's concern.

Tait had hardly arrived in Orkney before he found himself pitched into this hornets' nest, in the shape of a deputation accompanied by the agent for the Northern Counties League for the Repeal of the Contagious Diseases Acts.

From what Tait said later, it was the first he had heard of the Acts, which he thought must have been smuggled through Parliament. However, he was quick to see that the advantage lay in going with the flow, and said that, should his candidature for a seat in Parliament be successful, he would use all his influence to secure the total repeal and abolition of the Acts.

Laing, on the other hand, who had been an MP until 1868, and would have seen the first two Acts pass through Parliament, although he met the same deputation, would not give a definite answer as to whether, or not, he would support the repeal of the Acts.

The other issue of public concern was very different and was one that would have found an echo in Tait. This was the Permissive Bill introduced into Parliament in 1864 by Mr (later Sir) Wilfrid Lawson. Its object was to enable the ratepayers of any parish or township to forbid the sale of intoxicating liquors within their district by the vote of a two-thirds majority; taking the power of licensing public houses and liquor shops out of the hands of the local magistrates. It was generally accepted that excessive drinking was a scourge of the poorer classes, but the Bill was in fact supported mainly by those who saw it as a means of introducing prohibition on the American model. The Bill was thrown out by the House of Commons. However, the problem which it sought to address did not go away and eventually Parliament passed the Licensing Act 1872, an Act for regulating the Sale of Intoxicating Liquors, which provided that licenses should be granted by licensing committees composed of justices or stipendiary magistrates.

Notwithstanding this, support for a Permissive Bill persisted and it was something Tait mentioned at his public meetings. He said that, being an abstainer himself, and from his opportunities of observation well able to judge of the great blessings which followed temperance, and of the many evils which were only too commonly the result of intemperance, he would give a Permissive Bill his cordial support.

On the subject of the Permissive Bill, Laing was equivocal, though in this case perhaps it was he who was going with the flow.

Tait charters a steamer

To enable him to visit as many people and places as possible during the campaign, Tait not only chartered the steamer *SS Queen* for a month, but embarked on her with four horses and two cabs. It was not the best time of year to be conducting an election campaign in Orkney and Shetland, particularly in Shetland, where the sun rose over the horizon for only a little over five hours. Added to this, the weather was particularly inclement, with storms at sea to delay the *Queen* and in places on land strong winds and snow to impede travel; indeed there is no mention of the horses and cabs being disembarked at any of the ports of call.

Once embarked on the *Queen* at Aberdeen, Tait sailed first to Orkney. One of his first public meetings there was at Firth on Friday, 22 November, where he expressed a hope that as the polling could not take place for some little time, the electors in the various districts would hold themselves unpledged until he could have an opportunity of addressing them, when he would be happy to answer any questions that any of the electors might desire to put; and he trusted they would not forget that they now had the protection of the secret ballot.

After the meeting at Firth, Tait left for Lerwick, in Shetland, where he had been expected to arrive the following afternoon. However, stormy weather delayed his arrival until the Monday morning, when, as soon as it was known in the town that Tait had arrived, flags were hoisted on shore and vessels in the harbour were decked out with bunting. At a meeting called for 8 o'clock in the evening, Tait addressed the electors in the Old Wesleyan Chapel, where he was received with repeated hearty rounds of applause, and cries of "Tait for Ever", which continued for some time. He said that he need not say how much gratified he was at the enthusiastic welcome that he, as a Lerwick boy, had received from his fellow townsmen.

He said he did not come there asking them to send him to Parliament merely for his connection with the county; and he felt it his duty to give expression to his political opinions. He asked them on political grounds to return him as their representative to the House of Commons.

He thought it right to notice the subject of religion which, though omitted from his address circulated in Shetland, was inserted in that distributed among the electors of Orkney, and which he considered of importance to every one. The Orkney people were strong supporters of the separation of the Church from the State, and his opinions were in accordance with theirs. He was in favour of a voluntary Church; not to be supported by the State or under the control of the State. He thought that the Established Church in Scotland was free from many of the evils which were alleged against the Established Church in England. He had seen the disestablishment of the Church in Ireland carried out, and believed that much good had thereby been done to the country. The movement for the disestablishment of the Church in England and Scotland would come in the future and he would prefer that it was commenced by the people themselves, as they could best feel the evils which were opposed to Christianity. He was opposed to anything like a revolution.

On the subject of taxation, he considered that at present it was not equally levied. He did not think it right that the income tax should be imposed on persons receiving less than £300 per annum; and considered persons in receipt of £3,000 far more able to pay 1s than those receiving £300 were to pay 1d. It should be more equalised, so as not to press so heavily on persons in receipt of small incomes.

He spoke about the state of trade and thought that, because the interests of Orkney and Shetland were identical, their importance could be increased by union, aided by an energetic representative. He had long entertained the idea of starting some manufactory for the benefit of his native town and, if were to be returned, nothing would gratify him more than seeing it become a temple of industry.

After some reference to the policy of retrenchment and economy in regard to the army and navy, Tait said they all knew what he had been and what he was. He was the son of a poor, though honest, father and he attributed his success in life to the principles instilled at the fireside and at the Sabbath School. As there were many young men present, who would soon be leaving their homes to push their way in the world, he considered it his duty to give them some advice - and that was, to put their firm faith in the truth of God. All other trusts would fail. He would also advise them to have nothing to do with the glass. Many a young man, starting with good prospects, has come to an untimely end by trifling with drink. The principles which he annunciated to them, if attended to, would prove a bulwark through life.

He then touched on a constant theme. He said he was not an orator, but a worker like themselves; and though honoured by Her Majesty with the title of Knight, he preferred plain Peter Tait. For his services to the town of Limerick, the Lord-Lieutenant of Ireland did not think him unworthy of appointment as Deputy Lieutenant and High Sheriff; while for three times in succession his fellow townsmen had elected him Mayor of the third city in Ireland and he would now like, if they considered him worthy of the honour, to be able to put 'MP' after his name for his native county. He had told them what were his opinions and if these were in accordance with theirs, he hoped they would join together, and declare that he was worthy of the honour to which he aspired. What they wanted as their representative was a man of stamina and youthful energy and if returned as their representative to Parliament he would do all within his power to forward their interests.

The death of Barbara Irvine

By a strange coincidence, Barbara Irvine, who had been nurse to Tait in his infancy, died in Lerwick that night. She was a very old woman and although her exact age was not known, she was supposed to be over ninety. For some time her faculties had been failing but she constantly spoke about Tait, who, it was said, had always been very mindful of her. However, some days before her death, she had met with an accident, but on hearing of her boy's return to Shetland, she was much excited, which probably hastened her end - so that she died before Tait could visit her.

Tait's bankruptcy becomes an issue

Tait later received a letter from Laing, which referred to a circular put about by his supporters on the subject of Tait's bankruptcy -

Kirkwall
Dec 3rd. 1872.

DEAR SIR,

On my return from Shapinshay this morning, I found the inclosed hand-bill, which had arrived during my absence.

I lose not a moment in writing to say that I am in no way responsible for it, and have instructed my agents to do all in their power to prevent its circulation, as the first paragraph refers to matters of a personal nature, which never ought to be imported into a political contest. I remain, Yours faithfully,

S.LAING.

On 5 December, again in Orkney, Tait addressed a large meeting in the Parish School of Evie and Rendall. Although he covered much the same ground as he had covered in his earlier address at Firth, he dealt rather more with the political issues at stake in the election.

He returned to the subject of disestablishment, saying, in reference to Established Churches, that he believed them to be subject to many evils in consequence of their connection with the State. They had doubtless all heard of the disestablishment of the Irish Church some four years ago, and he could tell them, from his experience during his stay in Ireland, that the disestablishment of that Church had been productive of the greatest good; indeed, far more had been done for the cause of Christianity since that remaining mark of bondage or serfdom was withdrawn from Ireland than during its whole previous history. He wished to see the State treat all denominations of Christianity with perfect equality. The Episcopal Church of England had many evils which the Church of Scotland was to a large extent free from. There was the burning of candles, burning of incense, and other signs of Ritualism - which some of the more evangelical of the Episcopalians wished to suppress, though the High Church party opposed it. He was, however, happy to say that he had met with as godly men in the Church of Scotland as he had found in any dissenting body in the kingdom. Disestablishment had to come in the future, and all Established Churches must go together, and when this came to pass he was fully convinced that true religion would flourish all the better by being released from State control. The people would then take a greater interest in religious concerns, seeing that all of them would have the selection and support of their own ministers placed in their own hands; but whatever might be done in the matter of disestablishment he would protect vested interests, and he did not doubt but that

Established clergymen would be as acceptable then as now, and as well off.

Another subject of local interest was taxation and what he said perhaps reflected his experience in Limerick as the champion of the poorer classes. He said that he advocated even-handed justice to all. He knew that taxes were often levied so that they frequently fell upon those least able to bear them, and any measure calculated to equalise taxation would receive his earnest support. He instanced the tax on shepherds' dogs, also the tax on horses and carts, which fell so heavily on the poor farmer. No doubt the revenue had to be maintained, but those gentlemen who could afford to keep their packs of hounds and other unnecessary luxuries were better able to pay such taxes than farmers and shepherds whose very existence was greatly blended with that of their helpmeets - the horse and dog.

However, Tait had little to say on other local concerns, beyond saying that he would use his best exertions to extend and improve the telegraph and postal services, and steam communication throughout the islands and other parts of the nation.

Then the following notice appeared in the editorial columns of the *Orcadian.* It also appeared as an anonymous advertisement in the *Zetland Times* of 9 December, the paper having refused to carry it in its editorial columns.

FAILURE OF TAIT & CO.

The following letter has been received from an eminent London Merchant and is confirmed by Mr Cash, of the London firm of Messrs Cash, Edwards, & Stove, the official assignees, who also states that in 1868 Tait & Co, under the signatures of the four members of the firm, wrote to Mr Armstrong the Secretary of the Westminster Conservative Association desiring to be entered on the Register as Conservatives.

I have ascertained that the failure of Messrs Tait & Co occurred on the 24th July, 1869.

The *Standard* of the 29th July, contains the following:-

"The balance sheet prepared by Messrs Cash, Edwards & Stove shows a total of liabilities amounting to £133,000 beyond those covered by other parties. The assets are represented to be £202,000 including the surplus of securities held by creditors and the partners' private estate and a portion of that of Mr Cannock."

And the following is taken from the *Irish Times* of 30th July, 1869.

"Although a surplus of £5,000 only was shown on the estate of Cannock & Tait, the estate of Tait & Co together with the private property shows a margin of £80,800."

Notwithstanding the alleged surplus the estate of Tait & Co has hitherto paid 3s 6d in the pound to the creditors, and it is not expected that it will pay any more.

London, 3rd December, 1872.

Tait and his supporters did their best to try and discredit this information.

John Thomson, who had worked for Tait since arriving in Limerick in the early 1850s and was now a manager in the clothing factory, wrote a letter to the Editor of the *Orkney Herald* that might well have been composed by Tait himself -

Victoria Terrace
Limerick, December 11th, 1872

Dear Sir,

A native of Kirkwall, and I hope not quite forgotten by the school-fellows and friends of my boyhood, amongst whom I had the pleasure to number yourself, I cannot refrain from addressing you on the subject of the candidature of Sir Peter Tait for his native county of Orkney and Shetland. It seems to me here in Limerick that the independent Liberal electors of Orkney and Shetland cannot fail to appreciate the success of a native - one who, leaving his home in early youth, has, by his business-like energy and enterprise, attained so honoured a name in the ranks of commercial men.

Sir Peter, being such an extensive employer, might be of great service to such an honest, hard-working community as I remember to have known, with proud pleasure, in my young days. I believe you would agree with this could you see the successful manufacturing enterprise which has sprung up here under his auspices, often giving comfortable, well remunerated, employment to as many men and women as there are inhabitants in the brave old burgh of Kirkwall, and to a seafaring people such as the inhabitants of Orkney and Shetland are of necessity, such a man could not fail to be of great service, having had large experience in this noble branch of commerce, in which the empire holds so high a place.

Further, Sir Peter comes not before the electors without some experience of public life. Having been unanimously elected on three successive occasions Mayor of Limerick, in token of the esteem in which he is held by all classes for his public and private worth; and in further evidence of the wish of the people of Limerick to do him an honour for his acts towards so many of them, and in appreciation of his well known independent Liberalism, the Liberal electors, against his own express wish, put him forward as their candidate at the general election in 1868, and were within thirty of winning, against all opposition - even his own. There is yet one phase of his character I would venture to touch upon - a delicate one, because it is private, yet at the risk of offending him I must, it being that which endears his name above all else to us, the Nonconformists of Ireland. He is known amongst us in Limerick, and, indeed, throughout Ireland, and is therefore esteemed by many who differ widely from him in their religious opinions as the steady, straightforward, Christian advocate of those religious opinions, which he holds to be founded on the teaching of the scripture; and we, the members of the Independent Church in Limerick, have cause to mourn the absence of one who was a member and Sunday school teacher, deacon and Sunday school superintendent, and highly esteemed in all. To write of his pecuniary aid, is to mention that which continues to this day.

In venturing to write on these matters, I have mentioned nothing that is not known to me personally, having been acquainted with Sir Peter for well nigh twenty years. Taking all together, I would say that the electors of Orkney and Shetland would find in this enterprising, intelligent and, above all, Christian man of business, one who, as their representative in Parliament, will do all that in him lies to forward their interest and develop the industries of the county. The instincts of the native must be my apology to you and my fellow town and county men for venturing to trouble them, through your kindness, with these crude remarks. Yours, etc.,

JOHN THOMSON

Thomson's 'noble branch of commerce' seems to have been a reference to Tait's shipping interests, about which it would perhaps have been wiser to say nothing. However, as noted above, this aspect of Tait's affairs was not raised by his opponents during the campaign.

Another letter arrived from Limerick, dated 12 December, and signed by the Mayor, the High Sheriff, the Town Clerk and the Treasurer of the city, as well as by two clergymen, three J.P.s, and a banker. After referring to Tait's Protestantism, they went on to say that 'notwithstanding the financial position of the late firm of

Tait & Co with which Tait was connected some years since, his honour and integrity remain unimpeached'.

And yet a further letter came from Limerick; this time from John Morrison, an Aberdeen man living there. He also lauded Tait's qualities, but, like Thomson, and the Mayor and others, he could only speak from what he had seen of Tait in Limerick, where, it has to be said, he was unquestionably a very large fish, although in quite a small pool.

And none of them seemed aware of the true causes of the failure of Tait & Co, perhaps because the clothing factory had carried on as though nothing had happened.

The principal creditors were banks and discount houses, who were left holding unpaid bills of exchange, and they were all a long way from Limerick, or, if not, did not care to advertise the extent of their involvement.

However, the allegations surrounding the failure of Tait & Co were not about to go away.

The *Orcadian* returned to the attack on 21 December by publishing a copy of a letter received by Ashurst Morris & Co, who had been Tait's solicitors before the bankruptcy and were creditors in the liquidation -

1, Tokenhouse Yard, London, E.C
13th. Dec. 1872

DEAR SIRS,

Since writing you this morning we find that you are yourselves creditors of the estate and as such are entitled to the information which you seek.

Accordingly, we beg to inform you that Tait & Co stopped payment in July 1869, with liabilities to a very considerable amount - a deed of inspectorship was filed on the 31st December 1869 and ultimately the partners viz, Sir Peter Tait, George Cannock, Robert Thomas Tait, and Balfour Logie, executed an assignment to the inspectors for the benefit of the creditors.

Under the liquidation the creditors have received two dividends of 2s 6d in the £ and 1s in the £ respectively, and it is possible that further dividends have been [may be?] declared to the extent of from 2s 6d to 5s in the £; but such further dividends can be derived exclusively from the surplus of the private estate of George Cannock, the estate of Tait & Co having been already exhausted, and the private estates of the other partners, viz., Sir Peter Tait, Robert Thomas Tait, and Balfour Logie, not realising any surplus.

Any further information you may desire we shall be happy to supply.

Yours faithfully,

JAMES, EDWARDS, CASH & STONE.

What James, Edwards, Cash & Stone could not know was that Ashurst Morris & Co were only to receive a further 2s 6d; 6s (or 30%) in the pound altogether. On the basis of the debts disclosed in December 1869, that represented a final deficiency following the failure of Tait & Co of over £137,000 [*about £6,000,000*].

After this, there was a further letter, which, on the face of it, contradicted James, Edwards, Cash & Stone's assertion that the creditors of Tait & Co had been paid only 3s 6d in the £.

It was from David McBirney JP of 14 -17 Aston's Quay, Dublin, and dated 16 December. He was the owner of a very large establishment in Dublin, described in the local directories as 'wholesale and retail woollen and linen drapers, hosiers, silk mercers and haberdashers'.

McBirney said in his letter -

After Sir Peter Tait's retirement from [Tait & Co] the estate was handed over to inspectors for liquidation. I was one of the largest creditors, to the extent of over £8,000.

I was present at the meeting of creditors when inspectors were appointed to wind up the estate, and a statement of accounts was submitted, showing a large surplus after paying all liabilities in full; and I now have pleasure of stating that, although I held no security save the word of Sir Peter Tait, I have been paid in full, as my books can show ....

There is no doubt that, by December 1872, the estate of Tait & Co had only paid two dividends totalling only 3s 6d in the £. McBirney's letter therefore presents a puzzle. There seem to be two possible explanations. First, that he was a creditor, not of Tait & Co, but of the separate estate of Cannock Tait & Co, whose creditors were paid in full. Alternatively, if he was indeed a creditor of Tait & Co, and bearing in mind that the creditors of Tait & Co had asked Tait to complete the contracts outstanding in July 1869, the Inspectors might have had to pay McBirney in full, as a means of persuading him to continue providing Tait with essential supplies. And it would have been very much in the interest of the creditors for the clothing factory to continue in business, as it did, since there is no reason to doubt that, as it had always been, it continued to be profitable.

Whatever the answer to the question as to whether McBirney was a creditor of Tait & Co or of Cannock Tait & Co, there is no question but that he had invested £1,000 in shares in Tait's Steamship Company, the whole of which was lost; which makes one wonder why he should have been so ready to come to Tait's assistance in 1872.

Tait's response to the publication by the *Orcadian* of the letter addressed to Ashurst Morris & Co was to meet Dr Still, the Chairman of his election Committee, and three other members of the Committee, who, following this meeting, published the following statement -

SIR PETER TAIT having submitted to us a number of documents with reference to the alleged failure of Tait & Company, and having given us the fullest information in regard to the position of the late firm and the liquidation of the assets, we have great pleasure in certifying to the Liberal electors of the county that the charges brought against him and so extensively circulated by Mr Laing's agents, are false and malicious and the most scrupulous need not have the slightest hesitation in recording their votes for Sir Peter as the Liberal candidate.

We would further in the strongest terms impress on the Liberal portion of the constituency the great importance of remaining true to their principles, and earnestly uniting to defeat the attempt on the part of the Conservatives and Mr Laing to break up the Liberal ranks on the present occasion.

(Signed) CHARLES S. STILL, Chairman, Sir Peter Tait's Committee
JOHN STANGER, Depy. Chairman
JAMES MOWAT, Member of Committee
AND. GOLD, Convr. of Committee

KIRKWALL, 23d December 1872

But worse was to come. On 28 December the *Orcadian* published a letter written to Dr Still by Laing on 25 December, which as the *Orcadian* so rightly said, 'speaks for itself'-

Castle Hotel, Kirkwall,
25th December 1872

SIR,

I see your name, with those of three other members of Sir Peter Tait's Committee attached to the following circular:-

[Here he quoted from Dr Still's circular of 23 December]

As the charges referred to have been made on the authority of official documents forwarded to me, I assume the responsibility of them.

The documents are the following:-

1. Office copy, under seal of the Court of Bankruptcy, of Deed of Inspection, dated 28th December, 1869, under which the insolvent estate of "Tait & Co" was wound up.
2. Schedules annexed thereto, under the Bankruptcy Amendment Act, sworn to by Peter Tait, R. T. Tait, George Cannock, and Balfour Logie, and authenticated by the seal of the Court, showing:-
   Amount of Debts £196,207 14s 7d
   Estimated Value of Assets 76,359 12s 8d
3. Official extract from Perry's Bankrupt and Insolvent Registry Office, 37, Walbrook, City, London, recording the failure of Tait & Co, with a certificate from Messrs James, Edwards, Cash & Stone, 1, Tokenhouse Yard, London, the official Accountants employed, of the dividends paid, viz:- first Dividend of 2s 6d in the £, and the second dividend of 1s.
4. The following letter from the same Accountants to Messrs Ashurst, Morris & Co, Solicitors, Old Jewry, London, who, being Creditors of Tait & Co, had written to ask for information.

[Here he quoted the letter to Ashurst, Morris & Co of 13 December, reproduced above]

These documents are all in my possession and open to your inspection or that of any other Elector.

As you say that you have seen a number of documents which enable you to certify that these charges are "false and malicious", I hereby challenge you to specify and produce them.

If you can either disprove the authentic and official documents above quoted, or prove by documents equally authenticated and official, that *all* Sir Peter Tait's creditors have been paid in full, I shall be ready at once and publicly to withdraw the statement made on the authority of the Accountants who wound up the estate.

If you cannot do so, I have a right to call upon you to retract your statement that this charge is "false and malicious", and admit the truth.

As you say the documents are here, I call on you to give me an immediate reply to this letter, so that the vague contradiction you have given to the above specific statements based on official documents, may not be allowed to influence Electors on the eve of the poll unless it can be substantiated. I remain, Sir, your obet. Servt.,

S. LAING.

The *Orcadian* then went on to print a letter from the Thames Iron Works & Shipbuilding Co (Limited) dated 21st December 1872 which stated quite clearly that 'to this date we have only received 3s 6d in the £'.

On 26 December, Tait, having received a copy of Laing's letter, wrote to Dr Still -

KIRKWALL, December 26th, 1872.

DEAR SIR,

On my return to town this evening I have been handed a printed letter, addressed to you by Mr Laing, and I lose not a moment to say how deeply I regret that he should have sent you such a communication in consequence of the circular addressed to the electors of the county, by you and the three other gentlemen of my committee, at our meeting on Monday last.

Mr Laing and some of his party have never ceased to slander my character since I became a candidate for the representation of the county. That I have ever defrauded any man, is one of the grossest falsehoods that could have been fabricated and could only have been done maliciously, to damage my candidature. I positively assert that I have paid in full all my own creditors, and I defy Mr Laing, or Messrs James, Edwards, Cash & Stone, to disprove this.

As you will remember, the documents submitted to the meeting of the Committee established, among others, the following facts, viz:- That in June 1869 I retired from the firm of Tait & Co, in consequence of one of the partners becoming involved in a mining speculation, whereby the sum of above £40,000 was withdrawn from the business of the late firm, and lost; that some time after my retirement, the remaining members of the firm finding themselves unable to carry on the business, a meeting of the creditors was called, and the estate placed in the hands of five of the principal creditors, as inspectors for liquidation; that the statement of affairs submitted to the meeting by the accountants, Messrs James, Edwards, Cash & Stone, shewed a surplus of upwards of £114,000 after meeting all possible liabilities in full; and that the liquidation of the estate has not been completed in consequence of a large portion of the assets remaining in bank, pending a suit in Chancery.

I am proud to say that my character, position, and all my transactions, will bear the strictest investigation; and I may be allowed to remark that I think Mr Laing would have come into this contest with cleaner hands, had he found it convenient to explain away the observations of the Judges in the notorious Turkish case, charging him and his confederates with immoral practices, and deciding against them.

I am, Dear Sir,
Yours very truly,
PETER TAIT.

to which Dr Still replied -

ORPHIR, 27th Dec. 1872.

DEAR SIR PETER,

I have just received your letter of yesterday.

Considering that Mr Laing in his letter to you of 3rd inst., published in the *Orkney Herald* of Wednesday last, assured you that the allusions to your connections with the late firm of Tait & Co had been imported into the present contest without his knowledge, and that he would do all in his power to suppress them, thus throwing you off your guard, I do not think you should take further notice of the matter.

I for one, was perfectly satisfied with your explanation, and the documents produced at our meeting on Monday, and all the other members of your Committee who were present expressed themselves to the same effect.

You may rely the Liberal electors of Orkney and Shetland are shrewd enough to see that the attacks now made upon you are simply a bit of electioneering capital.

With best wishes for your success.

I remain, Dear Sir Peter,
Yours very truly,
C. S. STILL.

On 31 December P S Heddle, Tait's Agent in Kirkwall, addressed a letter to the electors. He said that 'with reference to the many grossly contradictory statements which have appeared in the *Orcadian* in regard to the failure of Tait & Co, he had in his hands for inspection on the part of any of Sir Peter Tait's supporters who may desire to see them' statements prepared by James, Edwards, Cash & Stone 'showing a balance of over £114,000 in favour of the firm, after meeting the liabilities in full'.

Tait had the final word, which took the form of a printed circular addressed to the Electors of Orkney, dated 2 January 1873, in which he said –

I have just seen a printed circular of yesterday's date, with Mr Laing's name appended ... again referring to the affairs of Tait & Co, with which I have ceased to be connected for four years. I strictly adhere to the statements in my letter to Dr Still of 26th December, and I solemnly reassert that I have paid all my creditors in full, and have never defrauded any man. I challenge Mr Laing to disprove these facts.

When the result of the election was declared on 7 January, Laing had polled 646 votes; Tait 621. Tait had lost by just 26 votes.

Failure and its possible causes

Various reasons were suggested for Tait's failure to obtain more votes. His late entry into the contest was put forward as one; a good three weeks after Laing, to whom a number of electors, who might otherwise have supported Tait had they known he was to stand, had by then committed themselves.

It was also felt that Tait was insufficiently known in Shetland, and not at all in Orkney, which is where Laing's strength lay. Although Tait made much of the fact that he was a native of Shetland, he had after all left home when he was only sixteen, and he was now forty-four. He had not so much as visited in the interval.

There were also Tait's Protestantism and his strongly held views on disestablishment, which would not have pleased everyone, but about which he said a great deal more than he said about the other political issues, which perhaps would have been of more interest to the electors.

And then there was the failure of Tait & Co. In his letter to Dr Still of 26 December, and in the circular of 2 January 1873, was Tait telling what he believed to be the truth? It is certainly difficult to reconcile what he said, or at least implied, with such of the evidence as has survived.

First, he assured Dr Still that he had paid in full all his own creditors and in the circular he said 'I have paid all my creditors in full'. It was a feature of the arrangements which had been made under the Bankruptcy Acts, following the failure of Tait & Co, that, although the partners of the firm were responsible for its debts, this responsibility extended only to the extent of any surplus remaining after they had first paid their own personal creditors. In their letter to Ashurst Morris & Co of 13 December 1872, James, Edwards, Cash & Stone said that the private estate of Sir Peter Tait had not realised any surplus. Except in the unlikely event that his liabilities were exactly matched by his assets, that must have meant that there was a deficiency. The only information available to test the matter is from the papers in the liquidation of the Steamship Company.

On 13 October 1870, David Swayne, the secretary of the company, swore an affidavit as to the then assets of the company. One of those assets was described as 'Calls due on shares held by Sir Peter Tait. The claim has been admitted by the Inspectors of his Estate which is in liquidation under an Inspection Deed. No dividend has yet been declared. £2090'. Eventually, on 23 May 1876 the liquidators of the Steamship Company received from the Trustees of the Separate Estate of Sir Peter Tait a first and final dividend of £647 3s 7d, which suggests a dividend of a little over six shillings (or 30%) in the £.[6]

If this evidence is to be believed, Tait had not paid his own creditors in full.

But even if this deduction from the papers of the Steamship Company is wrong and Tait had paid his 'own' creditors in full, what he said to Dr Still was surely specious, since it was Tait's fault that Tait & Co had failed and only a legal nicety that its creditors were not his own creditors.

Second, Tait went on to say that he had retired from Tait & Co in June 1869 'in consequence of one of the partners becoming involved in a mining speculation' as a result of which £40,000 of Tait & Co's money was lost; a reference to Cannock's mining adventure in Glamorganshire. But that money had already been lost by the middle of 1868. It was the later fiasco of the Steamship Company that brought about the failure of Tait & Co, as Tait would have known only too well.

Third, Tait said that it was 'some time' after June 1869 'that, the remaining members of the firm, finding themselves unable to carry on the business, a meeting of the creditors was called'. The meeting of creditors was called as a result of the firm's inability to pay bills of exchange which fell due on 26 July 1869. Strictly speaking, from June 1869 to 26 July 1869, was 'some time', but not, surely, what a fair-minded person would understand by those words.

However, what is beyond doubt from the Deed of Inspectorship is that, at least for the purposes of the Bankruptcy Acts, Tait had still been regarded as a partner in Tait & Co on 26 July 1869. Had this not been the case, he would not have been personally involved in the firm's failure at all.

Fourth, Tait referred to 'a surplus of upward of £114,000, after meeting all possible liabilities in full', as being shown by the accounts submitted to the creditors' meeting in July 1869; a figure £45,000 greater than that reported at the time. But, whatever the explanation for that discrepancy, Tait would have known that by the time the Deed of Inspectorship was executed in December, more accurate accounts had revealed that a deficit of nearly £120,000 was by then anticipated. His further comment that 'the liquidation of the estate has not been completed in consequence of a large portion of the assets remaining in bank, pending a suit in Chancery', seems to have been a tacit admission that the dividends so far paid amounted to only 3s 6d in the £ as alleged by Laing. The suit in Chancery was presumably Tait v Collie. Whether, even if that case had succeeded, it would have produced enough to enable the creditors to receive 20s in the £, seems in retrospect to have been wildly optimistic; but then the electors in the far-off isles of Orkney and Shetland could not know that.

In the event, as noted above, the creditors of Tait & Co lost more than £137,000, or the equivalent today of not far short of six million pounds. And that does not include any losses suffered by the creditors of the partners' private estates, the total amount of which is not known.

There was an interesting footnote. Following Tait's defeat, The Army and Navy and General Outfitting Company Limited, which had been formed at the start of Tait's campaign, was quietly forgotten.

19

The Laxfirth Estate in Shetland
1873-1878

Although Tait returned to London following his defeat in the Orkney and Shetland by-election, it seems likely that he intended to contest the constituency again at the general election expected either later in 1873 or, at the latest, in 1874. And he evidently realised that it would increase his chance of success if he were to establish a presence in Shetland and become better known locally.

An opportunity for him to acquire a local estate soon presented itself. The Laxfirth estate had been offered for sale at auction at the Queen's Hotel in Lerwick in March 1873 by James Davidson, but had not sold. Tait subsequently bought it for £4,500 [*almost £200,000*], with possession at Whitsunday 1873.[1]

The estate was in the parish of Tingwall, about four miles north of Lerwick, on the west side of the tidal creek known as Laxfirth Voe. The property also included the western bank of the freshwater Loch of Strand, which is fed by a small burn, and which flows into the southern extremity of Laxfirth Voe. It extended to 1,287 Scottish acres, the equivalent of 1,636 Imperial acres, in all; about one quarter being arable land and the remainder peat moor, with a total annual value of £134.[2]

The mansion house itself, once called John Tait's house, and later Scottshall, was by 1873 known as Laxfirth House, and stands close to the western shore of the Voe. It was surrounded, in 1873, on the south and west by an area known as the garden park. Whatever might have been his original intention, Tait himself was never to live at Laxfirth, which was occupied instead by his uncle, Robert Linklater, until his death in April 1874. Robert Linklater was a younger brother of Margaret, Tait's mother. He was seventeen years her junior and only seventeen years older than

Tait himself. When Robert died, his estate included not only furniture, silver plate and other household effects at Laxfirth, but also nineteen ponies and a gig and harness.

However, once again there were financial problems, and on 31 March 1874 Tait had given his bankers, Brown Janson & Co, his personal bond as security for advances to Sir Peter Tait & Co of £10,000 and upwards, together with interest at 5% per annum, limited to a total of £11,500. And on the same day he had charged the lease of the clothing factory in Limerick, together with the fixed and movable plant and machinery, as collateral security with the bond, subject to the C of E Institution's mortgage of 4 October 1871.

And on the following day he charged the Laxfirth estate as further collateral security with the bond.[3] Then, only a few months later, doubtless at the instance of the bankers, Tait put the estate on the market, either for sale or to let. His agents, Duncan and Galloway, could not find a purchaser, and in October they accepted an offer from David Inglis, a farmer at Flemington, to lease the land for one year from 11 November 1874 at an annual rent of £180. Inglis was to occupy the land as a sheep farm, but was allowed to use from fifteen to twenty acres for growing corn and turnips. It was a condition of the agreement that Inglis would only cultivate for crops, either land which had already been cultivated, or which was overgrown with weeds and thistles; other than this, none of the old grass was to be broken up.[4]

Before Inglis took possession Tait sold at auction the contents of the farm buildings, together with some animals which remained on the property: wheelbarrows, rakes, hoes, forks, harrows, a cart, a riddle, sheep scissors, a clipping machine, 3 milch cows, and 2 young mares.

Poached fish

Tait's ownership of some of the land bordering the Loch of Strand gave rise to a dispute over fishing rights in March 1876.

The opposite shore of the Loch formed part of the lands of Gott, the property of George H B Hay. Tait and Hay who, by virtue of the fact that the Loch was not tidal, were jointly entitled to the rights to salmon and other fishing in the Loch, inserted a notice in the *Shetland Times* saying that anyone fishing in the Loch without permission would be prosecuted. The notice also offered a 'handsome reward' to anyone giving evidence to the owners' agents of any offender. In the event, John McLeod wrote to the agents to say that he had seen Thomas Connon, an hotel keeper from Lerwick, fishing, and claimed the reward. He was probably paid, because Tait and Hay successfully prosecuted Connon, and were granted an injunction restraining him from repeating the offence.[5]

Presumably the fishing was let by Tait and Hay, who were afraid that their income would be damaged if the Loch were fished without permission.

Laxfirth re-mortgaged

In September 1876, under increasing financial pressure, Tait borrowed £5,000 at 4½% interest from Thomas M Adie of Voe, Delting, repayable on 11 November 1877.[6] The loan from Adie was secured by a charge on the Laxfirth estate. Since the general charge in favour of Brown Janson & Co was made subject to the new charge in favour of Adie, it is reasonable to suppose that the loan from Adie had been used to repay Brown Janson & Co, at least in part.

Meanwhile, Inglis's tenancy had been renewed from year to year.

But at the beginning of 1877 Inglis started to break up the grass in the garden park, whereupon Tait applied for, and was granted in the Sheriff Court an injunction to restrain Inglis from carrying out any more work there.[7]

However, this dispute did not prevent Tait from granting Inglis a new lease for fourteen years from Whitsun 1877, at an annual rent of £300.

This arrangement was welcomed in the local community because Inglis had a reputation as an improving tenant, in addition to which Tait was to undertake improvements himself, including cleaning out the existing, and putting in new, sheep drains, as well as rebuilding the dry stone walls. The *Shetland Times* of 20 January 1877 hoped that 'ere long what was formerly a standing disgrace to the agriculture of the beautiful valley of

Tingwall will become the most fertile and smiling'. But it was not to be.

Although Tait had expected his latest financial problems to be solved before the loan from Adie fell due for repayment, they were not, and the loan remained outstanding until Adie, by virtue of the power of sale contained in his charge, eventually caused the Laxfirth estate to be offered for sale by auction in September 1878. Not for the first time, it failed to sell. However, it was offered again on 31 October, with a reserve price of £5,000, and this time it was apparently bought by a John Robertson. What then happened seems to suggest, at this distance of time, that the sale and purchase on 31 October was not a genuine transaction at all.

It was not until 27 September 1880 that the disposition transferring the title to Robertson was entered into, and on the following day Robertson executed a disposition transferring the estate back to Adie for £5,000.[8] But the rating records show that Adie himself paid the rates as proprietor throughout the whole of 1878, 1879 and 1880 and continued to do so until the estate was sold to the Leslie family in 1891; perhaps following the expiry of the lease granted to Inglis by Tait in 1877.

A Notary Public certified on 18 October 1880 that it appeared, from a statement subscribed as authentic by Adie, that there was no surplus remaining for Tait's other creditors, which, had there been a genuine sale at £5,000, would have been the case.

Only two other aspects of Tait's adventure into Shetland call for notice.

A new Commission of Peace for the County of Orkney and Shetland, issued in June 1878 showed that Sir Peter Tait, Knight, of Laxfirth, had been added to the former list of Justices of the Peace. JPs were appointed by the Crown, usually on the recommendation of the Lord-Lieutenant of the County, and had important powers and duties in the County. That Tait should have been appointed a JP for Orkney and Shetland in 1878 is surprising, as he had been living in Constantinople since 1875.

And shortly following his appointment as a JP it emerged that Tait still owed the Collector of the local tax imposed by the United Parishes of Tingwall, Whiteness and Weisdale £9 7s 6d for the year 1877 and £11 5s for the year 1878. The Collector, who said that

Tait had 'left Scotland in or about 1876 and was now in London or elsewhere', petitioned the Sheriff Court for the Grant of Letters authorising the Arrestment of 'debts and effects due and belonging to' [Tait] 'in the hands of sundry persons within' [the Court's] 'jurisdiction which he intends to withdraw to the prejudice of the Petitioner'. The Petition was granted on 25 September 1878.[9] Whether or not the Collector eventually got his money is unfortunately not known. In any case, Tait himself was by now well beyond the jurisdiction of the Court and, not for the first time, had other, more serious, financial difficulties to worry about.

20

Financial Difficulties in Limerick
1873-1880

In spite of the Shetland interlude, Tait was still involved in Limerick.

In March 1874 a general election was held. But, instead of contesting Orkney and Shetland again, Tait entered the contest in Limerick, again in favour of Home Rule, or so he said, although it was generally thought that he was in reality a Unionist. There were, in addition to Tait, four other candidates: Isaac Butt, the sitting member, and Richard O'Shaughnessy, both Home Rulers, together with Sir James Spaight and Col Charles S Vereker, both Unionists. Butt and O'Shaughnessy were elected with 856 and 848 votes respectively; Spaight, Vereker and Tait securing 557, 242 and 291 votes respectively.

To give him his due, Tait's attention may well have been elsewhere at the time, as his mother, Margaret Linklater, or Tait, died on 21 March. She was 79 years old and had been ill for about eight weeks. She was living with Barbara and Balfour Logie and their family at Oakleigh Park in north London. Margaret was buried in the same grave as Tait's father, at Kensal Green.

It will be remembered that in October of 1871 Tait had bought back the lease of his clothing factory from the Inspectors in the bankruptcy of Tait & Co; having borrowed £5,000 on mortgage from the C of E Institution to enable him to do so. The first repayment, of £1,000, became due in October 1873, but Tait was unable to pay it and the Institution agreed to defer it for three months. In June, when it had still not been paid by Tait, the Institution agreed to a further postponement, provided the full £5,000 was repaid in the following October. But, come October, Tait still had no money, although he did manage to repay £1,000;

the Institution agreeing that the balance of £4,000 should be repaid in equal half yearly instalments.[1] There is no record of the intended amount of these instalments, but, in any case, none of them was ever paid.

Meanwhile, the clothing factory continued operating, sometimes busy, sometimes less so, depending, as it did, on the fluctuating demand for uniforms, whether from the British or foreign Governments. Although the value of army clothing being bought from the trade as a whole by the British Government had recovered from the level of £30,000 in 1870-71, to £84,000 by 1873-74, it had fallen again to £50,000 in 1875-76. Even though orders for the major part of this clothing were secured by the Limerick factory, it was far too little to keep it fully occupied. However, a substantial order from the Prussians has already been noticed, and in January 1874 there was an order for uniforms for the Spanish army. There were almost certainly orders from Turkey. The Canada Militia was still being supplied, as, once more, was the Royal Irish Constabulary.

However, not only was Tait still unable to repay his loan from the C of E Institution, whose 1871 mortgage was still outstanding, but Sir Peter Tait & Co still owed money to Brown Janson & Co, in respect of which Tait had of course given, as collateral security for his personal bond, a charge over the 1858 lease of the clothing factory, including all the fixed and movable plant and machinery on the premises.

The closure of the clothing factory

Then, in November 1875, the clothing factory was closed without notice and all the six hundred employees were put out of work.

The news was given by William Abraham and the ostensible reason for the closure was Tait's 'failure to obtain a contract for the clothing of the Turkish army'. It seems unlikely that this can have been the reason, because the factory was already working on contracts for the clothing of the Turkish army, some of which had been finished and the goods delivered before the factory closed. On the other hand, to put it the other way round, the closure of course prevented Tait from obtaining any further contracts for the supply of uniforms, whether from Turkey or anywhere else, because he no longer had a manufacturing facility.

The real reason for the closure was almost certainly another financial crisis, the proximate cause of which may well have been the spectacular failure of Alexander Collie in June 1875. With that went the 'assets remaining in bank', or the case of Tait v Collie, which in 1872 Tait had hoped would produce a very large sum of money; indeed he seems to have hoped that its result would be that, instead of Tait & Co owing Collie some £43,000 as claimed by Collie, Collie would owe perhaps the same amount to Tait & Co. That might have meant that creditors in the bankruptcy could be paid in full, with something over for the firm's partners as well.

It is not clear for how long the factory remained closed, but it was probably for not more than a few months. It was re-opened by a new company formed in Ireland, the Limerick Army Clothing Company Limited, which became the tenant of the factory in place of Tait; the Institution, whose 1871 mortgage was still outstanding, granting it a lease for seven years, no doubt on the same terms as to the payment of rent as had applied to Tait.

Nothing is now known for certain about this company beyond its name, and that Thomas Hamilton was its Secretary, because all the official records were destroyed when, in May 1921, the IRA set fire to the Custom House in Dublin, where they were kept.

However, since Thomas Hamilton continued as manager of the factory and both Tait and Robert Tait continued to be very closely involved, it seems likely that it had been formed to give the Taits the benefit of limited liability. It would not have been surprising if Tait had wanted to avoid involvement in another bankruptcy.

When the factory opened again, the crisis seems to have been overcome, at least for the time being, and by 1878, if not before, there were again some five or six hundred employees. Also, by 1879, Robert Tait had taken over as manager from Hamilton. However, it had become more difficult, if not impossible, to obtain foreign orders, due to a dearth of major military conflicts throughout the world. It was therefore more than ever important for the factory to obtain a significant share of the increasing number of orders for clothing now being placed by the British Government. These orders had recently been fixed at two-sevenths of the total requirement for clothing in each year and were worth in total £196,000 in 1878-79, £98,000 in 1879-80 and £125,000 in 1880-81. Fortunately, early in 1879 the factory had received an order for 100,000 uniforms, which kept it busy until the end of that year, and a further order for 60,000 garments at the beginning of 1880.

Beyond that, things did not look so hopeful.

Although it was important for Tait that the factory should be busy, it was even more so for the city of Limerick, where there was, by 1880, considerable poverty and distress, caused by unemployment among the men and a depression in trade generally.

In June 1880 a deputation from Limerick called on Mr Childers, the Secretary of State for War, at the War Office in London. The deputation included the Earl of Limerick, Deputy Lieutenant for the County of Limerick, Messrs O'Shaughnessy and Gabett, Members of Parliament for the City, Mr O'Sullivan, one of the Members for the County, and Robert Tait. They impressed upon Childers the vast importance of the factory to the working class of Limerick, particularly during the present distress. They also pointed out the considerable saving to be gained by the public service which would be effected by giving the factory a regular and secured supply of work to do. Childers indicated that it would be one thing to give the factory an order to relieve the present distress, but quite another, and one which would require careful consideration, to promise a regular supply of work for the future.

However, Childers was not slow to act in the case of the present need; he immediately wrote to the Local Government Board for Ireland, in Dublin, asking whether there was exceptional distress in Limerick, as represented on behalf of the clothing factory. The Board's report confirmed that such distress existed and went on to say that 'the hands engaged in the army clothing factory have no prospect ... of obtaining suitable employment from any other source if discharged from the factory, and ... on previous occasions when this has happened the girls employed have sunk to the lowest depths of poverty and privation'. The report went on to say that on this occasion 'their sufferings ... would I fear be severer than usual owing to the general want of money in the city and the deficiencies of trade'.[2]

The result of this was an agreement that the existing contracts should be renewed; an order for 40,000 garments being issued immediately.

As well as writing to the Local Government Board for Ireland, a letter went to Mr W E Foster at the Irish Office, where tenders had just been received for the supply of 12,000 helmets for the Royal Irish Constabulary, for the period ending 31 March 1882. The lowest tender, at 5s 11¾d each, had been received from a supplier in London. The Limerick factory had tendered 6s each; an extra cost over the whole of the contract of £12 10s. Foster was asked whether, in view of the distress existing in Limerick, the contract should be given to the Limerick factory. His answer was that in his opinion it should.[3]

Again, in October 1885, Thomas Hamilton wrote to the Lord-Lieutenant, pressing the claims of the Limerick factory to a larger share of the orders for clothing for 1886 issued by the War Department. The Lord-Lieutenant took the matter up with the Secretary of State for War, with the result that orders for 132,000 garments were received.[4]

How might the course of history have been altered, if the cries of help from Ireland during the famine years had received the same sympathetic responses?

21

Constantinople: the Early years
1874-1878

On Wednesday 28 May 1873 Tait had again attended the annual dinner of the Royal Literary Fund, held on this occasion in Freemasons Hall. He went as an ordinary member, paying one guinea for a dinner ticket, but again, he failed to complete the cheque on the back of the menu.

The Prime Minister, William Gladstone, was in the chair, and it is interesting to note that among the stewards were Samuel Laing, the victor of the recent by-election in Orkney and Shetland, William Monsell MP, still one of the Members for the County of Limerick, and Jonathan Pim MP, the Member for Dublin City since 1865 and who had been a shareholder in Tait's ill-fated Steamship Company.[1]

I think it is not too fanciful to suggest that the significance of this dinner, for Tait, may have been the presence of the Turkish Ambassador among the guests. Did they meet and thus sow the seeds of Tait's ultimately disastrous relationship with the Sublime Porte?

The clouds of war were gathering about the Ottoman Empire and Tait will have foreseen the opportunity for substantial business. What he could not foresee was the Empire's impending bankruptcy; that he would not receive payment in full for the goods he supplied. A Government which defaulted on its obligations was outside his experience.

Without entering upon a study of the financial affairs of the Ottoman Empire in the second half of the nineteenth century, it may be helpful to look very briefly at the circumstances prevailing during the period of Tait's involvement and at how they arose.[2]

When the Sublime Porte declared war on Russia in October 1853, an event which led to the Crimean War, in which Turkey was joined by Britain, France and Sardinia, and which lasted until 1856, the finances of the Ottoman Empire were already in a parlous state. The costs of the war meant that things became worse and, almost immediately, the Sublime Porte was forced, for the first time, to look outside the Empire for funds and over the next twenty years it was to contract an increasing number of foreign loans.

But in spite of this, the Empire was never for long out of financial difficulties; it simply spent beyond its means.

Insurrection in the Balkans

Then, in July 1875, two of the nations subject to Ottoman rule, Herzegovina and Bosnia, revolted; soon to be followed by other neighbouring states.

But, although the expenses involved in restoring order in the Balkans put yet further strains on the Empire's finances, the world was not prepared for what happened next.

Bankruptcy of the Ottoman Empire

In October 1875 the Ottoman Council of Ministers announced that, for five years, the interest on the Empire's external loans, by now totalling some £200,000,000, would be paid, only one half in cash, the other half in securities paying interest of 5% per annum. Financial disaster was complete when, after only one payment on this basis in the following January, payment stopped altogether. The Ottoman Empire was, to all intents and purposes, bankrupt.

The situation was now desperate and, finding itself unable to raise further funds abroad, the Government determined on a desperate solution; the printing of paper money. But this could only be done with the concurrence of the Imperial Ottoman Bank.

The Imperial Ottoman Bank had been founded by an Ottoman Act of Concession in 1863 as the State Bank of the Empire. Although it had its head office in Constantinople, control rested with two Committees, one British in London, the other French in Paris. The Bank had been granted, inter alia, the exclusive privilege of the issue of paper money. As a corollary, the Ottoman

Government, by Article 12 of the Act, had expressly undertaken not itself to issue any paper money.

However, in the circumstances that had arisen, the Bank agreed to the waiver of Article 12 of the Act of Concession, in return for a commission equal to one per cent of the paper money issued and the agreement of the Government that the issue would be controlled by the Bank. It had little choice.

Existing currency

Since 1844 the coinage of the Empire had consisted of the gold *lira,* or Turkish pound (abbreviated as £T), divided into 100 silver *piastres,* the twenty *piastre* coin being known as the *mecidiye,* although there were also still in circulation throughout the Empire, much debased, pre-1844 coins. Paper money had been experimented with in the past, but it had all been withdrawn some years before 1875. During the whole period of Tait's involvement in the Ottoman Empire, the Turkish pound traded at a rate of approximately 110 to 100 pounds sterling.

However, there was also in circulation a considerable Government debt in the form of *sergis.* These were in effect acknowledgements of debt issued by the Porte or by Government Ministries either in respect of loans or in respect of goods supplied. They seem to have differed little from paper money and there was no limit to the number outstanding from time to time.

Although *sergis* could not themselves be exchanged for cash, they could, for example, be used as security for bank advances. To obtain cash, *sergis* had to be exchanged, in the case of a merchant such as Tait, for commercial *havales,* or exchequer drafts drawn by the Government on provincial treasuries and payable out of specified local revenues; for example the sheep or goat tax, the tithe of grain tax and so forth. Because merchants rarely had agents in the provinces to act for them in the collection of *havales,* they were frequently sold, at a substantial discount, to *sarrafs,* who were money lenders and brokers, generally of non Muslim origin, known locally as 'Galata bankers' from the area of Constantinople in which they operated, and who then arranged for their collection. Alternatively, if an *havale* was not sold to a *sarraf,* but collected in person by a merchant or his agent, substantial backsheesh, or 'commissions', would have to be paid to the various local officials concerned in the transaction, for making the necessary arrangements. Another difficulty, which frequently occurred, was that the Government would issue, against the tax revenues of a particular year, *havales* vastly in excess of the amount of the tax collected, so that the *havales* of the less fortunate holders - or perhaps the holders who had paid the least amount of backsheesh to the local officials - were paid only in part, or not at all; the balance, or the whole amount, being carried forward to a later year, or sometimes indefinitely.

The issue of paper money

Agreement having been reached between the Imperial Ottoman Bank and the Government for the proposed issue of paper money, a Government decree followed on 16 August 1876 setting out the terms governing the issue of the equivalent of a maximum of £T3,000,000 in the form of 300,000,000 paper *kaimes*. Initially, 200,000,000 *kaimes* would be issued; one month's notice to be given before the issue of the remaining 100,000,000. The decree contained the important stipulation that, in respect of any contract entered into before 16 August 1876, settlement would still take place in the currency indicated in the contract; presumably to afford protection against any depreciation in the value of the new *kaimes*. But it appears that, in spite of this stipulation, any *havales* already issued in exchange for *sergis* became payable in *kaimes*, notwithstanding that the *sergis* themselves had been given in payment for contracts entered into before 16 August 1876.[3]

However, although there were nominally 100 paper *kaimes* to the Turkish pound, the *kaimes* rapidly became devalued; even at the outset the rate of exchange between the *kaime* and the Turkish pound was only about 115 *kaimes* to the pound.

For example, although an *havale* for £T100 could be encashed for 10,000 *kaimes*, with an exchange rate of 115 *kaimes* to the £T, the recipient of the *kaimes* immediately suffered a loss, since his 10,000 *kaimes* would only be sufficient to buy £T87; and that ignores the costs of actually getting the *havale* encashed in the first place. As the value of *kaimes* depreciated further, the discrepancy between theory and fact became ever greater.

Notwithstanding this first issue of *kaimes,* the Government was soon again in financial crisis, and on 5 January 1877 a second decree announced the issue of a further 700,000,000 *kaimes;* making, with the first issue, a total of 1,000,000,000 *kaimes.*[4] But this was not to be all. Between August 1877 and December 1878 a further 600,000,000 *kaimes* were issued. Not surprisingly, the effect of these further issues was to accelerate the depreciation in the value of *kaimes.*

The rate of exchange, which had already fallen to 147 *kaimes* to the Turkish pound by the end of 1876, was to fall to 256 by the end of 1877, 500 by the end of 1878 and 1,000 by the end of 1879.[5]

Such was the financial state of the country with which, and in which, Tait started to do business in 1874.

Sources

What follows is based upon the following sources, which are remarkably complete –

1 the files of the British Embassy and Consulate in Constantinople;

2 the papers of the British Supreme Consular Court in Constantinople (the Consular Court); and

3 the journals and ledgers of the Imperial Ottoman Bank; the Bank principally used by Tait.

Except to the extent that they are reflected in one of these sources, there are no records of Tait's activities in Constantinople surviving from C S Hanson & Co or the Bank of Constantinople, two other banks used by Tait.

I have not found it possible to access the archives of the Ottoman Government, either in Istanbul or in Ankara, which has made it impossible to present other than an incomplete picture of the extent of Tait's dealings with the Sublime Porte.

Tait visits Constantinople

It appears that Tait, accompanied on this occasion by his wife, first visited Constantinople towards the end of May 1874. On this and on his other early visits, Tait stayed at the Hotel d'Angleterre in Pera, the modern quarter on the northern side of the Golden Horn.

He secured substantial orders, both from the Minister of War and from the Minister of Marine, probably for made up army and navy uniforms; perhaps also for other supplies, such as boots. We know that Tait was able to execute these orders, if not in full, at least in part, before his Limerick factory closed in 1875, and that by early in 1876 he was again in Constantinople, when he was to obtain further large orders.

The contracts obtained by Tait in 1874

From the surviving evidence, two things can be deduced about the contracts Tait obtained on his visit to Constantinople in 1874; first, the approximate value of the contracts, and, second, the loss Tait suffered as a result of having to accept payment for them, not in cash, but in *sergis* exchangeable for *havales,* one of which itself became payable in *kaimes.*

By June 1876 Tait had in his possession at least two *sergis;* one for about £T5,800 received from the Seraskerate, or Ministry of War, and one for about £T2,900, the source of which is not known. Taken together, these two *sergis* were for the sterling equivalent of about £7,900 [*about £320,000*], which must have been the minimum value of the goods already delivered by Tait.

Tait was eventually to receive the sterling equivalent of only about £5,700 for these two *sergis* and it may be of interest to follow the, unfortunately somewhat complex, steps which led to this result.

The sergi for £T5,800

In June 1876, Tait evidently needed to raise some money without waiting for the *sergis* to be exchanged for *havales* and for those to be collected. He therefore resorted to the method for raising cash which had initially proved so successful, but ultimately so disastrous, in his dealings with Alexander Collie ten years before. To do this, he first granted Erskine Foster, who was a lawyer and the son of the General Manager of the Imperial Ottoman Bank in Constantinople, a Power of Attorney, which was registered in the Consular Court on 9 June. Tait then accepted bills of exchange for £2,500 drawn by Foster, which Foster discounted with the Imperial Ottoman Bank, depositing Tait's *sergi* for £T5,800 with the Bank as security. There is nothing to show what Tait did with the £2,500, although he almost certainly sent it to Robert Tait in London, where the need was greatest.

Tait then arranged for Foster to exchange this *sergi* for two *havales*,[6] each for £T2,800 payable out of the revenues of the *vilayet*, or province, of Rustchuk, the collection of which was entrusted by Tait, not to the Imperial Ottoman Bank, but to C S Hanson & Co. The town of Rustchuk itself (now Ruse) is in Bulgaria on the south bank of the Danube about two hundred and fifty miles north west of Constantinople.

The two *havales* were duly collected by Hanson and produced a total of about £3,600 net; out of which £2,500 was paid to the Imperial Ottoman Bank in settlement of the £2,500 owed by Tait on the discounted bills of exchange; £500 was paid to the Bank in settlement of a further loan of that amount which Tait had contracted, the proceeds of which had been sent to Robert on 8 November; and the remaining £600 was credited to Tait's account with Hanson.

The sergi for £T2,900

At the same time as Foster had exchanged the *sergi* for £T5,800 for the *havales* on the province of Rustchuk, he had, at Tait's request, also exchanged the *sergi* for £T2,900 for an *havale* for £T2,800, payable in this case out of the revenues of the *vilayet* of Broussa, which borders the Asiatic shore of the Sea of Marmara. The town of Broussa (now Bursa) is about fifty-seven miles south south east of Constantinople. This *havale* was evidently an example which could only be exchanged for *kaimes*.

In August 1876 Tait borrowed, in addition to the £2,500 he had earlier received from the discounting of the bills of exchange, a further £2,500 directly from the Bank. This was sent to Robert Tait in London in two instalments, each of £1,250, one on 20 August , the other on 27 August; repayment to be made out of the proceeds of the encashment of the *havale* on Broussa, which on this occasion was entrusted by Tait to Foster. It gave rise to an extraordinary episode.

On 30 August, Tait wrote a letter to Foster authorising him to obtain payment of the *havale* and, if he succeeded, authorising him to 'deduct twenty per cent from the proceeds and apply them to your own use'. Foster proceeded to Broussa and obtained payment of the *havale* about six weeks later.

However, because the *havale* was the Bank's security for its loan to Tait, Foster had to give the proceeds to the Bank, which credited them in full to Tait's account without anything being deducted in respect of Foster's twenty per cent commission; this Tait subsequently refused to pay.

Eventually, in November 1876, it was agreed by all concerned that the dispute over the payment of the commission should be referred to three arbitrators, the award of all, or of any two of whom, was to be final and without appeal. After much deliberation, extending over almost three months, and having heard Counsel for both Foster and Tait, the arbitrators held their final meeting on Saturday 3 February 1877. Two of them were of the opinion that Tait should pay the commission to Foster, but the third, Thomas Nasmyth, requested that the award should not be drawn up until the following Monday and that, meanwhile, he would consider the matter. However, Nasmyth became ill and died twelve days later without having indicated whether or not he could concur in the opinion of his colleagues. Notwithstanding this, the remaining two arbitrators went ahead and made their award.

Tait still refused to pay and the matter came before the Consular Court, where it was decided that Nasmyth's death had rendered the whole arbitration, including the award made by the surviving two arbitrators, null and void. And, since the agreement for arbitration, reached the previous November, had made it a condition that Foster should initiate the arbitration within three days of the agreement, it was held to be too late for him now to seek a fresh arbitration.[7]

So Tait did not pay the commission, a large part of which Foster had no doubt paid to the local officials in Broussa to 'facilitate' the payment of the *havale*. Perhaps Tait had good reason to act as he did; we are not in a position to judge.

However, even without paying any commission to Foster, the proceeds of the collection of the *havale* on Broussa were insufficient to cover the cost of the sums sent to Robert in August and the shortfall was made good by Tait from his account with Hanson, as follows -[8]

Sums remitted to London –			
20 August 1876 - £1,250 @ £T110 to the £1			£T 1,375.00
27 August 1876 - £1,250 @ £T110 to the £1			1,375.00
Bank commission			12.50
			2,762.50
Proceeds of the *havale* on Broussa -			
280,000 *kaimes* @ 114½ *kaimes* to the £T		£T 2,445.41	
Less: Bank charges	£T 53.33		
Bank interest @ 10%	37.31	90.64	2,354.77
Shortfall paid to the Imperial Ottoman Bank by Tait			£T 407.73

Thus, by the time the *sergis* in Tait's possession in June 1876 had actually been exchanged for *havales,* and, in the case of the smaller one, the *havale* had been paid not in Turkish pounds but in *kaimes,* at the rate of 114½ *kaimes* to the pound, Tait had received the equivalent of only about £5,700; £2,500 following the discounting of the bills of exchange by Foster in June 1876, £2,500 advanced by the Bank in August, the further £500 advanced by the Bank in November and the net payment of £200 to his account with Hanson.

It had taken Tait a year to obtain settlement from the Ottoman Government of his invoices for goods supplied prior to November 1875, and that settlement had produced only three quarters of the amounts due.

A move borne of desperation

It is easy with hindsight to see that it was unwise of Tait to make his next move, even though he desperately needed to make some money.

On 28 November 1876 he entered into a contract with Hassan Pasha, then Chief of the Intendancy of the Seraskerate, to supply 300,000 metres of English woollen cloth at a price of 30 *piastres* a metre, for which he would receive *sergis* redeemable in *kaimes,* which then stood at 120 *kaimes* to the Turkish pound.[9] There was a lot involved. The Imperial equivalent of 300,000 metres is 186 miles, and the sterling equivalent of 300,000 metres at 30 *piastres* a metre (payable in *kaimes* at 120 *kaimes* to the £T) was £68,200 [*nearly £2,800,000*]. The potential for error was enormous.

Not surprisingly, Tait had been reluctant to enter into a contract for payment in *kaimes,* but Hassan Pasha had said that the contract could only be made in that currency. He had assured Tait that no further issue of paper money would be made, beyond the 3,000,000 liras authorised by the decree of 16 August 1876, and that the issue, being tied to the rate of the *beşlik* and the *metalik,* it was impossible that there could be any depreciation of it.

Tait had still hesitated, but having taken the advice of leading bankers, as well as legal advice, he became convinced that, without a violation of the Imperial decree regarding the issue of the paper money, there was no reason to anticipate danger. After all, the decree said that the repayment of the value was to be guaranteed and amortised, by coal mines, chrome mines and other valuable property, handed over by the Civil List to the Imperial Treasury.

Also, because the *sergis* were to be redeemable directly in *kaimes,* rather than having first to be exchanged for *havales* and then into *kaimes,* Tait would not have to incur the costs involved in the discounting or redemption of *havales,* which had cost him so dearly before.

And so he had signed the contract.

There are no records to show why Tait supplied cloth and not complete uniforms, as the army clothing factory in Limerick had by now re-opened following its closure in 1875. However, there were army clothing manufacturers in Constantinople and so presumably, even if it was not less expensive for the uniforms to be made up there, rather than in Limerick, there would have been a useful saving of foreign currency by the Ottoman Government.

The first signs of trouble

By the time Tait was due to start delivering cloth, the second issue of *kaimes* had taken place and the value of *kaimes* had fallen below 150 *kaimes* to the Turkish pound. Tait therefore went to see Hassan Pasha and said that, unless some satisfactory arrangement could be reached regarding the rate at which he would receive *kaimes* under the contract, he could not deliver the cloth. Upon which Tait was promised by Hassan Pasha that the question of the price of the *kaime* would be satisfactorily settled; a promise repeated by him on several subsequent occasions. He begged Tait to deliver the cloth, 'it being most urgently needed for the soldiers, it being the depth of winter and the weather very severe'. Tait therefore began to deliver the cloth, although on several occasions he asked Hassan Pasha for a letter confirming what he had promised regarding the price of the *kaime,* to which the answer was always that his word was quite sufficient.[10]

When, in May 1877, Tait had delivered nearly 67,000 metres of cloth, for which he had accepted *kaimes* in payment, and by which time he had sold about 1,258,000 of those *kaimes* in exchange for Turkish pounds at ever worsening rates of exchange, he arranged for the Imperial Ottoman Bank to sell a further 200,000 *kaimes.* By then the price of *kaime* was 178¼ *kaimes* to the Turkish pound and so, after deduction of the Bank's commission of one eighth per cent, Tait received only £T1,120; a loss on exchange of £T880.

The British Embassy becomes involved

This seems finally to have brought home to Tait the need to take some positive action to obtain an agreement as to the price at which he would receive *kaimes* under his contract with the Seraskerate. He therefore refused to deliver any more cloth until this was achieved. Tait then not only engaged the interest of the Right Hon Austin H Layard, the British Ambassador, but also obtained an opinion from Hassan Fehmi Effendi, a local lawyer,[11] which was favourable. The Ambassador, meanwhile, sought the opinion of J H Fawcett, the Consul-General and Judge of the Consular Court,[12] and wrote as well to the Sublime Porte in support of Tait's case.

This activity culminated in a meeting held on 27 June 1877, between Tait and Hassan Pasha, at which Hassan Fehmi Effendi (now Hassan Fehmi Pasha, Minister of Public Works), as well as Tait's English barrister, Edwin Pears, were also present. At this meeting, after much discussion, Hassan Pasha agreed to settle the price of *kaime,* by way of compromise, at 130 *kaimes* to the gold lira. The meeting ended on Hassan Pasha's assurance that the matter was finally arranged.

However, barely two hours later, Tait was sent for to be told by Hassan Pasha that his superiors felt that the settlement agreed upon earlier should be submitted to the Sublime Porte for confirmation. Hassan Pasha had therefore written a strong letter to the Prime Minister in support of what had been agreed. When Tait expressed his deep regret on receiving this intimation, Hassan Pasha replied 'What can I do with a Council comprised of seventy or eighty Pashas?'.[13]

Notwithstanding this unexpected setback, Tait resumed delivery of the cloth.

It later turned out that Hassan Pasha's letter had been referred by the Prime Minister to the Council of State, which had refused to sanction the agreement which had been reached, on the ground that it would create a precedent for others having similar claims.

This was no doubt the case, and the Porte maintained this stand throughout the whole of the subsequent negotiations. But Tait was advised that it did not affect the position in law, under which he was entitled to compensation for the depreciation in the value of *kaimes*, which had been brought about by the actions of the Ottoman Government.

By the time Tait learned of the Council of State's decision, he had delivered 106,927½ metres of cloth altogether, but he then again stopped, and was never to resume, the delivery of the remaining 193,072½ metres.

In October, Layard wrote again to the Porte, asking for the matter to be reviewed, but again the answer was the same.[14]

By then, Tait had actually received from the Seraskerate *sergis* for £T32,078, payable in the form of 3,207,800 *kaimes*, which was the total amount due in respect of the whole of the cloth delivered. But, as we have seen, he had only exchanged *sergis* for £T14,580 (for 1,458,000 *kaimes*), leaving *sergis* for £T17,498 outstanding. Perhaps he felt that if he exchanged any more, at the rapidly depreciating current market rate for *kaimes*, his chances of obtaining any adjustment later would be lessened.

At much the same time as Tait entered into the contract with the Seraskerate in November 1876, he entered into a contract with the Minister of Marine for the supply of merchandise, which he delivered at the end of that year and at the beginning of 1877. I do

11. James Tait, son of Robert Tait and Ellen Hinchy

Sity Goal May 14th 1867,
Limerick

To His Excelency
The Lord Leintenant of Ireland
been here as a prisoner. I beg
of you to See me justified. I
am the mother of two children
the Father of them. is the Mayors Brother
of this Sity. He wishes to have
me put into a madhouse. I am
not insain. if such things
can take place. why they may
make laws themselves. for
State Fact the Mayor, has a
Kept me to London,
they put me in the hands

12. The letter written by Ellen Hinchy to the Lord-Lieutenant of Ireland on 14 May 1867.

of a Doctor my child
died in the Doctors hands.
My health since then has
been very bad. They then took
away my Child 18 years and
a halfe now old, and it is
for asking to see him that
I have been imprisoned. it is
onely by trying to baffel justice
that they are trying to put me to
a Madhouse. May it please
your Excelency to see me
justified you will have
The prayers of your humble
Servant Ellen Hinchey

13. A recent photograph of Laxfirth House in Shetland.

14. The Arms granted to Peter Tait in 1868, and photographs of Sir Peter and Lady Tait taken in Constantinople in 1874.

15. A photograph of Sir Peter Tait, thought to have been taken in Australia in 1882.

16. The staircase at 27 Rue Venedik in Constantinople.

17. The Hôtel de France in Batoum, where Tait died in 1890.

18. The author at work in the Ottoman Bank Archives and Research Centre, Istanbul, in 2002.

not know what this merchandise was. Tait himself referred to 'goods supplied under very pressing exigencies of the Government, the sailors being about to proceed to the Black Sea'.[15]

As in the case of the contract with the Seraskerate, there developed a lengthy dispute over payment. It seems as though the point at issue was the same in both cases, since Tait asserted that in this case the Minister of Marine and the President of the Council of the Admiralty had promised to be responsible to him for any depreciation in the value of *kaimes.* Negotiations took place throughout 1877, without reaching a satisfactory conclusion, and in April 1878 Edwin Pears began proceedings on Tait's behalf in the Commercial Tribunal of the Tidjaret, the Ottoman Commercial Court, claiming payment based on the value of *kaimes* at the time the contract was entered into.[16]

However, in spite of, or perhaps because of, his problems with the Ottoman Government, Tait was evidently turning his hand to new lines of business, with mixed success.

Russia declares war

Meanwhile, compounding the Ottoman Government's difficulties, Russia had declared war on the Sublime Porte on 24 April 1877. Advancing through the Balkans, the Russians took Adrianople (now Edirne), within 135 miles of Constantinople, in January 1878. The war did not finally end until the Treaty of Berlin was signed in July 1878, although it was not until after the conclusion of the definitive Russo-Turkish Treaty in February 1879 that the Russians retired from the territories they had occupied during the war.

Peter Tait Son & Co

The proceeds of the sale of the *kaimes* in May 1877 seem to have been used to establish a new firm, Peter Tait Son & Co. The son must have been Peter, junior, who had been born in 1860 and who had presumably joined his father in Constantinople.

There is little to show what this new firm did, although it entered into a contract with the Russian Military Authorities, following the end of the Russo-Turkish war, for the purchase from them of surplus war materials. This contract was to give rise to an incident, described in the next chapter, which occurred at the end of 1878.

At least initially, the firm had two employees, John Stark and a man called Isaacson. Stark had been born in Londonderry in 1840 although he had been baptised at St Margaret's, Westminster. He was an engineer and had lived in Turkey since 1870. It is not known for how long he worked for Tait, but by 1885 he was manager of the Small Arms Department of the Ottoman Government Arsenal at Tophane. Of Isaacson nothing is known.

The account of Peter Tait Son & Co with the Imperial Ottoman Bank shows that in 1877 its expenditure amounted to about £T3,000, in 1878 to £T2,600, in 1879 it was negligible, but in 1880 it was about £T1,400, in 1881 £T2,300 and in 1882 about £T400; a total for the six years of £T9,700 [*about £470,000*].

There is no information about the firm's income, although it probably made at least some contribution towards Tait's expenses in Constantinople. After 1882 there is no mention of the firm in such records as I have seen.

Domestic arrangements

By this time, Tait was no longer staying at the Hotel d'Angleterre, but had settled into a house in the Rue de Pologne (now Nuri Ziya Sokagi), a turning off the eastern side of the Grande Rue de Pera (now Istiklal Caddesi) just north of the church of St. Antoine. The house itself, which was almost opposite the English High School for Girls and backed onto the yard of a small joinery workshop, has now disappeared as part of a particularly ugly development.

There is nothing to show whether Tait and his son were lodgers or whether they had their own apartment in the house. In the latter case Tait presumably had a servant, since Rose, apart from her first visit in 1874, remained in England throughout the whole of what was to be Tait's lengthy stay in Constantinople. Tait had given up Tingwall House in Clapham and his family lodged at Boston Villas, Mount Ararat Road, in Richmond.

He must also have had some secretarial assistance, because his letters were very seldom, whether in English or French, written in his own hand. Although there is nothing to show whether Tait could speak or write French, he probably had at least a working knowledge of the language, which was the principal commercial and diplomatic language used in Constantinople at that time. For his numerous meetings with officials of the Ottoman Government, he was accompanied by one of the Embassy dragomans, or interpreters.

A family wedding

Meanwhile, back in London, on 4 May 1878, Tait's third daughter, Rose, had married James Bryan; she was 20, he 36. Witnesses to the marriage were James's brother, Frank, and on Rose's side her mother, Barbara and Balfour Logie, and Robert Tait.

James Bryan was a partner in Bryan Bros & Co, who were described in Kelly's trades directory as 'curriers, japanners, leather merchants, manufacturers of accoutrements, helmets, busbies, shakos and saddlery etc' and were no doubt business associates of Tait & Co.

22

A Diplomatic Incident
1878

When, on 7 December 1878, Edmund Calvert, HM's Acting Consul in Adrianople, sent a letter to Sir Henry Layard,[1] with a copy to Lord Salisbury, the Secretary of State for Foreign Affairs in London, Adrianople was still occupied by the Russian army following the recent Russo-Turkish war. The letter speaks for itself - [2]

Sir,

I have the honour to report to Your Excellency the following particulars of the outrage on Her Majesty's Consulate and the forcible seizure of Mr Stark, announced by my telegram of this morning.

The day before yesterday Mr Isaacson, who is in the employ of Sir Peter Tait, called to enquire whether I could inform him what had become of Mr John Stark, a British subject, also employed by Sir Peter, who was known to have left Yeni Zaghra by rail on the 3rd instant, who had not made his appearance here, and who, it was rumoured, had been arrested by the Russian Authorities.

As this was the first I had heard of the matter I at once made enquiry of it of the Vice Governor, who is specially charged with all police matters. Major Oboukhoff replied that he knew nothing of any such affair, that he was perfectly aware that it was the duty of the Authorities, in cases where a foreign subject was charged with any offence, to apprise at once the Consulate under whose protection such subject might be placed, and that as no arrests were effected without his cognizance I might rest assured that there was no foundation for the rumours in question. I have no reason to doubt that the Vice Governor was sincere in this declaration.

Yesterday, towards the evening, Mr Stark drove up to the Consulate in a carriage, under the charge of a Russian soldier. I must here explain that Mr Stark's employer, Sir Peter Tait, some time ago passed a contract with the Russian Military Authorities for the purchase of useless war material. Mr Stark, in leaving Yeni Zaghra brought with him among other purchased material a considerable quantity of gunpowder without having, as he admits, made the declaration required by the rules of the railway company. For this offence he was arrested on his arrival at the Adrianople station (Karagatch). He was kept under close confinement in a room at the station, and prevented from holding communication with any person outside, during that night and the day and night following. He had not however, he says, cause to complain of his treatment otherwise. On the 5th instant he was conducted to town and lodged in a room at the "Hotel d'Amerique" but kept always under close guard by two soldiers who, as before, would not allow him to hold communication with any one. In this condition he passed that night also. It was only on the following (yesterday) afternoon, that his state of arrest was so far relaxed that he was allowed to move about under the surveillance of a single soldier. Thus was Mr Stark enabled at last to apprise me of his situation, which he did at once in person, as already stated.

I immediately sent the Dragoman of the Consulate with a message to the Governor, General Molostvoff, demanding the release of Mr Stark, for whose appearance, I added, the Consulate would in case of need be responsible. Mr Stark, still under guard, accompanied the Dragoman. The Governor replied that as he had nothing to do with the arrest it was not in his power to comply with my wish, but he would be happy to do what he could to that end. I then repeated my demand in writing, again reminding His Excellency that the Consulate was now answerable for Mr Stark, should he be wanted, and that requesting that the soldier under whose guard he was placed might be immediately withdrawn from the Consulate, where, I added, Mr Stark would for the present remain.

Before my written demand could reach him at the Government Konak, General Molostvoff had gone out, nor could His Excellency be found until about midnight, when he sent a verbal message in reply, to the effect that nothing could be done till next day (today). As I could not call upon the soldier to disobey orders and leave his prisoner, I made arrangements for his passing the night at the Consulate.

Whilst this was being done a Russian soldier appeared on the scene and demanded that Mr Stark should be given up to him in order to be conducted back to his quarters at the hotel. It is needless to say that I flatly refused. The sergeant then sent the soldier away with a message, himself remaining at the Consulate. My first Cavas [an armed attendant], who understands Russian a little, then informed me that he heard the sergeant telling the soldier to bring a guard of soldiers to carry off the prisoner by force. Upon this I caused the front and back doors of the Consulate to be locked inside, and kept the keys myself. Presently the guard came up, with fixed bayonets, and knocked at the door. I asked through the Cavas whether any officer or person with a message from the Governor was with them. They replied in the negative. I rejoined that the door could not in that case be opened, and told them to apply to the Governor. They remained outside. After a time the sergeant asked to be allowed to go out. By my order the Cavas complied with his wish, letting him out by the back door which had been left unguarded. About two o'clock in the morning when all in the house had retired to rest the front door of the Consulate was knocked at, but I ordered no notice to be taken of it, and after a time the knocking ceased.

Nothing further happened until half past eight this morning when a violent knocking at the front door was heard, accompanied by vociferations in Russian and Turkish to "open the door". I presented myself at a window on the ground floor close to the door, and found that the uproar proceeded from a large party headed by a person in civilian dress and a Bulgarian bonnet, and whom I afterwards learnt was the secretary of the "Bureau de la Police". He was accompanied by three policemen and eight or ten Russian soldiers. I asked the Secretary (in Turkish) what he wanted. He answered by calling out in a peremptory tone, "Open the door". I rejoined, "The door will certainly not be opened to you. Who sent you?". He replied, "I have orders to enter the Consulate". I said "I have already told you the door will not be opened to you, nor will it be opened to any person who does not bring an answer from the Governor to whom I have written". He repeated in a yet louder and more excited tone, "Open the door, I say!" and as I turned away to leave the window he bawled out, "If the door is not opened to us, we will break it open". I said, "I have no force to prevent you. Do as you choose". The party then began to push violently against the door endeavouring to burst it open. Not succeeding in this, a hatchet was brought with which one of the lower panels was soon cut away, and the Secretary, followed by the police and the soldiers, entered the Consulate through the opening thus made. I met them as they came in and asked what they meant to do. The Secretary passing on, answered in an insolent tone, "We are going to look into the rooms". Going upstairs, he opened one or two rooms until he came to the one where Mr Stark had been sleeping and where he was putting on his clothes. On seeing him the Secretary shouted to him, "Make haste!". Mr Stark did so and as soon as he was dressed the party conducted him downstairs. I asked the Secretary as he was going, "By whose orders do you act?". He replied

"By order of the Chief of the Police". The whole party then left the Consulate taking with them Mr Stark.

At 9.15, three quarters of an hour after the above occurrence, Mr Stark was brought back to the Consulate under the charge of a Russian officer who in a profoundly respectful manner handed me at the same time a letter dated yesterday the 6th inst. and signed by the President of the Court Martial; and a copy of which I beg to inclose. If anything were wanting to complete the illegality of the whole of the above outrageous proceedings it would be furnished, as your Excellency will observe, by the fact revealed in that letter, that "the Russian Authority having no further cause to retain Mr Stark", he had been placed, yesterday, by order of the Commander in Chief, "at my entire disposal".

No further incident has occurred.

I at once, as a matter of form, officially notified the circumstances to the Commander in Chief by a letter a copy of which I have the honour to inclose. Your Excellency will observe that I have confined myself to recording the facts in the simplest and briefest terms.

The Chief of the Police, a Russian Major named Vulpios, who by his own admission gave the immediate order under which the outrage was committed, has made in the course of the day several endeavours directly and indirectly to induce me to accept his humble excuses for the "mistake".

I have declined to hear anything this official might have to say. Whether he really acted on his own responsibility as these overtures would imply, or by superior orders, I am unable at present to conjecture.

In any case I regard the matter as one which it is now competent for your Excellency and Her Majesty's Government alone to deal with; and I earnestly hope that my conduct in this emergency may meet with the approval of my superiors.

I have the honour to be, with the highest respect,

Sir,

Your Excellency's most obedient,

humble servant,

Edmund Calvert

Acting Consul.

The letter of 6 December from the President of the Court Martial, referred to by Calvert, revealed that Stark had carried in one of the compartments of the train from Yeni Zaghra 280 ocques, or about seven hundredweights, of gunpowder and that it had been confiscated.[3]

On 7 December Calvert had also written a letter of complaint to General Todleben, the Commander-in-Chief of the Russian Army, who, the following day, sent an orderly officer to express great regret at what had occurred and to say that Major Vulpios had been dismissed from his post and placed under arrest.

But Calvert subsequently learned that, far from being under arrest, Vulpios had gone the previous night to a private soiree which was attended by Todleben and other officers of distinction, and to which it was known Calvert was invited. It was only on being spoken to by General Molostvoff, that Vulpios withdrew.[4]

On 10 December, Tait went, or perhaps was summoned, to an interview with Layard, following which Tait wrote him a letter.[5]

In this letter, Tait agreed that Stark should not have taken the gunpowder on board the train without giving proper notice to the authorities; adding that Stark's taking of the gunpowder to Adrianople was itself directly at variance with Tait's instructions. He went on to say that Stark had been treated throughout with consideration and courtesy, both by the Russians and by Calvert. Tait hoped that the matter might be regarded as closed, since Todleben had expressed his deep regret for the incident. Tait added "that Mr Stark being naturally very proud of his nationality was rather indiscreet in his conversation", about which Tait had reprimanded him on a previous occasion.

Had Stark perhaps said something indiscreet to the Russians, when he was found out with the gunpowder, which caused the matter to develop as it did?

Tait was, of course, in a difficult position. He could not afford to upset the Russians, from whom he had evidently purchased the gunpowder as 'useless war material', or Layard upon whose help he relied to obtain payment of the amounts he was owed by the Ottoman Government. Least of all could he afford to upset the Ottoman Government, from which he hoped to obtain payment of the amounts due to him.

Was Tait telling Layard the whole truth? He had no doubt bought the gunpowder from the Russians, hoping to sell it to the Ottomans. But was it Russian gunpowder to sell, or was it really Ottoman gunpowder seized by the Russians in their advance through Bulgaria?

Certainly, when somewhat later Tait applied to the Sublime Porte for permission to export some 'old irons' which he had bought from the Russians, the Porte refused him permission on the ground that 'it resembled material from the foundry at Samakov and the Grand Master of Artillery was unable to satisfy himself as to either the Russians' or Sir Peter Tait's title to it'.[6]

Both Yeni Zaghra (now Nova Zagora) and Samakov (now Samokov) in Bulgaria, like Adrianople, were Ottoman towns which had been occupied by the Russians during the recent war.

23

Constantinople: the Later Years
1879-1885

For the next seven years Tait's life in Constantinople was dominated by his efforts to obtain from the Ottoman Government payment for the goods supplied to it by him; a soul-destroying, time-consuming, and ultimately largely fruitless, task in which he depended heavily upon the British Embassy to bring pressure to bear on the Sublime Porte.

Tait was not of course the only British subject owed money by the Porte. As we shall see later, by 1881 a total of some £T280,000 [*nearly £12,000,000*] was owed to British subjects. One is left with the impression that a great deal more might have been achieved in a great deal less time if, instead of relying solely upon polite diplomatic exchanges which, perhaps not surprisingly, achieved little or nothing, the Embassy, representing as it did the most powerful nation on earth, had felt able back up these exchanges by some more forceful action. But to return to the sorry tale.

In 1878 Tait entered into his last contract with the Ottoman Government. This time he thought he was taking no possible risk, as payment was to be made in silver *piastres* and *mecidiye*.

The contract was for the sale to the Grand Master of Artillery, for the Arsenal at Tophane, of 118,903 ocques (just over 150 tons) of lead at the price of 2½ *piastres* an ocque, a total value of about £T3,000 [*about £130,000*], for settlement in four instalments on 18 March, 8 April, 29 April and 20 May 1879.[1]

The lead was delivered on time in December. Where it came from is not recorded. Perhaps Tait had acquired it from the Russian Military Authorities under the contract already referred to. Tait had supplied it at the special price of 2½ *piastres* an ocque, which the Grand Master accepted was 25% below the market price, only on condition that settlement would be made promptly on the agreed dates, although it need hardly be said that payment was not made when due; indeed more than a year later only £T250 had been paid.[2]

But in September 1879, there had been what appeared to be good news. Judgement was finally given against the Minister of Marine in the case begun in the Commercial Tribunal of the Tidjaret in April 1878, for the full amount of Tait's claim for £T7,002, with interest. However, nothing having been paid by November, Edwin Pears wrote to Layard asking him to use his influence to obtain payment. Layard therefore wrote to the Minister of Marine, who replied that the Ministry 'had found itself in the necessity of referring the matter to the Sublime Porte, with which it was presently in correspondence'.[3]

Diplomatic exchanges

On 31 December 1879 Layard therefore penned to Salisbury the first of a number of stately diplomatic exchanges. He said -

I regret to have to report to Your Lordship another instance of the bad faith of the Turkish Government in its dealings with British subjects.

At the commencement of the late war the Turkish Admiralty being in need of materials for clothing their navy, entered into an engagement with Sir Peter Tait who in consequence furnished them with materials to be paid for in *kaimes* or paper money then standing at 130 *piastres* to the gold *lira.*

Soon after these events and as the war progressed the fall in the value of paper money was such that it would have been simple ruin for Sir Peter to have accepted payment in the depreciating currency.

After vainly endeavouring for a year to arrive at an amicable settlement with the Turkish Admiralty Sir Peter was left with no other course but to sue the Admiralty before the Commercial Court of the Tidjaret. After a delay of another year he succeeded in obtaining a judgement against the Admiralty for the full amount of his claim, namely 700,210 *piastres,* with expenses, which was duly communicated to the Admiralty by the Minister of Foreign Affairs. Upon this the Admiralty appealed against the judgement by way of a "requête civile" or Revisory Court which after another year's delay confirmed the previous judgement. But up to this date, although the decision was final and there is no other legal course open to Sir Peter, the judgement has remained without effect.

On a personal representation to the Minister of Marine which I caused to be made it was pretended that the continued delay in settling the claim arose from a difficulty of deciding whether the money should be disbursed by the Dept. of Marine or of Finance. The former accusing the latter of causing depreciation of the paper currency by repeated emissions while the latter retorts that it has nothing to do with a contract to which it was not a party. And thus the matter stands with every possibility of continuing to do so unless Your Lordship will instruct me to insist on an immediate settlement of a claim which it is no more than justice to demand.

I did not take up this case officially, although frequently appealed to by Sir Peter Tait to do so, until he had brought the matter before the proper tribunals within whose competence it was. But now that he has received an ultimate judgement in his favour it appears to me that we are entitled to demand that it should be put into operation.

The question as to which Turkish Dept. should disburse the money does not concern us and may be left to the Porte to decide as it may see fit.

Salisbury replied, in his own hand, on 21 January -

I have received Your Excellency's despatch relative to a claim of Sir Peter Tait against the Turkish Admiralty, which has been decided in his favour by sentences delivered in two of the Ottoman Judicial Courts, but the settlement of which, notwithstanding, he has been unable to obtain.

I request that Your Excellency will support this case energetically and represent to the Porte the necessity for promptly carrying out the legal decisions pronounced by the Ottoman Tribunals in this case.

On 10 February Layard took up the matter with the Sublime Porte -

HM's Embassy has made repeated representations to the Sublime Porte relative to a claim of Sir Peter Tait against the Turkish Admiralty which has been decided in his favour by sentences delivered in two of the Ottoman Judicial Courts including that of ultimate appeal but the settlement of which, notwithstanding, he has been unable to obtain.

HM's Embassy has now the honour to inform the Sublime Porte that it has been instructed by HM's Principal Secretary of State for Foreign Affairs to support this case energetically and to represent to the Turkish Government the necessity for promptly carrying out the legal decisions pronounced by its own Tribunals in this case.

HM's Embassy trusts that the Porte will enable it to inform Lord Salisbury that the necessary measures have at once been taken to give effect to these decisions.

Having had no response, and Tait having asked for a report on progress, Layard tried again a month later -

On the 10th of last month HM's Embassy had the honour, in conformity with instructions received from HM's Government, of making again representations to the Sublime Porte on the continued delay on the part of the Imperial Government in giving effect to the decisions of its own Tribunals with reference to the claim of Sir Peter Tait.

HM's Embassy request the honour of a reply to the note above alluded to.

Of course the Porte still paid no attention; not even the courtesy of an acknowledgement. Why should it? Tait had served his purpose. Now that the war with Russia was over, the Porte no longer needed a supplier of military uniforms, or cloth for their manufacture. But, on the other hand, it was probably politically impossible for the Porte to ignore altogether the case of a British subject who had the active support of the Embassy behind him.

Meanwhile, in October 1879, encouraged by the decision in Tait's case against the Minister of Marine, Pears had taken his case against the Seraskerate, in which nothing had happened for more than a year, to the same Commercial Tribunal of the Tidjaret. Since the point at issue in both cases was the same, Tait was confident that he was in sight of success at last. He might have been less sanguine, if he could have foreseen that, even if he was successful in the Courts, this did not mean that effect would be given to their judgements by the Sublime Porte.

And in November 1879 Pears started a case on Tait's behalf in the Consular Court, seeking to enforce payment of the amount still owing by the Grand Master of Artillery in respect of the lead delivered the previous December.

The boot on the other foot

In February 1880, Tait found himself in the unusual position of being himself on the receiving end of a lawsuit. The Bank of Constantinople issued a summons alleging that Tait owed it

£2111 11s, as security for which it held 10,000 metres of English woollen cloth. However, in his reply Tait said that he owed only some £870. He also said that he had arranged eighteen months before for a sale of the cloth to the Turkish Government for 200,000 silver *piastres* but that the Bank refused to agree and the sale was lost. Furthermore, Tait said that the Bank held as security, in addition to the cloth, *sergis* for 290,000 *piastres*. In the event, the parties to this dispute must have settled their differences as the matter did not proceed to trial.[4] But the episode is interesting as it highlights the fact that Tait was again using several banks at the same time; these were the Imperial Ottoman Bank, Hanson and the Bank of Constantinople locally, as well as Brown Janson & Co and the National Provincial Bank of England at home. It also highlights the apparently still parlous state of Tait's financial affairs.

The Commercial and Maritime Club

By 1880, if not before, Tait had become a member of the Commercial and Maritime Club in Pera and his letters were now often addressed from there.

Tait's claims summarised for a new Ambassador

In May 1880 Layard was succeeded, as Especial Ambassador, by George J Göschen who, shortly after taking up his appointment, asked Tait for particulars of his claims against the Ottoman Government. Tait explained that he was owed about £T2,500 by the Arsenal, £T7,000 by the Ministry of Marine, and £T17,500 by the Seraskerate; equivalent in today's money to about £1,130,000 sterling altogether. The claim against the Arsenal was before the Consular Court, the claim against the Ministry of Marine had been decided by the Ottoman Tribunals in Tait's favour, but nothing had been paid, and the claim against the Seraskerate was before the Commercial Tribunal of the Tidjaret, as it had been since October 1879.[5]

Tait was becoming ever more anxious, not to say desperate, and he must have been lobbying for support at home, because in July 1880 Earl Granville, who had by then succeeded Salisbury as Foreign Secretary, forwarded to the Embassy a forthright enquiry from Mr O'Shaughnessy, one of the MPs for the City of Limerick, as to the position regarding Tait's claims.[6] Astonishingly, it took the Embassy until July of the following year to reply to this enquiry, by which time Göschen had himself been succeeded as Ambassador by the Earl of Dufferin. However, the reply might as well have been sent straight away; nothing had changed in the intervening year.

In October 1880 there was an amusing incident, illustrative of the difference between the bureaucratic mind and the mind of an entrepreneur.

It was necessary, in connection with his case against the Seraskerate then before the Commercial Tribunal of the Tidjaret, for Tait to be able to produce to the Tribunal copies of certain of the letters which had passed between the Embassy and the Porte in 1877.

However, the Embassy refused to release the copies to Tait on the ground that it would be 'contrary to custom', although the truth which emerged later was that the 'copies' on the Embassy files were always in the form of the drafts from which the actual letters had been copied and it was not possible, so the Embassy said, to be certain that the letters actually sent were in identical form to the drafts.

But Tait was not one to let a little local difficulty stand in his way, and a few days after this exchange had taken place, the various copies which he had been refused were in his possession. Although when questioned he said that the copies 'must have come into his hands in September 1877 from Sir Henry Layard himself', it seems more likely that he had a mole in the Embassy.

Outflanked, the Ambassador wrote a letter to Tait, for production in Court, confirming that the correspondence had been sent, but including a further letter addressed to Tait personally saying that his request for copies was 'quite unusual, and if acceded to would establish a very inconvenient precedent'.

Fresh hope

The Spring of 1881 saw a renewed flurry of activity to try and get settlements with the Minister of Marine and the Grand Master of Artillery. But the impression given by a reading of the correspondence, in this as in other instances, is that if Tait had been left to sort out the problems on his own, with only occasional pressure from the Embassy in support, he might have had more success. As it was, the Embassy was very much involved, but their approach lacked the drive and determination, as well as the subtlety, that were surely necessary in dealing with the Sublime Porte. The correspondence between Salisbury, Layard and the Porte in 1879 is an example of this. And because a number of different Embassy officials were involved at any one time their efforts lacked focus.

Or perhaps Tait should have left things entirely in the hands of the Embassy, which must sometimes have found that his initiatives, usually made without consulting, and sometimes without informing, the Embassy, made the problems less, rather than more, susceptible of resolution. But someone had to take the initiatives.

The Minister of Marine has no cash

At the beginning of April, the Prime Minister had told the Embassy that the real reason for the Minister of Marine's failure to pay Tait was that he had no cash with which to do so. Tait therefore saw the Minister and said that he would accept in settlement scrap iron, of which sufficient was available, but the Minister responded by saying that he needed to sell this for cash, which indeed he subsequently did, although he did not use any of the cash to pay Tait!

An ingenious proposal by Tait

Then, on 12 April, knowing that the coal mines at Heraclea (now Eregli), which were close to the Black Sea coast about 150 miles east of Constantinople, had been idle for the previous four years for want of money to pay the workpeople, Tait wrote to the Minister of Marine with an ingenious, if somewhat audacious, proposal for a settlement of the amount due to him, which he said would not involve the Ministry in the payment of any cash; in fact quite the opposite.[7] The amount which had been awarded to Tait by the Commercial Tribunal of the Tidjaret was 700,210 *piastres*, although there is some evidence to suggest that Tait had by now accepted a payment of about 180,000 *piastres* in *kaimes,* leaving only 520,000 *piastres* outstanding.

Tait's proposal was that he should advance to the Ministry, in silver, the difference between the amount now due to him and 1,000,000 *piastres;* an advance of 480,000 *piastres.* Tait pointed out that this advance would enable the Ottoman navy to buy iron which it could not otherwise afford to do for lack of funds. In return Tait would receive, during the following two years, 50,000 tons of coal from the mines at Heraclea, at a price, payable by Tait weekly, of 62½ *piastres* a ton to cover the cost of extraction and transport to the sea coast - a total cost to Tait of 3,125,000 *piastres.* Tait no doubt thought that he would be able to sell the coal for at least 82½ *piastres* a ton, which would be sufficient to cover, not only the 62½ *piastres* he would have paid for extraction and transport (3,125,000 *piastres*), but also the amount owed to him by the Minister of Marine (520,000 *piastres*), as well as the amount of the advance (480,000 *piastres*); a total of 4,125,000 *piastres.*

There is nothing in the correspondence to indicate where Tait was going to find the advance of 480,000 *piastres* [*about £200,000*].

But did Tait really expect the Minister to spend the advance of 480,000 *piastres* on iron, or was Tait at last coming to terms with the way business had to be conducted in the Ottoman Empire? Either way, the possibility that the Minister, having received the advance of 480,000 *piastres,* might fail to deliver the coal, seems not to have occurred to Tait.

Meanwhile, the Minister of Finance had suggested that payment of the amount due to Tait should be made in the form of three *havales.* But Tait had written to Göschen to say that this was quite unacceptable, since two of the proposed *havales* were worthless and the third would have to be encashed at 25% to 30% discount. He sent with this letter a copy of the proposal he had made to the Minister for payment to be made in coal from Heraclea. His final request of the Ambassador was that, if he could not obtain a settlement either in cash or by acceptance of Tait's proposal to take coal, the Ambassador would 'see his way to have this claim settled out of the Cyprus revenue'.[8]

Nothing came of any of this, and so Tait made yet another suggestion. He was now willing to accept from the Minister of

Marine one half in cash and one half in *havales* (on the corn tax of 1881 and on provinces to be selected by Tait himself); or even all in *havales* if to an amount 10% or 15% greater than his claim, to allow in part for the discount payable by him on encashment.[9] However, this idea does not seem to have found favour, because, by the middle of June 1881 Tait was still owed about £T2,500 by the Grand Master of Artillery (outstanding for two years), about £T5,500 by the Minister of Marine (outstanding for four years) and, of course, about £T17,500 by the Seraskerate (also outstanding for four years); some £T25,500 altogether [*about £1,070,000*]. Tait's continuing efforts to obtain settlement of these amounts, lasting for the next four years, gave rise to a huge number of letters and memoranda passing between the various protagonists, only some of which need be noticed here. The whole thing had become like a game of snakes and ladders, but with the dice loaded very heavily in favour of the snakes.

A recapitulation

On 26 June Tait sent to Plunkett, the Chargé d'Affaires at the Embassy who was now handling Tait's case, the following *cri de coeur*, with which he enclosed, yet again, statements of his claims against both the Minister of Marine and the Grand Master of Artillery -[10]

Sir, You will remember that some time ago I showed you a telegram from my solicitors requesting my attendance in London at the trial of an Insurance Case in which I am interested to the extent of £4,000 - after that interview I wrote to say that it would be impossible for me to leave here until I got some settlement of my present claims, by today's Post I have a letter to say that the Case cannot go on in my absence and that they throw the responsibility on me. May I therefore beg that you will do me the favour to bring my Case under the notice of His Excellency - for independent of this Case in London I have very pressing engagements here early next month and the consequence to me will be very serious if some arrangement is not soon made, as I have mentioned to you the large lock up of my Capital here is very seriously interfering with my business at Limerick as to which you will see by the Times of Friday last a very complimentary reference was made by Mr Childers in the House of Commons. ... it is most important that [my claims] should be settled without further delay. I will do myself the pleasure of calling on you on

Wednesday morning. I hope it will also be convenient for His Excellency to grant me a short interview.

P.S. My friends at home cannot understand how it is possible for a British Subject to receive such injustice as I am receiving from the Turkish Govt.

I am, Sir, Your most obt servant,
Peter Tait

An Insurance Case

The 'Insurance Case' referred to was almost certainly in some way connected with Tait's continuing inability to repay in full the amount he had borrowed in 1871 from the C of E Institution to buy back from the Inspectors in his bankruptcy the lease of the Limerick factory; £4,000 of which was still outstanding. Tait had no doubt been referring to the same matter when he had told Plunkett on 30 May that it was of the 'utmost importance' that he should be 'enabled to return to England at the very earliest possible moment'. The Case was evidently being brought by Tait, as surely otherwise it would have proceeded in spite of Tait's absence. On the other hand, I have found no surviving reference to it other than in Tait's correspondence with Plunkett; there is no reference to it in the Institution's Minutes, which are otherwise remarkably complete in relation to its dealings with Tait. But since there does not seem to have been any reason connected with his business in Constantinople why Tait could not have left there, if only briefly, for a matter of the 'utmost importance', one is bound to ask whether there was perhaps some reason of even greater importance why he could not visit England? It is an intriguing question, but one to which I can only guess at an answer.

It will be remembered that, at the time of the Orkney and Shetland by-election in 1873, Tait had confidently predicted that the liquidation of Tait & Co would produce a surplus after meeting all liabilities, and referred to 'a large portion of the assets remaining in bank, pending a suit in Chancery'; sufficient indeed to enable the firm's creditors to be paid in full. I have surmised that these 'assets' were what Tait hoped to recover from Alexander Collie. But with Collie's bankruptcy in 1875 went any hope of Tait's creditors receiving anything from that source.

On the other hand, by 1875, Tait himself had begun to recover from the failure of Tait & Co; he once more owned the lease of the clothing factory and was a partner in Sir Peter Tait & Co which owned the business.

Might the creditors turn to him to recover their losses? Did he anticipate this possibility, and not only go abroad, but have to remain there for at least six years, to obtain the protection of the Statute of Limitations relating to civil debt?

A meeting with Lord Dufferin

The interview with Dufferin requested by Tait took place at Therapia, the Embassy's summer quarters on the shore of the Bosphorus. Following the interview, Tait told Plunkett that he 'was charmed with Lord Dufferin's kind interest in my affairs'. Dufferin had told him that Plunkett was going to the Porte the following day and would do the very best he could in Tait's case. However, Tait reminded Plunkett 'that the Prime Minister hates all Europeans especially the English so that you know what weight is to be given to his words'. Nevertheless Tait entertained the confident hope that some satisfactory settlement might be reached.[11]

The Minister of Marine still has no cash

Plunkett saw Said Pasha, the Prime Minister, who admitted that the delay in settling in the case of the Minister of Marine was that there was no money, but Plunkett drew the Prime Minister's attention to the fact that Tait was willing to settle by means other than cash. The Prime Minister eventually promised to write to both the Minister of Marine and the Grand Master of Artillery, to see what might be done.

It was this information which was given to London on 23 July, by way of reply to O'Shaughnessy's enquiry, passed to the Embassy by the Foreign Secretary in London almost exactly a year before.[12]

Tait wrote to Plunkett on 4 July saying, inter alia, 'I beg to assure you that in addition to the great loss I am sustaining by being kept here without benefit, the letters I am receiving by every post inform me of the difficulty of my company in the business at home [which] with the large lock [up] of capital here is becoming most serious'.[13]

This letter seems to show that Tait was by now, perhaps not surprisingly, becoming obsessed by what he saw as the injustice to which he was being subjected. He spent much of his time visiting the various Government Departments involved in his problems and recently, when he had run into Dufferin and Sir Alfred Sandison at the Porte, it does not seem to have occurred to him that they might have been there on other business than the settlement of his claims.

Shortly after this Tait had succumbed to an attack of fever, brought on no doubt by worry, which had lasted for several days, during which time he was confined to his room. This had prevented him from keeping an appointment at the Embassy with Mr Preziosi, who evidently had now taken over day-to-day charge of Tait's case.

Then on 15 July, following several communications with the Minister of Marine, Tait told Plunkett that 'if the promises made are carried out, my business with that department will be very soon settled'. He asked Plunkett 'to instruct Mr Preziosi to get the letters which were promised by the Prime Minister to the Minister of Marine and the Grand Master of Artillery sent at once'. If only it had been that simple!

It then turned out that the Prime Minister had written to the Grand Master of Artillery but that the latter had affected not to know to what it referred. Tait was therefore asked by the Embassy to prepare a concise memorandum of his claim, which could be presented in Turkish to the Ministry of Foreign Affairs to be forwarded to the Grand Master. If Tait was becoming a nervous wreck, it is hardly surprising.

The Embassy reaches an agreement with the Porte

In August 1881 an agreement was reached between the Embassy and the Ministry of Foreign Affairs for the settlement of all outstanding claims by British subjects. This was to be effected by the issue of *havales*. Although Dufferin evidently regarded Tait's claims as outside the terms of this settlement, he sent a copy of the agreement to Tait for his information.[14]

In spite of Dufferin's view that Tait's claims did not fall within the terms of the overall settlement reached with the the Porte, Tait was not so sure. He had therefore gone to see the Grand Master of Artillery and the Minister of Marine to say that it would be impossible for him to accept *havales* in settlement of his claims. Each of these officials had given him a very strong letter addressed to the Minister of Finance requesting an immediate cash payment to enable them to settle Tait's claims, which Tait took straight to the Minister of Finance. He was accompanied by Preziosi 'who displayed great ability and tact in explaining the matter to the Minister', who promised an answer within the week as to how they could arrange the matter.[15]

A further letter which Tait sent to Dufferin on 10 September, covering five pages of foolscap, was in an entirely different vein to Tait's recent letters. Although clearly based on Tait's own views, it was almost certainly put together by Pears. It started by explaining why Tait could not accept the basis of settlement agreed between the Embassy and the Ministry of Foreign Affairs for the settlement of outstanding claims against British subjects. No time was fixed for the encashment of the *havales* proposed to be given to them in settlement of their claims and Tait had spoken to the Imperial Ottoman Bank who said they would not advance 'one *para*' [the fortieth part of a *piastre*] on them; a view confirmed by one of the leading Galata bankers to whom he had also spoken. The letter also pointed out that of the £T280,000 stated to be due to British subjects, £T245,000 was due to only two; the Varna Railway and Messrs Cuppa. These large concerns, being able to employ agents in the provinces, which Tait could not afford to do, would be in a much better position to obtain encashment than Tait, who, because the banks would not advance money on the *havales*, would have to discount them himself locally at a discount of 30 to 40 per cent. The letter went on to 'remind Your Excellency that the two claims together are for about £T8,000; and that I have already expended in law costs over £T1,500; that during the five years that I have remained here to settle these claims, and not to speak of my own personal time during the best five years of my life, I have incurred for personal, dragomans and other incidental expenses a sum of more than £T2,500 and if I am now called upon to make a fresh sacrifice of 30 to 40 per cent, the merchandise which I have supplied goes for nothing, in addition to the loss of my time'.

He distinguished his claims, which were judgement debts, from the ordinary business debts of the other claimants. And he said that he had 'received the most reliable information through a private source that more than three months ago more *havales* had been issued on the provinces than the amount of the revenue for the present year; and that while it is possible that small payments may be made by way of a show of good faith, still it is quite sure that a very considerable time will elapse before these *havales* will be encashed'.

This was about as close as Pears and his client could decently come to telling the Embassy that the Agreement, reached with the Porte in August, was not worth the paper on which it was written.

Tait went on to hope, as he has hoped on so many previous occasions, that 'Your Excellency will be able to see your way to make a very strong representation to the Prime Minister in the interest of justice to a loyal British born subject and a large tax payer who has shown every consideration to the Turkish Government in their time of need, for the immediate payment of these claims'.[16]

The reference to himself as 'British born' seems to have been a dig at the Cuppa family who were Ionians by birth, sons of an Ionian who had commanded as a British Naval Officer a 'Scamparia', or gunboat, in the war with France; presumably when the Ionian Islands were taken from France by the British in 1809. They had claimed accordingly to be British subjects under an Act passed in the reign of George II; a claim which had been allowed by the Secretary of State. They had been registered as British Subjects in 1864 by Sir Edmund Hornby, then Judge of the Consular Court.[17]

Following receipt of this letter, Plunkett told Tait that, although Dufferin could not recognise officially any difference between his claims and others who had judgements, he had again spoken to the Porte in his favour and urged an early settlement.

Yet another recapitulation

A month later, Dufferin again saw the Prime Minister, who asked to be provided with a *pro memoria* on the subject of Tait's claim against the Minister of Marine, which had therefore been prepared and sent to the Under-Secretary of State.

On 19 November Dufferin wrote to Said Pasha, the Prime Minister, regarding Tait's claim against the Grand Master of Artillery, in respect of which Tait had evidently accepted *havales* on Broussa. The draft, translated into French before despatch, read -

Highness, I am sorry to say that after two journeys to Broussa, Sir Peter Tait has met with an absolute refusal on the part of the Vali to cash the *havales* with which he was furnished by the Treasury. I therefore venture to make an earnest appeal to Your Highness on behalf of Sir Peter Tait. His case is a peculiarly hard one, and his claim is one of those which it is most incumbent on the Porte to pay, and the total amount is comparatively small - something like £7,000. I would beg Your Highness almost as a personal favour to give orders that it may be satisfied in cash, say in two or three instalments.

The Right Hon Earl of Dufferin, KP, KCB, GCMG, to give him his full title, was a quintessential English gentleman and in his world this letter would not have fallen on deaf ears. But Said Pasha was a wily Turk, from another world; he knew that if he ignored Dufferin's pleas, as he had before and as he did on this occasion, nothing worse would happen than more of the same. Tait seemed to be getting nowhere.

Indeed, in the event, it was to prove a fatal error for Dufferin to have introduced into the negotiations the notion of payment by instalments.

A settlement with the Minister of Marine at last

Nevertheless, by the end of December 1881 the Prime Minister had eventually directed the Minister of Marine to settle Tait's claim by the supply of coal from Heraclea. Tait told Dufferin that 'the conditions they propose are very onerous, but I think the Minister is disposed to address a letter to the Prime Minister, so to modify them that I may be able to conclude the matter'. How this was achieved I do not know; whether on the lines which had been suggested by Tait in April 1881, or otherwise; although presumably some compromise acceptable to both sides was arrived at, since there is no further reference to this claim in the correspondence.

On the other hand, there was of course as yet no progress with the claim against the Grand Master of Artillery. Tait wrote to Dufferin with various suggestions as to what *havales* he would or would not accept, in the absence of cash, and again sought help from Dufferin, who again did his best. However a note which Dufferin endorsed on Tait's letter suggests that he was becoming exasperated by Tait's continual importuning. He wrote -

> The Prime Minister was stepping into his carriage when I went to call on him, so that I was unable to comply with Sir Peter's request - how indeed can I undertake to negotiate these details for him.

They might have seemed like 'details' to Dufferin, but they were rather more than that to Tait; by now on the verge of ruin.

A visit to Australia?

It is interesting to note that, after this, there is no further letter either to, or from, Tait in the Embassy archives, until Tait wrote again to Dufferin on 1 August 1882.

Had Dufferin indeed given up? Or was Tait away from Constantinople for the first seven months of 1882? The former would not have been surprising, but the answer appears to have been the latter.

There is some evidence to suggest that Tait had gone to Australia where he may have visited his sister Jean and her family, as well as Robert Tait's son James. Perhaps, also, he was beginning to look for some way of recouping his Turkish losses and was considering taking an interest in the Australian gold mining industry.

It was probably when he returned to Constantinople following this absence that Tait took a suite of rooms at 27 Rue Venedik (now Erden Han, 34-35 Balyoz Sokak), a street off the western side of the Grande Rue de Pera. This was an altogether more modern building than the house in Rue de Pologne, where he had been living before.

It consisted of purpose built apartments, on four floors served by an impressive cantilevered marble staircase.

Failure in the Commercial Tribunal of the Tidjaret

Surprisingly, Tait's case against the Seraskerate, which had been started in the Commercial Tribunal of the Tidjaret in October 1879, and the outcome of which Tait confidently expected to be favourable, was still before the Tribunal.

However, on 21 October, after deliberating for three years, in a matter, to use the words of Pears,[18] 'which an English or any other fairly constituted court would certainly have decided in one sitting after the matter had been fairly brought before it', the Court expressed itself as being incompetent to decide as to the validity or invalidity of acts of the Ottoman Government; a conclusion against which no appeal was allowed.[19]

This was a body blow for Tait, who found himself back where he had been when the dispute first arose in 1877.

A settlement with the Grand Master of Artillery

In addition, Tait's claim against the Grand Master of Artillery was still partially outstanding in the Consular Court at the end of 1882, in spite of the fact that he had been given a partly paid *havale* on the *vilayet* of Erzerum (now Erzurum); a *vilayet* some 600 miles distant from Constantinople, bordering on Russia, in which lie the two sources of the River Euphrates. Tait therefore sought, and received, an order from the Court for payment of this balance, plus interest and costs.

The only other reference to this claim in the archives is in December of the following year, when Tait gave the Imperial Ottoman Bank authority to dispose of the unpaid balance of the *havale* on Erzerum on his behalf,[20] although some further payment must also have been made by the Grand Master following the Court order, as in September 1883 Tait told the Embassy that all his business with the Imperial Government was now finished except for his claim against the Seraskerate.

Negotiations for the settlement of that remaining claim had been renewed by Tait with a letter to Hugh Wyndham, who was now the Charge d'Affaires at the Embassy dealing with Tait's case, on 16 December 1882. He set out yet again the history of the claim and asked for the application of diplomatic pressure to obtain a settlement.

In response, Wyndham wrote to Aarify Pasha, the Minister of Foreign Affairs, suggesting arbitration, or the appointment of an intermediary, or a willingness to consider any other means of settlement which Aarify Pasha might suggest, with a view to 'the smoothing out of this unfortunate matter'.[21] Tait had seen and approved this letter before it was sent, although he said that 'in consequence of the intrigue and corruption existing here' he had little faith in arbitration.

By August 1883, no reply having been received from the Porte, Tait recalled to Wyndham the events of the intervening months. Aarify Pasha had referred Wyndham's letter to his Counsellor, HE Goescher Effendi. He, following a meeting with Pears and Tait, had reported that the matter should either be settled in a friendly manner, or by arbitration. The papers were then passed to the Prime Minister, who, in turn, passed them to the Seraskerate, where they had remained until recently, when they went back to Aarify Pasha. Tait told Wyndham that he had seen Aarify Pasha several times, only to be told that the matter rested with the Prime Minister.

And so it went on, until December, when Tait wrote to Dufferin to say that the Prime Minister had referred the matter to the Council of Ministers, which had rejected the claim on the ground that to accept it would create a precedent for others having similar claims; a decision confirmed by Aarify Pasha in his reply to Dufferin's letter of a year earlier. Back, once more, where it all began!

In the same letter to Dufferin, Tait referred, 'as regards the question of precedent', to the case of an American merchant, who had a disputed claim for £T6,000 against the Grand Master of Artillery, and whose case was taken up by the American Minister directly with the Sultan; as a result of which payment had been made in cash.[22] Tait said that there seemed no valid reason why his case should not be dealt with in a similar manner. Which, of course, illustrates what the Council of Ministers had in mind.

When nothing further had happened by March 1884, Dufferin wrote again to Aarify Pasha to express his astonishment that a question so clear and so simple should be the object of a lengthy diplomatic controversy without resolution.

A most unsatisfactory compromise

However, in May, a settlement of Tait's claim against the Seraskerate was reached, or so it was believed.

But Tait wrote to Wyndham on 28 January 1885 explaining the sequence of events that followed, and seeking further help.

Early in May the Grand Vizier had appointed the Minister of Justice to look into the claim and have it amicably settled. Mr Stavrides, one of the Embassy dragomans, and Tait had several interviews with the Minister with this in mind. As a result, the Minister proposed that Tait's claim should be compromised in the sum of £T5,000. This Tait regarded as most unsatisfactory, but, since it was accompanied by an assurance of immediate payment in cash, he agreed to accept; notwithstanding, as he said, that it 'would entail upon me a loss of 25,000 *liras* and considering the position of the Imperial Treasury, and my having wasted 8 years about this affair incurring very great expense'.

He said that the settlement had been approved by the Council of Ministers and the Grand Vizier, and obtained the Imperial *Irade*. This had been sent to the Minister of Finance in August, who immediately made a payment of £T300 and had told Tait that the balance would be paid in sums of £T200/300 every 8 or 10 days.

On these assurances by the Minister of Justice and the Minister of Finance as to payment, Tait 'being most anxious to return to England to visit my family after an absence of more than 8 years', disposed of about half of the total payable, to the Imperial Ottoman Bank, which, as part of a financial operation between itself and the Minister of Finance, received settlement in cash.[23]

But not so Tait, to whom the Minister had made no payment by the end of December, beyond the first payment of £T300 in the previous August. So Tait wrote yet again to the Embassy for assistance. Dufferin thereupon wrote to the Minister of Foreign Affairs, who replied to say that the Grand Vizier denied having directed periodical payments following the initial payment of £300 and said that the outstanding balance 'is to be discharged by degrees in such sums as the Minister of Finance can find at his disposal'.[24]

Whether the Minister ever found any sums at his disposal, or whether Tait finally gave up, I have been unable to discover.

Either way, taking everything into account, Tait must have lost the equivalent today of well in excess of £1,000,000 as a result of his dealings with the Ottoman Government; although this was very much less than his own creditors had lost in the bankruptcy of Tait & Co and the shareholders had lost in the failure of the Steamship Company.

But it is a sobering thought that had Tait known in 1877 what he knew in 1885, he might well have done better to have written off the Turkish debt at the outset, and spent the intervening years, at least with his family; possibly engaged in some profitable enterprise as well.

Or was it the case, as I have suggested above, that the collection of the Turkish debt was not the reason, but the excuse, for Tait's long absence abroad.

24

The Sale of the Army Clothing Factory

1881-1884

In 1881 Tait still owed the C of E Institution the balance of £4,000 secured by the mortgage created by him on 4 October 1871, and the Limerick Army Clothing Company Limited was still the tenant of the clothing factory.

Orders were still hard to come by. Indeed, the Report of the Director of Army Contracts for 1880 noted that in that year the Limerick factory did not obtain the same amount of work at tender as usual; their principal competitor being a Mr Bamberger who had premises in Whitechapel in London's East End.[1]

However, in March 1881 Robert Tait tendered successfully for a new three-year contract from the British Government to supply garments for the artillery, the cavalry and several line regiments. This was expected to 'afford ample and continued employment to over six hundred operatives for the next three years'. The estimated weekly wages expenditure of the factory for six hundred operatives was calculated at close to £400 and the *Limerick Chronicle* noted that 'the benefit derived by the city from the diffusion of so much money among the most helpless class must be regarded as very considerable'.[2] 1881 was the first year in which the Government had awarded three-year contracts, which they had decided to do on a trial basis. The Limerick factory had conceded 1.09% for the sake of a three-year contract, rather than have the uncertainty of annual contracts.[3]

In June there was a debate in the House of Commons on the subject of Army Contracts and it was during this debate that Mr Childers said of the contracts being undertaken in Ireland 'that this work is being well done at Limerick, under an improved system'; the comment which had not passed unnoticed by Tait in

Constantinople. Childers also said that the uniforms for the Post Office were largely being made in Limerick;[4] as indeed were all the head-dresses, greatcoats and tweed frocks for the Royal Irish Constabulary.[5]

In September Robert Tait was reported as saying that, with sufficient capital, the factory would be in a position to employ twice the present number. He spoke of the factory as employing families who could not be employed at other pursuits, and helping them to live in comfort.

There were no reports during the following two years to show what further orders the factory might have received, but perhaps no news was good news.

The sale of the clothing factory

However, Tait had still not been able to repay the remaining £4,000 [*nearly £200,000*] which he owed on his mortgage. And it was increasingly apparent, following the rejection of his claim against the Seraskerate by the Commercial Tribunal of the Tidjaret in 1882, that, even given more time, he was unlikely to be able to do so.

And, although there is nothing in its minutes to indicate that the C of E Institution, which of course had power under its mortgage deed to sell the clothing factory on the open market, was putting any pressure on them, Tait and his brother Robert no doubt realised that they had to find a long term solution to their financial difficulties.

The result was that, early in 1883, they found a group of army officers, with good connections in the War Office, who agreed to form a limited liability company to buy the clothing factory as a going concern.

The next step was the formation on 9 March 1883 of the new company, which was called the Auxiliary Forces Uniform and Equipment Company Limited (the Auxiliary Co), with a nominal capital of £250,000 in 50,000 shares of £5 each.[6] The principal object of the company was 'to supply to the Auxiliary Forces, and to persons connected therewith and others, uniform clothing and equipment of every description'. The first Directors of the company at its formation were Maj-Gen W M H Dixon CB,

Maj G W A FitzGeorge, Maj C A Cooper, Capt W E Heath and Maj W J Elliott. Heath was the Secretary.

Dixon had been Superintendent of the Royal Small Arms Factories at Enfield from 1855 to 1871, when he had retired on full pay.

It had been intended that the next step should be the purchase by the Auxiliary Co of the clothing factory, comprising the 1858 lease of the factory premises, together with the plant and machinery, as a going concern, for £15,060 [*about £800,000*] in cash.

As part of this transaction, the £4,000 owed by Tait to the C of E Institution, and the money owed by Sir Peter Tait & Co to Brown Janson & Co on overdraft, was to be repaid.

However, whatever efforts were made to find subscribers for the company's shares, they failed; only 790 shares, or £3,950, being subscribed for, over half by the Directors themselves. As a result, there was insufficient cash available for the proposed purchase of the clothing factory to take place.

The next recorded event, on 23 January 1884, was the Institution's agreement to grant a lease of the factory premises to Robert Tait; presumably for assignment by him to the Auxiliary Co. But, hardly had this agreement been reached, when, on 6 February, the Institution agreed to sell their interest in the factory premises to Robert. Thus, on 9 April 1884 the Institution, in purported exercise of the power of sale in the mortgage deed of 4 October 1871, sold its underlease of the factory premises, not in the open market or at its market value, but to Robert Tait for £6,270 [*about £330,000*]. This sum was probably made up of the outstanding balance of Tait's original loan, amounting to £4,000, plus unpaid interest, and costs. To enable the transaction to take place, Robert borrowed £5,770 from the Institution. This loan of £5,770 was secured by the grant by Robert to the Institution of a new underlease of the factory premises, for a period fifteen days shorter than the unexpired term of the 1858 lease.

However, a significant advantage of the sale by the Institution was that it gave rise to the trust, referred to in the mortgage deed of 1871, in favour of Robert, as the purchaser. Arrangements could therefore be made for the 1858 lease to remain in place, subject to Brown Janson & Co's 1874 security for the overdraft of

Sir Peter Tait & Co, which both Tait and Robert, as partners in the firm, were liable to repay, and for the plant and machinery to be released from the charge to enable them to be acquired by Robert.

Then on 14 May 1884 Robert conveyed to the Auxiliary Co an underlease of the factory premises, for the unexpired term of the 1858 lease, less the last ten days thereof, (subject to the Institution's latest mortgage to secure £5,770), together with absolute title to the plant and machinery. Although this was not the 1858 lease, which it had been intended to sell to the company, it was after all only ten days shorter than the 1858 lease.

The consideration for the conveyance was the payment by the Auxiliary Co of £60 in cash and the issue, credited as fully paid up, of 1,846 shares of £5 each in the capital of the company with a nominal value of £9,230. The total of the mortgage, £5,770, the cash, £60, and the shares, £9,230, was equal to the originally proposed sale price of £15,060. As the Chairman of the first general meeting of the company on 26 March 1885 explained, 'We did not get the required capital, and consequently ... [the vendors] ... took the whole in shares'.

There is now no record of the shareholders of the company in 1884, so we do not know in whose names the 1,846 shares acquired by Robert were registered.

All that can be said is that the only family holdings in 1953, the earliest date for which a list of shareholders now survives, were those of Robert's daughter Isabel Maud, and those of Logie's descendants; none of Peter Tait's descendants then holding any shares.

To turn briefly to the history of the Auxiliary Co itself. By March 1885, the Directors had changed; FitzGeorge, Cooper and Elliott had gone and Maj-Gen Mathew C Dixon VC, Mr George H M Ricketts CB, Mr F H Balfour and Mr Edward Taylor had been added. Robert Tait continued as manager of the clothing factory; becoming a director later in 1885, when he was described in the company's annual accounts as 'Captain' R T Tait. Heath was succeeded as Secretary by Logie in 1886. The company's offices were at Vauxhall Bridge House in London.

Among later changes in the Directors were the retirement of Robert Tait in 1889 and the addition in his place of Major

Daubeney; the addition in 1890 of William Abraham; and in 1891 of Logie, who nevertheless continued as Secretary.

All that need be said further about the Auxiliary Co is that, if the Limerick factory was short of capital in the 1870s and 1880s, it was no less so under its new ownership, in spite of the fact that Ricketts in 1890, and Mathew Dixon in 1895 lent it money; obligations taken over by Taylor in 1898. The company went from crisis to crisis for many years, before achieving relative prosperity in the first half of the 20th century. In 1969 it was acquired by Aquascutum and was closed by them in 1975.

The Auxiliary Co's interest in the premises was eventually purchased from a subsequent owner by Limerick City Council for £2,500,000 in 2001, although little now remains of the historically and architecturally important clothing factory built by Tait in the 1850s and 1860s, following a disastrous fire in 2003.

25

Cigarette Maker
1885-1887

Less is known about Tait's involvement in the manufacture of cigarettes than about any other of his business ventures, except perhaps for Peter Tait Son & Co, referred to in chapter 21, and his journeys to Russia, described in the next.

It is part of Limerick tradition that Tait attempted to establish a factory for the manufacture of Turkish cigarettes in Salonica, or, according to some, in India.

On the other hand, when Tait's younger son, Thomas William Tait, was married in 1893, he described the rank or profession of his late father as 'Cigarette Maker', which suggests that cigarette making had been, for a time at least, a significant, if not the major, business activity in Tait's life.

Also, we know that when Tait and Peter junior returned to Constantinople in 1885 from a visit to London, the latter was by then working as a clerk with the *Régie des Tabacs*,[1] an organisation recently established by the external bondholders of the Ottoman Empire to manage the state monopoly over the cultivation of tobacco for internal consumption. The *Régie* had no jurisdiction over tobacco for export.

Although not published until 1895, The Tobacconists Handbook by E B Alexander says that, although imported cigarettes made of Turkish tobacco were too expensive for ordinary trade, Turkish tobacco in leaf was imported into England in immense quantities for the manufacture of cigarettes, of which some commanded a very good price and yielded a good profit.

Presumably, as well, the manufacture of cigarettes would have been susceptible to the same principles of mass production as were pioneered by Tait in his army clothing factory.

And the Index of Brands covering the years 1876 to 1893, published in the Tobacco Year Book for 1894, contained an entry for 'Turkish Cigarette Co: Sir P Tait & Sons'. This is the only mention of this firm in the records. Could both Peter jnr and Thomas have been involved by now?

As to what went on, there are some records to help us;[2] the first being an agreement entered into in April 1886 between Tait, 'trading as the Turkish Cigarette Company', and William Abraham, by now the Parnellite MP for Limerick County West, which recited that Tait had 'for some time past carried on the business of a cigarette manufacturer' at 58 St Mary Axe in the City of London.

The agreement contemplated the formation of a limited liability company to purchase from Tait 'the business, goodwill, assets and effects' of the business and to take over the tenancy of the premises at 58 St Mary Axe, for which the rent was £250 per annum. The consideration for the purchase was to be £10,000 [*about £600,000*], payable as to half in the form of 5,000 fully paid up shares of £1 each and as to half in the form of 100 8% debentures of £50 each, secured on the company's undertaking, property and assets.

The agreement went on to provide that Tait, 'having resided for ten years in Turkey and having great experience in the business' should become Managing Director at a salary of not less than £500 per annum.

On 4 May the Turkish Cigarette Company Limited was duly incorporated with a nominal capital of £50,000 divided into 50,000 shares of £1 each. There were seven subscribers to the Memorandum of Association, each taking one share. They were Robert Banks Lavery, a merchant, William Abraham, Peter Tait, George Briggs, an accountant, and Laurence Nicoll, WD Liddell and W Henderson, merchants' clerks. Lavery became Chairman but there is nothing to show what was his connection with Tait or the manufacture of cigarettes, if any. Perhaps he was just a figurehead to add respectability to the proceedings.

It is difficult to know when Tait first occupied the premises in St Mary Axe; the only guide being the street and commercial directories of the period. These were of course prepared somewhat in advance of the beginning of the year in respect of which they were published, but, even bearing this in mind, it seems that Tait cannot have been in St Mary Axe before 1885. However, what is interesting is that Chas E Goad's Insurance Survey of January 1887 shows 58 St Mary Axe to have been a tobacco warehouse and number 56 a cigarette warehouse. Since the street directory does not show a separate tenant for number 56 after 1884 and before 1889 it seems fair to assume that Tait actually occupied 56 as well as 58. These two buildings together had a ground floor area of about 1,600 square feet, the same area on the first and second floors and a smaller third floor under a mansard roof, with dormer windows.

However, the next recorded event, after the formation of the company in 1886, was an agreement, in February 1887, between Tait and the company. This recited the fact that the value of the assets upon which Tait's debentures were charged were then of much less value than was the case when the debentures were issued. It was therefore agreed that Tait would surrender his 100 existing debentures in exchange for half that number and that shares in the company should be issued 'to such members of the public as shall subscribe for the same'. A strange conjunction; whereas the assets had apparently halved in value in less than a year, it was considered an appropriate moment to ask the public to subscribe for shares. Whatever happened next, the only further shares ever issued were to a Mrs S A Hunt, who acquired just 100.

Separately, in August 1887, the company itself had resolved to issue 5,000 preference shares of £1 each, although there is nothing to show that any were ever issued.

Circumstantial evidence suggests that, probably late in 1887, the business of the company was sold by Tait to the Scaramanga family, from St Petersburg, who became the occupiers of 56 St Mary Axe in the name of the Levant Cigarette Manufactury; number 58 becoming vacant. The proceeds of the sale were probably used to reduce the amount which was still owed to Brown Janson & Co by Sir Peter Tait & Co, notwithstanding the sale of the underlease of the army clothing factory in 1884. Indeed Sir Peter Tait & Co were still indebted to Brown Janson & Co at least until 1898, and probably beyond.

26

A Speculative Purchase in the Caucasus

1886-1893

In May 1886 Tait and his wife travelled to Batoum (now Batumi), a port on the eastern shore of the Black Sea, which had been ceded to Russia by the Ottoman Empire following the Russo-Turkish War of 1877/78. They remained in Batoum at least until August before returning to London.

Then Tait made what was probably a brief second visit alone in July 1889. We do not know what Tait did on this visit, but it was while he was away that his daughter Mary Jane married Osborne Limrick, a surgeon from Liverpool.

Then, in May 1890, both Tait and his wife went to Batoum on what was to be Tait's final journey.

During their time in Batoum Tait and his wife stayed at the *Hôtel de France.* A traveller, who passed through Batoum in 1883 on his way to Baku, said of the *Hôtel de France* that it occupied an extensive and commodious building about three minutes walk from the landing stage and close to the station. He went on to say that 'the rooms are well furnished; the charges high, but not exorbitant; and a decent dinner can be had any time up to midnight'.[1]

The Georgian Oil Fields

At the time of Tait's visits, Batoum was in the Russian province of Georgia, which covered the whole of the territory south of the Caucasus mountain range from the Black Sea to the Caspian Sea. It was in Georgia that, in the last quarter of the nineteenth century Ludvig and Robert Nobel, brothers of Alfred, who later established the Nobel Prizes, were largely responsible for the development of the oil fields in Baku, which at that time were the most productive in the Russian Empire. Baku is situated close to the point where the Caucasus Mountains run into the Caspian Sea; at the boundary between Europe and Asia.

The Rothschilds were also active there, and in 1888 sought permission from the authorities in Batoum, already given to the Nobel brothers, to build a pipeline to carry oil from the oilfields to Batoum, where it could be loaded directly onto ships. However, they were refused permission on the ground that it would be unfair competition for small traders.[2]

Towards the end of the nineteenth century and in the early years of the twentieth century, oil was found, not only in Baku, but to a greater or lesser extent throughout Georgia; at its extreme north-western tip, in the area between Batoum and Poti stretching inland to Kutais (now Kutaisi) and in the Chatma Valley south-east of Tiflis (now Tbilisi). Oil was also found in Chechnya, mainly in the vicinity of Grozny on land belonging to the Cossacks.

Not surprisingly, there was an 'oil rush'. And this seems to have been what took Tait to Batoum. But, unfortunately, such records as survive are insufficient to tell us much of the circumstances of Tait's activities there; our only knowledge being derived from records held in the Kutaisi State Archives, themselves seriously depleted as a result of a fire in 1905.

Control by the Russian Government

The extraction of oil in Georgia was controlled by the Russian Government through the Mountain Area Development Board, part of the Ministry of State Properties.

Once the Board had declared a district to be oil-bearing, it allowed prospectors to choose square plots of land, each of about 101 acres, known as *zaiavki,* which were then surveyed by the Government's mining engineer. The prospector was then allowed up to two years during which time he could make pits, or bore, to prove his property, before choosing a square or rectangular area of just under twenty-seven acres as his 'claim', or o*tvod.* This then became his property, subject to the payment of an annual rent to the Government, not for a certain period of time but until any oil was exhausted, although subject to forfeiture if no development took place within a further two years. The balance of each *zaiavka,* not forming part of the o*tvod,* was then let by the Government in claims subject to an annual rent and a royalty on the oil extracted. Some of the original *zaiavki* were Imperial grants to senior soldiers or other servants of the Empire.[3]

Tait's involvement

On 5 April 1885 a *zaiavka* in the Jacobi area of Guriantskaya dacha, in the Ozurgetskiy district of the Kutais region, was granted to retired Guards Col Pavel Dmitrievich Davydov,[4] within which he had evidently established a claim to an o*tvod,* with the reference number 756.[5] The Guriantskaya dacha, which had been acquired by the State in October 1883, was about six miles north-west of the town of Ozurgeti, between the Supsa and Skurduba rivers, and about seventeen miles from the Black Sea coast. The town of Ozurgeti itself is some thirty-five miles north east of Batoum.[6]

Davidov's o*tvod* was subject to a rent of 100 roubles per annum payable to the Russian Government, but the records show that fines and interest for late payment were levied by the Government in addition to the rent. It is not clear what gave rise to the fines.

At the then current rate of exchange, the sterling equivalent of the annual rent of 100 roubles would have been about £12 10s [*about £700*].

Davydov, who paid the rent from 5 April 1885 to 30 June 1886, transferred his *otvod* to Tait on 1 July,[4] and Tait is recorded as having paid the rent, fines and interest in each year from then until 9 November 1893,[7] by which time the records show that Tait had paid to the Government a total of nearly 1,000 roubles [*about£7,000*].[8] Although the only record of the transaction is silent on the point, I think we should assume that Tait had needed to pay Davidov a capital sum for the initial transfer of the o*tvod* on 1 July 1886. Did this perhaps give rise to the following matter, which arose later?

It is recorded that on 24 July 1890 Henry McCarthy, an American, and Tait wrote to the Kutais Circuit Court asking for McCarthy's action against Tait for the sum of 6,300 roubles [*about £45,000*] to be discontinued; the matter having been amicably settled between them on Tait's undertaking to pay McCarthy 6,300 roubles out of the first proceeds received for the oil produced by the Syndicate (see below).[9]

Although there is no record as to why Tait should have owed McCarthy 6,300 roubles, could it have been because McCarthy had provided some, or all, of the money for Tait to pay Davidov for the o*tvod*?

Notwithstanding the transfer of the o*tvod* to Tait, Davydov seems to have remained involved thereafter as Tait's agent.[5]

The development rights transferred to a Syndicate

When Tait went to Batoum in 1890, it appears to have been as the representative of a Syndicate which had been formed to exploit the oil-bearing potential of the *otvod* acquired by him in 1886.

On 8 June 1890 he entered into a contract with Davydov for the transfer to the Syndicate of all the rights for oil extraction and the development of the o*tvod*. This transfer required the payment by the Syndicate to Davydov of the sum of 3,500 roubles [*about £25,000*] in five instalments, the last of which became due on 18 October 1890. The transfer was for a fixed term of thirty years at a rent of five hundred roubles a month, payable by the Syndicate, presumably to Davidov.[10]

There is nothing to indicate why the Syndicate should have had to pay Davidov for the transfer of the rights for oil extraction and the development of the o*tvod* if Tait was already its owner; could it possibly have been that Davidov was acting as Tait's undisclosed agent?

As for the Syndicate, I have been unable to discover who were its members, or indeed how Tait came to be involved.

It appears from the correspondence that the o*tvod* was eventually taken back from Tait by Davydov in November 1893, and transferred by him to Prince Alexander Zeelovich Chelokayev, but there is no surviving record of the circumstances in which this change took place.[11] We do not know whether the Syndicate retained, or sold, or forfeited its interest in the o*tvod*, following its transfer back to Davidov in November of that year. Nor do we know how Tait's interest was dealt with.

It is disappointing that it has not been possible to find out more about Tait's activities in Georgia. However, there are no doubt records somewhere which may in time give up their secrets. It will be interesting to see if this is the case.

However, there is a footnote to the foregoing. All of the financial dealings with the Russian Government relating to the *otvod* were meticulously recorded, down to the very last copeck, by various agencies of the Russian bureaucracy and these records exist today in the Kutaisi State Archives; having survived the fire of 1905. But it is a curious aspect of them that, although they continue to record Tait's involvement until November 1893, they reveal no awareness of the fact that, as we shall see in the next chapter, Tait had died in 1890.

27

Tait's Death
1890

On 27 November 1890, Sir Peter Tait JP DL made his last Will. And on 15 December, at the *Hôtel de France* in Batoum, he died.

The death certificate issued by the British Consul in Batoum gives no cause of death, but an announcement in the deaths column of *The Times* said that Sir Peter died 'after six weeks' illness, of inflammation of the lungs'. In spite of this reference to the length of his illness, it is clear from his signature on the request to the Kutais Circuit Court in the previous July, that even then he was very frail.

Sir Peter was almost certainly buried in the English cemetery in Batoum, although there are now no written records of burials there and any gravestones were destroyed in the 1930s during the Stalinist era. But Batoum was a far cry from Kensal Green, where he had hoped eventually to be laid to rest beside his parents, and where his elder sister, Barbara, had been buried in 1885 and where his elder son, Peter, was to follow all too soon in 1902.

What might have happened if Sir Peter had not died in 1890, at the early age of 62, we cannot know.

We do know, however, that, when his widow, Rose, proved his Will in the following March, the total value of his Estate was only fifty pounds.

When Sir Peter died, apart from his sister Barbara Logie, all the other members of his family who had played parts in his career survived him, as did his nine children.

Some of these people had played significant roles during Sir Peter's lifetime and, by way of tying up the loose ends, I tell in the following brief biographical notes, so far as it is known, what became of them all after his death.

Sir Peter's widow

After Sir Peter's death, his widow, Lady Rose Tait, stayed briefly in London before moving to Ashton Cottage, Waverton, in Cheshire and later to Bournemouth, where she lived with her daughter Evelyn, until she died, in 1906, aged 72.

Sir Peter's children

Nothing is known about any of Sir Peter's children until they were grown up; there is, for example, no record of what formal education, if any, they received. And indeed little is known about most of them in later life.

Perhaps the most striking thing was the fate of Sir Peter's two sons, which contrasts starkly with that of his daughters.

Of Sir Peter's eldest daughter, Elizabeth Anna (Lizzie), nothing is known, until she was living with her mother at Waverton after Sir Peter's death, and was living with her sister Rose when she died unmarried in 1930, aged 75.

Similarly, nothing is known about Sir Peter's second daughter, Margaret (Manna) although she lived at a succession of addresses in the West Country; suggesting that she perhaps worked as a housekeeper or nurse companion. She died in 1933, aged 76.

The marriage of the third daughter, Rose (Posy), to James Bryan in 1878 has already been noticed. They had four sons. James died in 1907 and Rose married secondly Salmon Linton. She died a widow in 1946, aged 89.

The next daughter, Mary Jane, who had married Osborne Limrick in 1889, had three daughters and a son. The son was killed in action in France in 1916 while serving in the 8th Battalion, the Liverpool Regiment. Mary Jane died a widow in 1932, aged 73.

As we have seen, Peter, the elder son, joined his father in Constantinople where he became involved in Peter Tait Son & Co and, latterly, worked as a clerk in the *Régie des Tabacs*. There is no further record of him until 1897, when at the age of 36 he married Emmeline Vavasour Macfarlane, who was thirteen years his junior. We do not know what went wrong, but by the time of the 1901 census Peter was lodging in East Ferry Road on the Isle of Dogs, working as a dock clerk, while Emmeline, describing herself as single, was working as a nurse at St Olave's Union Infirmary in Rotherhithe, where she lived in. In 1901 the Infirmary's staff of eighty-three were responsible for the care of seven hundred and fifty-one in-patients. On 17 May 1902 Peter was found dead in lodgings at 145 High Street, Whitechapel. He was just 41 years old. The inquest found the cause of death to be broncho-pneumonia accelerated by alcoholic excess; an ignominious end for Sir Peter's heir. Less than three months after Peter's death, Emmeline married Timothy Daley, described on the marriage certificate as a general labourer.

Barbara Isabella, my grandmother, married, in January 1891, the landscape artist Edward Wilkins Waite, whose work has become popular with collectors in recent years. They had two daughters and a son. Barbara died a widow in 1950, aged 88.

Thomas William, Sir Peter's younger son, only 26 when his father died, worked initially as a journeyman tailor. Then in December 1892 he had a son. He married the child's mother, Amelia Jane Harding in the following year and a second son was born in 1894. Thomas, was working for a timber merchant as a machine wood sawyer when he died of laryngeal consumption in 1904, aged 38.

Evelyn Rosina (Eva), Sir Peter's sixth daughter, who had been named after his boat, became a nurse; having trained at the Liverpool Royal Infirmary. Apart from appointments in the UK, she served in the Army Nursing Service in South Africa as a nursing sister from 1900 to 1902 and with Queen Alexandra's Imperial Military Nursing Service as acting matron on HMHS St George for a year from September 1914, when she left to take up the position of Matron of the newly opened King Edward VII Hospital for Crippled Children in Sheffield; a position she held until her retirement in 1925. Evelyn was a Founding Member of the Royal College of Nursing in 1916. She died unmarried in 1926, aged 61.

Alice Emily, the last child, was also a nurse. She joined the Army Nursing Service in 1896 and became a nursing sister at Woolwich in 1899. From early in 1901 until the end of the Boer War she served in hospitals in South Africa. She was mentioned in despatches by Lord Kitchener on 23 June 1902, by which time she had joined Queen Alexandra's Imperial Military Nursing Service on its formation in March of that year. Alice, by then a Matron, resigned from the QAIMNS shortly before her marriage to Lieut-Col Isaac Bomford Emerson in 1906. The couple had two daughters. Alice died a widow in 1944, aged 76. Tradition has it that Alice said of Sir Peter that he disappeared in Russia where he had gone in disgrace, and that when his son went to find him, he disappeared as well, which tends to confirm that, for whatever reason, and strange as it may seem, even his children did not really know what became of him.

Other members of Sir Peter's family

Balfour Logie, who was already a widower in 1890, ended his working life as a director and the secretary of the Auxiliary Co and died in retirement in 1915, aged 85. Although Barbara and Balfour had five children, none of them became involved in any of Sir Peter's various enterprises.

Of James Tait, Sir Peter's elder brother, nothing is known, either of him, or of his wife and children, after the end of the American Civil War, when he had acted as Tait & Co's agent in the Confederate States.

Of Robert Thomas Tait nothing further is heard, following his retirement as a director of the Auxiliary Co in 1889, until he died in a nursing home in Bournemouth in 1903, aged 64. His daughter, Blanche Edith, had married Francis Hoskins Pedroza, a surgeon lieutenant-colonel in the Indian Medical Service in 1896. They had no children and Blanche died a widow in 1933, aged 61. Robert's younger daughter, Isabel Maud, became the joint owner, with Miss Kate White, of Eversley, the well known and respected boarding school for girls at Folkestone in Kent. Isabel died unmarried in 1964, aged 86.

What Thomas Nicoll did after 1879 is not recorded. He died unmarried in 1915, aged 71. Of his younger brother, Laurence Nicoll there is no record after 1886, when he was one of the subscribers to the Memorandum of Association of the Turkish Cigarette Company Limited.

William Abraham, Sir Peter's brother-in-law, who was nine years younger than Rose, had been closely involved in the management of the clothing factory in Limerick before its sale to the Auxiliary Co in 1884. He then became involved in politics and at the general election of 1886 was elected unopposed as the Parnellite member for Limerick West, in spite of being a Protestant. Thereafter, with only a short break, William Abraham spent almost thirty years in Parliament, first as the member for Limerick West, then for Cork North-East and lastly for Dublin Harbour, the seat he held when he died in 1915, aged 75. William Abraham is remembered chiefly for his part in precipitating the split in the Parnellite party in 1890. When the party convened in Committee Room 15 of the House of Commons on 1 December, it was William Abraham who moved the motion that Parnell's chairmanship of the party be terminated. It was when Parnell refused to accept the motion, that Justin McCarthy and forty-four of his colleagues left the room; splitting the party.

Thomas Bruce Hamilton, who had married Rose Tait's eldest sister Margaret, is believed to have remained with the Auxiliary Co until he retired. He died in March 1896, aged 77.

Peter Thom, who had married Rose Tait's sister Mary Anne, and had been one of the partners in Cannock Tait & Co, left Limerick following the bankruptcy in 1869 and set up in business on his own account in Nenagh, in County Tipperary.

Appendix A

Extract from Minutes of Evidence taken before the Commissioners Appointed to Inquire into the State of the Store and Clothing Depots at Weedon, Woolwich and the Tower etc.

London, Tuesday 7 December 1858
Present: Henry Selfe Selfe Esq in the Chair
James Aspinall Turner Esq MP
Colonel Henry John French
Mr Peter Tait examined

(*Chairman*) You are an army clothier? - Yes, that is one branch of my business.
What other branches have you? - I am a general draper.
You live at Limerick? - Yes.
Have you been a contractor with the Government? - Yes.
When did you first become a contractor? - About 1856; perhaps towards the end of 1855, since the war broke out with Russia.
Did you ever furnish clothing under the old system? - To one regiment of militia.
Never to the line? - No.
What was the regiment of militia? - The Royal Limerick County Regiment.
Have not you been somewhat fortunate in tendering under the new system of open competition? - Yes.
What has been the extent, speaking generally? - I have supplied during the three years for the service of the line 120,000 suits of clothing in round numbers.
Did you furnish the cloth in the first instance? - For this year's service I have; formerly cloth was supplied from Weedon.
Then your contract was to make up cloth? - Yes, and furnish the garniture and trimmings.
Have all your supplies been the result of competition by tender? - Yes, all.
Have you reason to know that your tender has been the lowest? - I have reason to know that it has not been the lowest tender in any of those instances in which I have supplied this large quantity of clothing.
The general rule being that the lowest tender shall be accepted, how is it that you have been the person employed? - I have not been the only person employed. I believe the principle adopted is this, if the lowest tender is sent in by a

respectable firm, they get the largest portion of the contract; then the next in price is taken, according to the respectability of the house that tenders.
Have you tendered for larger quantities than your tender has been accepted for? - The quantity is not specified in tendering for line clothing; the price is given and the Director of Contracts allots to one person as many regiments as he thinks the price warrants him doing.
Do not you state how many you are prepared to take, because if that is not done you might have more apportioned to you than you could make? - We never got more than we were able to make.
Do not you say, "I will make 10,000 or 20,000, whatever the number may be? - No, not in all instances.
I presume you have hardly had an opportunity personally of comparing the old system and the new one? - I have gone a good deal into the question. I have samples with me which I shall be happy to lay before the Commissioners, of the clothing supplied under the three different systems which have been in operation during the last six years. I have also calculations, as to which I shall be happy to afford any information in my power.
Have you had opportunity, practically, of knowing the working of the old system? - No, not further than by statistics.
Then your statement would be merely a matter of opinion as regards the past? - No it would not; I am a practical tradesman, and so far as cloth goes, I have specimens; I know what they cost, and I am in a position to state the facts of the case on those points.
Do you use the sewing machine largely? - I do.
Do you use the American machine or Thomas's? - Thomas's.
Do you find that answer? - I do. I have samples of clothing which have been made by steam power, which I am prepared to lay before you.
You know the size rolls from information received from the Government? - Yes, and where the size roll is not supplied, I have a size roll, which I furnished to the Government, comprising about 45 different sizes for a regiment 1,000 strong. I have gone practically into the question, and measured several regiments.
(*Mr Turner*) I think we heard from Colonel Horne that you rather objected to make the coats according to the size of the men, and adopted your regulation sizes, and expected the men to fit them? - That is not the fact.
(*Chairman*) Colonel Horne says that you furnished the 13th regiment, 2nd battalion, with a certain number of suits; that he suggested that the tunics should fit the men, but that you wished the men should fit the tunics. Is it the fact that you objected to measure a man in the position that he placed him in? - I did not object to measure a man in the position that he placed him in, but I showed by my eye, that I disapproved entirely of the manner in which he wished the man measured.
(*Mr Turner*) Tell us why you objected to measure the man as he stood? - I received a telegram from the War Office requesting that I would send some practical tradesman to Winchester to have an interview with Colonel Horne relative to the clothes, and instead of sending anybody I went to Winchester myself. When I got there, Colonel Horne was not in barracks, and I was delayed till the following day, when the regiment was paraded for my inspection.

Colonel Horne stated what his views were with regard to the clothing, with which I entirely disagreed.
What were his views? - In fitting a man he took hold of him by the shoulders and expanded his chest, and he wished the cloth cut out of the back of the coat and put in the front of the coat. I told him that his notions were entirely absurd; as the mission which I had been commissioned to fulfil by the Secretary of State was a very important one. I would be very careful, in making my report, to state the principles upon which the clothing was cut for the general army.
(*Chairman*) What did you say to Colonel Horne? - I told him that the clothing was cut according to the pattern which had been approved after the measurement of several regiments, and had been found to answer well for the service, and had been approved by the War Office.
(*Mr Turner*) Whether the clothing fitted the men or not? - The clothing fitted the men.
Colonel Horne states that it did not fit the men? - He stated what is not correct.
(*Col. French*) Colonel Horne stated that the clothing did not meet by two or three inches across the chest? - That is not the case. If the clothing had been made according to Colonel Horne's plan, when the man got on his knapsack, or had his firelock on his shoulder, his coat would burst.
A soldier has to go through extensive motions; if you put a man into a coat that is merely to button up, it may not fit him; you are aware that a soldier requires to use very great exertion? - That was all provided for in the patterns adopted by the War Office. I supplied other battalions, and evidence was given by Colonel Elmhirst the same day, which entirely disagreed with the evidence of Colonel Horne with reference to the same clothing.
(*Chairman*) Did Colonel Horne put the right men into the right coats? - Would you allow me to state that when the second battalion of the 13th was raised Colonel Horne did not command the regiment; there were some 550 men in the regiment when Colonel Horne joined, and as soon as he joined he found fault with everything; the clothing had been passed by Colonel Faunce and Colonel Cathcart, and Colonel Horne disapproved of it. I made the clothing up in anticipation of the wants of the regiment.
Did you make the clothing which had passed the inspection of Colonel Faunce and Colonel Cathcart? - Most unquestionably.
Colonel Faunce was commanding the regiment in February? - Yes, and Colonel Horne succeeded after the regiment was 550 strong, on the 20th of July; it was the very same clothing. I told Colonel Horne that I should make a report to the Secretary of State stating that I saw no ground to alter the patterns; that the clothing had not been made on defective principles, and at the very time I had an order for 280 suits, 42 suits of which he complained of and referred to in his evidence given on the 21st of October. I went down to Winchester; and I have omitted to state, that when I was at Winchester on the former occasion I found that Colonel Horne's master tailor had deserted, and there was no person there to fit the men. I then suggested to the War Office, in order to meet the requirements of the service, that if the buttons were forwarded to me I would have them placed on the tunics, and that when I visited London the next time I would assist in fitting the men. I went down to Winchester and I fitted 143 men in about two

hours, and I found that the 42 tunics which the adjutant-general had ordered to be taken into wear also fitted.
Those which Colonel Horne objected to, and which he was ordered by the Horse Guards to take into wear, did fit the men? - Yes; the tunics ought never to have been rejected.
Colonel Horne says, that in the position in which the men would frequently have to stand, the coats would not meet by a couple of inches in the front. I understand you to attribute that to the fact that he threw the men's shoulders too much back? - He got behind the soldier and put him in a position in which it would be impossible for any man to walk, either with or without his knapsack.
Do you think that your experience upon the subject is to be put in competition with that of Colonel Horne? - I will meet Colonel Horne or any other officer, and prove that the clothing was not cut on defective principles. I will prove that it was the proper cut, and well made and fit for any soldier to wear. When I got the order for making up the clothing for that battalion there was not a single soldier in the battalion. I received the order in the month of September, and I delivered the clothing in the December following. It was inspected by the Government, and on their certificate I was paid. I heard nothing about the clothing till twelve months after I got the certificate.
When you send in clothing according to sizes, do you mark the size upon each coat? - Yes; there is a printed ticket with the tradesman's name and the size of the garment placed upon each coat.
As you had not measured the men, and were making clothes in Limerick for men in Winchester, must it not be, to a certain extent, a chance whether the man upon whom the garment was put would fit it? - There is no difficulty in it whatever. We make 45 sizes for a regiment; we commence with 5 feet 4, and increase to six feet. For every height we make four different widths. When a regiment is 1,000 strong, there are from 50 to 100 suits always supplied in material to meet the requirements of men who are out of proportion, as frequently occurs.
Have you anything more to say with regard to that interview with Colonel Horne? - When I had fitted the 143 men Colonel Horne wished to inspect them, but on account of the trouble I had had with Colonel Horne, I declined to inspect the men I had fitted unless two other officers were present with himself. After some difficulty, Colonel Horne agreed to that, because I stated that I should not inspect the clothing with Colonel Horne only. He, therefore, appointed two other officers to inspect the men with himself. I requested that I should get a certificate stating what I had done at Winchester. I had been at an expense of about 30*l*. for nothing, and I thought it was only fair to me, as a tradesman, that I should get a certificate, and this is it:-

"We certify that we have this day seen and inspected the 143 tunics supplied by Mr Tait, army clothier, for the 2nd battalion of the 13th foot, fitted by him in our presence. We are perfectly satisfied with the make and fit, little or no alteration being required.
Signed,
Arthur Horne, Lieutenant-Colonel
Thomas Faunce, Brevet Lieut.-Col.
A.M.Cathcart, Brevet Lieut.-Col."

That is dated the 26th of October, three or four days after Colonel Horne was examined. Those are some of the tunics which Colonel Horne stated in his evidence he had rejected for being bad and inferior.
Colonel Horne complained of the misfit some months before? - The tunics are cut on precisely the same pattern for every regiment. Colonel Horne's complaint was that the clothing was cut on defective principles. This clothing was cut precisely by the same patterns, and if they were defective in one instance, they must have been defective in another. I should have been very sorry to cut up 20,000 suits of clothing upon the principles laid down by Colonel Horne.
You say that the alteration of position that he suggested would have left too much cloth in front? - Yes; in fact no man that knew anything of his business would have made such a coat. If Colonel Horne had offered me 30*s*. a garment, which would be 10*s*. more than I am at present paid, I would not make them.
Why not? - Because I would not have my character as a tradesman disgraced. I was not dependent upon Colonel Horne for any character. I am anxious to show you the different coats under the old system. It has been stated by many witnesses that there never was any cause of complaint under the old system, but I can show by samples that the new tunic is fully 3*s*. 6*d*. more valuable than the former tunic, for which the same price was paid. I have here the coats supplied under the off-reckoning system; then the tunic under the patronage of the colonels; and now the tunic supplied by public contract.
(*Mr Turner*) Where did you get the specimen of the coatee made under the off-reckoning system? - At the War Office. I applied to them to allow me to have a coatee out of store, which they did.
(*Chairman*) When? - As soon as I communicated with the Commissioners. That is the coatee supplied under the off-reckonings (*producing a coatee*). I must observe, however, that this is a militia coatee, but it is just the same cloth as was cut for the line. There is the garment supplied when the colonel had the patronage, and gave the orders to his own tradesman; that the country paid 1*l*. for (*producing a tunic*). This is the garment which I am now supplying under my present contract for 19*s*. 9*d*. The whole of the coat is cut and made by steam power. The buttons are supplied by Government. The real cost of that tunic to the country is 20*s*. 5½*d*. My price is 19*s*. 9*d*. The buttons cost 6½*d*., and the regimental tailor is allowed 2*d*. for sewing them on.
(*Chairman*) Did you furnish any clothing to colonels before March 1857? - I supplied a militia regiment.
How did it come to pass that there was such an enormous difference in price between the double breasted tunic and the old coatee, both being made of the same cloth? - Because there is more cloth, and more facings.
There is an enormous difference apparently charged? - I believe the price charged for the coatee during the war was 14*s*. 10*d*.
Is there more or less cloth in the improved single-breasted tunic? - There is a little less cloth and a little less facing; but the real difference in value between these two garments is about 3*s*. 6*d*., so that there is a saving of 3*s*. 6*d*.
Do you mean to say that you could get the old cloth at 3*s*. cheaper? - Yes, the cloth could be supplied at 3*s*. cheaper than that.
Would you undertake to do it? - Certainly.

You now supply a tunic at how much? - 19*s*. 9*d*. is my price, but the real cost of the garment is 20*s*. 5½*d*.
Is this cloth furnished by yourself? - Yes.
How do you test the strength of it? - There is Hebdon's testing machine, but I do not use it. I trust more to the character of the manufacturers I employ. I pay the highest price that is paid in the market, and go to a respectable house.
(*Chairman*) From whom do you get your cloth? - From Joshua Ellis and Sons, of Dewsbury.
(*Col. French*) Have you always resided at Limerick? - No, I am an Irishman by adoption, but not by birth. I am a native of the Shetland Islands myself. This is a serge frock supplied this year for India, and is supplied for 7*s*.
(*Chairman*) Can you compare it with anything equivalent to it? - This is supplied in lieu of shell-jackets. Regiments in India have a tunic one year, and a shell-jacket the other. This serge frock is a cheaper article, and far more comfortable. (*The witness produced several pairs of trousers, and a tunic rejected by Colonel Horne at Winchester.*)
How much a yard do you pay for your cloth? - I pay for drummers' red, 8*s*. 3*d*.; for sergeants' scarlet, as sergeants are very particular, I am supplying a superior article that costs me 10*s*. 3*d*. a yard.
(*Mr Turner*) You say that you employ machinery; can you make all of the parts of a coat by machinery? - That coat is made by machinery, with the exception of the buttonholes and sewing on the buttons.
An objection has been raised by many other clothiers that sewing machinery is not applicable to many operations, though it may be useful in light descriptions of work? - All I have to say is, that I have proved machinery to be perfect. I have gone to a great deal of trouble with it, and I have now brought it to a great state of perfection. I can conduct many branches of business with it. I have a garment here which I believe could not be made as well by hand (*producing a quartermaster-sergeant's tunic*). That badge is put on by steam power, and every stitch, except the buttons and buttonholes, is done by steam power.
(*Col. French*) How long would it take, cutting out and all? - There are only four staff sergeants in a regiment; ordinary clothing we make at the rate of 4,000 a week. I am at present able to supply the whole of the British army with clothing; I have only been in the trade three years.
(*Mr Turner*) You have been very candid as to the price of your cloth, perhaps you will have no objection to state what is the saving between steam power and sewing machinery applied to the making of a coat of this kind and hand work? - This quartermaster-sergeant's coat is made very much superior to what a quartermaster-sergeant would be entitled to have it made if it were made by hand; that is the way I find machinery turn to advantage. The price paid for soldiers' clothing is not at all sufficient to have the clothing made properly. I was anxious to make this statement before you, that I am able to make the clothing far better for the same price by introducing machinery, and at the same time to raise the wages of my workpeople.
What would be the difference of cost to you, between making this staff-sergeant's coat by machinery and making it by hand sewing? - The difference in that

garment would be about 2*s*. in favour of machinery, besides the superior workmanship. The price of that coat is 3*l*. 5*s*.
Then there is a saving of something like 3 per cent. in the workmanship? - The saving would be 3 per cent. on the workmanship.
Besides giving a much superior article? - Yes; I made these garments specially for the Commissioners' inspection, and I have no objection to have them inspected by any tradesman in London if I am present. We have to thank Sir Thomas Troubridge for machine sewing being brought to perfection for army clothing. When it was first introduced the master tailors and colonels reported against the machine sewing. I bought a sewing machine, and I was so perfectly satisfied with the superiority of the sewing that I took it to the War Office and worked it before Sir T Troubridge, and he was perfectly satisfied that the sewing was sound and good. I first of all took pains to ascertain the perfection of the sewing machine. Early in 1856 I bought one, fastened it up in my own study and took it all to pieces, and I was satisfied that the machine sewing was better than hand sewing. There is one machine by which if one stitch is cut the work will run, but in Thomas's machine the stitch is perfectly the same on both sides. You will see that the sewing on that tunic on one side is green and the other side is scarlet; that is done at the same time with the same needle.
(*Chairman*) Are we to understand you to say that you have machine power by which you could clothe the British army? - If the Government will give me an order I can clothe the whole of the British army.
How many suits could you make in a year? - I calculate for about 250,000 suits. If the Government were ever in an emergency, whether I am in the army trade or not, by steam power I then could supply them with 10,000 suits a week.
(*Mr Turner*) Have you had an opportunity of looking at the prices quoted as the cost of the artillery clothing? - I have. I went down to Woolwich to see the establishment there.
The parties there rather impressed the Commissioners with the opinion that there was a good deal in what they said, and that they were making very excellent garments, of a better quality and cheaper than they had previously been supplied for the artillery? - That is quite the fact.
But the prices for artillery clothing were formerly very high. I understood that the contractor had a very excellent price for them, and therefore, perhaps it is not a fair comparison; we asked several of the clothiers, Mr Dolan particularly, and he pledged himself to produce an article equal to that made at Woolwich, and that he would contract for any quantity at the price which they professed to make them for. Have you had any opportunity of judging about that? - Yes.
Would you take a contract at the price they state to be their cost price? - Certainly.
Would you be glad to have a contract at that price? - I would not be glad to have the contract; the price would not be such as to give a large profit; the profit would be exceedingly small; but it could be done at the same price. They are doing their business very well at Woolwich. I was quite surprised to see the way they are turning out the tunics.

They turn the machinery by the feet of the workpeople? - That is only for trousers and for cap covers. I believe no person has attempted to use the machine in making tunics with the exception of myself.
(*Chairman*) Did you never hear of the London clothiers making use of machinery? - I did; but my impression is that they did not know how to use it, and it turned out a failure. Mr Dolan, I know, had Thomas's machine. I recollect Mr Thomas telling me that he had been with him on two occasions; but they could not get on with them somehow or another; and I should have had a difficulty getting on with them , only I made myself practically acquainted with them, and could work them myself.
Do you know any other London army clothier who has had sewing machines? - I understood that Messrs. Hebbert had them. I believe Mr. Bischoff stated so, and he found them not to answer.
Do you attribute that to their not knowing how to set to work? - Most certainly; it is a good thing for the country that we have more persevering tradesmen to supply our army now.
(*Col. French*) Does not the use of the sewing machine throw a great many people out of work? - No. I employ about 1,000 people, and I am enabled to pay them superior wages. I employ no man at wages lower than a guinea a week. I pay about 30 per cent. more than is paid in London for labour. I will give you an instance in which the introduction of machinery has been of great advantage to the public service; I received by telegraph an order from the War Office on Monday evening, the 22nd of May, for 800 suits. On receiving that telegram I imagined that unfavourable news had been received from India; the telegram stated that haste was of the greatest importance. I had not all the materials in stock, and I was obliged to telegraph to England for a portion of the supply, and request that I should have the material by express train. I had my people in attendance and we worked all night, and on Friday morning at 11 o'clock I forwarded 800 suits complete by express train to London.
(*Chairman*) Could you have done that without machinery? - No. Perhaps I may be permitted to read a certificate that I have received from Lieut.-Col. Maude:- "I certify that Mr Tait, of Limerick, has supplied the 2nd battalion, 3rd foot, during its formation, a considerable number of free kits, and the articles comprising them have been found, on close examination by the Board of Officers, to be very good. The promptitude with which Mr Tait executes an order, owing in a great measure to his extensive sewing machinery, added to his own business-like habits, cannot fail to gain for him extensive patronage. I gave Mr Tait an order for 100 free kits, and the next evening he supplied me with the greater part of all the articles, some of which, the trousers for instance, had been made up by him on that day; he seems to be a very enterprising respectable contractor, and as such I trust to hear of his success. W.F.Maude, Lieutenant-Colonel, Limerick, 16th November 1857."
Did you not send 200 forage caps to the 2nd battalion of the 13th regiment? - Yes; I shall be very glad to state the whole circumstances. I received an order on the 3rd of May for 200 forage caps, and I sent in error blue caps for green, not knowing that the 13th was a light infantry regiment. When I arrived in London soon after, I ascertained that the caps had been sent in wrong. I went into the City to the agent of one of the Kilmarnock houses, and asked to see their best rifle

green caps. They showed me a dozen. I opened a parcel and took out two caps. I stated that I could not give any order till I ascertained whether the caps were equal to the sealed pattern at the Board. I submitted them to Sir Thomas Troubridge. The caps were approved and sealed, and I sent down 200 green caps to replace the blue ones. Those green caps were rejected. But previously to my hearing that the caps were rejected I received an order for a second supply of 200. Those I forwarded immediately to Winchester. A correspondence ensued with the War Office, the adjutant-general and myself, making a delay of three months, and the caps were ultimately returned to Limerick. When they came to Limerick I compared them with the second sealed pattern, and on examination I found they were equal in every respect to the sealed pattern. I re-packed the caps and returned them to Winchester, and they were received by the regiment and approved of.

They were returned to you in August, were not they? - Yes; they were received at Winchester about the 1st of September. That was three months from sending the first green caps, till the caps were issued.

Were they received by the same regiment? - By Colonel Horne; Colonel Horne did not know anything about it, he did not know that I returned him the precise caps that he rejected. I was not fool enough to tell him that.

And he passed them? - Yes, because he was no judge of them. I dispute Colonel Horne's judgement very much. The mistake of sending blue for green arose because I was not aware that the 13th was a light infantry regiment. I had an order for kits for 2,000 men, all of which wore blue caps, and I supplied this regiment with blue as well as the other regiments.

You had an order for kits, shell-jackets, and various things, do you remember when you received that order? - I have all the particulars here of every article that I supplied Colonel Horne with, and with the exception of those caps, which were ultimately approved of, all my supplies were received; that is the date of the order, the date of the execution, and the particulars of the free kits that I received for Colonel Horne's regiment (*handing in a paper*).

(*Mr Turner*) You have given us some valuable information with regard to your enterprise as a commercial man, and the perfection to which you have carried manufacturing by machinery; do you think it is possible for any Government establishment to manufacture clothing so as to contend successfully against an enterprising man who is engaged in the business himself? - I do not; I think if the Government manufactured their own clothing, it would give rise to many grave objections; supposing they had establishments sufficiently large, and machinery in sufficient perfection, they would be more or less dependent on tailors; and if it was all confined to one trade, the trade could do just precisely as they liked. I think it is not a bad plan to have a small establishment if they wish to ascertain the cost of every article. They have an opportunity of doing that; they have an opportunity of knowing how soon or how long it will take to execute an order of a certain magnitude.

You think that for the bulk of the supply of army clothing it would be much wiser for the Government to trust to the commercial and manufacturing enterprise of the country, than to attempt to manufacture the whole of the clothing

themselves? - That is my decided opinion. I believe, however, that clothing supplied by public contract is the true principle.
(*Chairman*) Why do you think so? - Because competition is the life of business. If there is competition and the enterprise of Great Britain is brought to bear upon one particular branch of trade, it ought to be done pretty perfect.
Would you have competition as to quality or price? - As to price; I have read the paper put in by Messrs. Hebbert with reference to that subject, and I entirely disagree with it; that is, competition for quality instead of price. I think that plan would be a very difficult one to carry out; in the first place it could not obtain uniformity of pattern; if the War Office had in their pattern-room a perfect set of patterns, then competition is of no use. If we are anxious to give a good garment to the soldier, let us give it at a fair price; for instance, Col. Horne and I had great difference of opinion respecting clothing. Supposing the 2nd battalion of the 9th foot were lying at Winchester, and that regiment was clothed by Messrs. Hebbert; they do not much like me to be in the army trade, and they might say, "We can afford to throw away 100*l*. here to get Tait put out of this trade; we can order cloth of a superior quality, and get a superior make, so as to supply that regiment with clothing much superior to pattern." Very well, when Messrs. Hebbert's clothing is inspected by the general commanding in the district, it can easily be brought to the general's notice, that I am paid the same prices that Messrs. Hebbert are paid, and that Messrs. Hebbert have supplied the soldiers with a very much superior garment; and, of course, there would be a report sent to His Royal Highness to that effect. It does away at once with competition; there is no competition at all; as in an ordinary commercial transaction. When anything is introduced in the silk or any other trade, the price is brought down by competition, as I know from being engaged in general business.
I do not think Messrs. Hebbert's memorandum suggested that because one supply might be a little better than another, the contractors should be dismissed at the next contract? - Certainly not; if the colonel had the choosing or if the commander-in-chief represented to the Secretary of State-for-War, that one regiment had been clothed much better than another, and that Messrs. Hebbert were willing to supply the one regiment precisely the same as they had done the other, of course, the Government would be bound to accept the offer.
Are you not assuming that the contract is annual? Would you have annual contracts or triennial? - Triennial would be the best.
Then the suggestion that you made of Messrs. Hebbert throwing away 100*l*. must be carried out for three years? - No; for the Government have the power to terminate the contract, if satisfaction is not given.
(*Col. French*) If triennial contracts were carried out, would you take care to have such a supply of cloth on hand that you could meet a great emergency if it arose? - Most certainly. I have suggested to the Government that they ought to extend the contracts longer, and I believe the next contracts will be for two years. The tradesmen from not knowing whether they will receive a contract next year, are not able to hold a sufficient supply to meet urgent demands. There has been a good deal said in reference to delay in issuing clothing; I am now under contract for clothing for next year, and I have sent the clothing for 26 regiments complete to Mark-lane.

(*Chairman*) Where are those regiments? - At home. My foreign clothing is shipped. I think the clothing for the Indian regiments was delivered about the end of September or October.
Would that clothing be packed by Messrs. Hayter and Howell? - Yes.
Mr Hayter stated, on the 7th October, that he did not think that any of the clothing was then delivered complete for packing? - Our clothing for the Indian regiments is paid for. I have had the money for the 15 regiments that I supplied for India.
When did you get the money? - About a fortnight ago.
We have heard that the clothing ought to start nine or ten months before it is taken into wear? - Yes; under the new form proposed for the next contract, the clothing is to be delivered at certain periods for different stations, which will do away with the difficulty which has arisen, for the Indian clothing must be completed by the contractor in the month of March.
When did you enter into your contract for the supply of clothing for the Indian regiments? - Not till towards the end of May. The red serge frock being introduced, and this being the first year of its introduction, a difficulty arose which would not arise in subsequent years; the article had entirely to be manufactured. No person held a stock of that precise article. A similar article was very much used in the China trade, but not quite so good as that required for the army. The difficulty arose in getting the serge manufactured, and in the dyeing.
Which system, in your opinion, would be the most beneficial, assuming competition for price, to leave the colonels or the Government to fix upon the persons who should execute the contracts? - Most certainly the Government.
Why? - Because I find in this book (Parl. Paper, No. 269, 1857, Appendix No. 9, page 638,) that one house, Messrs. Hebbert's got 110 regiments and depots; and if the thing went back to the colonels, it would be in the same way through interest. I believe if the thing was back in the hands of the colonels, I should not get a single regiment to supply, but I have no objection to the system on that ground.
(*Mr Turner*) Would it not be to the interest of the colonel to have good clothing for his regiment? - I do not say that Messrs. Hebbert would not supply as good clothing as I would. The difficulty that arose during the Crimean war was in consequence of the army clothing trade being confined to a few houses. The business was most lucrative; almost everyone engaged in it had made large sums of money, and, of course, as is natural, they are anxious that the clothing should return to the same channel; but if we want the country to save money, and the soldiers to get good clothing, public contract is quite the thing in my opinion.
(*Col. French*) Do not you think you are arguing in your own favour? You having established your connexion may get a good proportion of the regiments yourself? - I have no more chance than anyone else. The Government can do without me as well as any other tradesman. I believe the Government are the trustees of the public money, and whoever will supply them with the best and cheapest article has a right to the business. I have laid out 4,000*l*. on machinery, although I have no claim upon the Government.
(*Mr Turner*) With reference to the subject of the inspection of these garments, have you any observations to make? Have you had any cause of complaint of the

way in which your garments were treated? - I believe I differ in opinion entirely from almost every other tradesman upon that subject. The inspection is very rigid; but when I look at the Government inspection, compared with that in ordinary commercial transactions, I find it is entirely a different thing. The viewers who inspect the clothing cannot be allowed any latitude. They may on the one hand do me an injury, or they may do the public service a very great injury. When I am called upon to tender I am instructed by the Director of Contracts to make an inspection of the specifications and patterns. If I do that, and am anxious to supply the precise article I tender for, I have no cause to complain.

In your experience have you not met with an inordinate number of rejections? - I have had rejections, but I have never had rejections for the quality of the material. I have supplied, if not a superior article, always the same as the pattern.

Did you not complain of Colonel Horne's rejections? - He did not make any rejection; the clothing had been passed, and I had been paid for the garments. I only went to Winchester as a matter of compliment; I was called upon to go to Winchester and make a report upon a certain subject.

Do you think that Colonel Horne was unreasonable in his criticisms of your garments? - I think he was most absurd.

Have you any reason to think that there has been the same absurdity displayed by the Government inspectors? - No; I have had no cause of complaint, as I have stated already. The inspection is very severe; but only such as will warrant the soldier getting proper garments. I cannot make any complaint of the inspection.

Have garments been returned to you for trivial reasons? - They have been returned for small things, such as stitches being wrong.

Those defects you could repair and send the things back, as you did the caps to Colonel Horne? - That always has been the case; they have put a chalk mark to denote the defects, which I have remedied and returned the garments.

Is it the fact that you have not had to retain in your establishment any number of garments that have been rejected? - I have not a single garment. I am able at this moment to go out of the army trade without any difficulty. When I have completed my present engagements, I shall not have 50*l*. worth of Government articles in my possession. I have not a garment of any description.

(*Chairman*) What do you do with the rejections? - I never have had them. I have remedied the objections.

Then I presume you would see no advantage in an appeal from the decision of the inspector? - There are great difficulties connected with the question of appeal. The question was raised the other day, at a conference of tradesmen, at the War Office, on the subject. The present system is, that supposing I have a difference of opinion with the inspector, I make a report to the War Office upon that subject; my letter or my report is referred by the War Office, and probably the same inspector reports; however, to obviate that, the Government are quite sensible that a practical tradesman, connected with the department, should look into it to see that no rejection is made, unless upon serious and real grounds. On that statement we are perfectly satisfied; I am perfectly satisfied to tender on those conditions. The conditions of the contract are very binding; we are obliged to give sureties.

You are content that the referee should be a person in the department? - Yes, different from the person who had already inspected the clothing.
Would that be better than giving a contractor with the Government the same right which every man has at common law, if he says that his contract has been fulfilled, and another man says it has not? - We have to bear in mind that the Government tender for 20,000 different articles, and if a clause to that effect was put into the contract there would be no end of appealing. My decided opinion is, that the complaints that we have had would never have been made if tradesmen tendering had determined on supplying the article they tendered for; I believe they have not supplied the right articles; they have gone in at a low price calculating on supplying an inferior article.
Supposing there were a power of reference, such as that which you say the trade are now content to accept, to a practical man connected with the department; not the same inspector who previously rejected the goods; would that be better; in your estimation, than allowing a man to have as against the Government the ordinary legal remedy which he would have as against an individual? - Yes, I think it is better on account of the questions that would arise. In tendering with the Government we are quite satisfied that we shall get our money, and from an experience of three years, I believe that vexatious rejections will not be made. There are some trifling things which we might account vexations, but when we make the contract we decidedly state that we will supply the precise article. We see the specification and the patterns before tendering, and I do not think we have any reason to grumble.
As you have no establishment in London, of course you have all the extra expense of transit from Limerick. That must be paid for somehow or other? - I pay for it; the clothing must be delivered free in London.
Do you find the distance any material objection? - I find that I pay a very large sum annually to the railway company, which I would save if I were in London.
Have you not other advantages? - I have no advantage; I pay more for my labour in Limerick than the clothiers in London.
You have handed in the prices that you paid, as compared with the prices of Messrs. Dolan and Messrs. Hebbert and Co. (as stated in Mr. Shaw's pamphlet), for making up clothing for the Indian army in 1857? - Yes I executed a portion of the contract referred to on the paper with Messrs. Dolan and Messrs. Hebbert.
For a sergeant's jacket they paid 1*s*., you paid 1*s*. 6*d*.; for a private's jacket they paid 10*d*., you paid 1*s*; for sergeant's trousers they paid 8*d*., you paid 10*d*.; for private's trousers they paid 7*d*., you paid 10*d*.? - The reason I put down those prices is because I saw the question was raised with respect to labour.
(*Col. French*) Was not your clothing made by machinery? - Those that I have produced were made by machinery; if you refer to that precise contract, the clothing for India for 1857, it was made by hand.
I suppose you pay according to the number the workpeople make? - Yes.
(*Chairman*) Is there not now an inspection by a regimental board besides the Government inspection? - Yes.
What is your opinion of that? - My opinion is, that if regimental boards are conducted on the same principle that I saw conducted at Winchester, by Lieutenant-colonel Horne, they are a complete farce. I should be sorry to think

that such is the case. I have come in contact with several officers who understand clothing practically, and who are very anxious to meet the views of the tradesmen, and receive any suggestion that may be made. But my opinion is, that there should be no regimental inspection further than this, - when the clothing arrives at the regiment and is unpacked, unless it is damaged by transit or in any way spoilt in the packing, there should be no appeal. The Government have now appointed two military inspectors in addition to the civilian inspectors, and I believe that those gentlemen are fully competent to judge of the supply, and I think there it ought to end.
(*Col. French*) What was the rank of the officers who sat upon that board at Winchester? - Three Lieutenant-colonels. Colonel Horne was the board himself; that is the precise way to say it.
(*Chairman*) What were the articles? - The tunics I have referred to.
(*Col. French*) Did they bring in the master tailor? - Yes, he had got a new master tailor then on approbation.
Was the quartermaster there? - Yes, the quartermaster was there, but he was not asked his opinion, nor did he give any opinion.
Nor any of the sergeants? - No; Colonel Horne asked no opinion.
(*Chairman*) Do you wish to make any other statement to the Commissioners? - The first year the clothing was to be supplied by the Government was April 1857. Sir Thomas Troubridge was then Director-General of Army Clothing, and he went very practically into the question. When that supply was made, the cut of the tunic was altered from the former tunic to a single breasted. I had a portion of that supply to make, but when the clothing was made, Sir Thomas Troubridge and Mr Ramsay being deeply interested in the matter, and very anxious that the clothing should be made complete, and that the colonels should have no complaint, requested that I should go, on my return to Limerick, to the different depots at Dublin, to the camp at the Curragh of Kildare, and the barracks at Limerick, and look through the regiments without going officially, to see whether I could suggest any improvement in the cut of the garment then supplied. I found, in consequence of the uniform being altered, an error had arisen to a small extent, and the clothing had been cut rather too round in the breast, something in the way that Colonel Horne wants it. I conferred with Lieutenant-colonel Tracy, of the 56th. And told him what my views were with reference to the cut that would meet the requirements of the soldier. He fully agreed with me; and when I returned to Limerick I made up such a coat and cut a set of paper patterns, and forwarded them to the War Office with my observations. Those were inspected by practical tradesmen and approved of, and those patterns have been adopted since. I gave the dimensions of every height. I have gone to a very great deal of trouble. I have measured several regiments myself, and entered into the matter as closely as it is possible for any tradesman to do. I also made out for the Government a statement of the quantity of material, when clothing is supplied in material for rifle regiments, for light infantry, infantry, and highlanders.
What proportion of clothing unmade do you now send to a regiment? - To a regiment 1,000 strong the supply of unmade clothing has been fifty privates, twenty band, and eight drummers; but it has been suggested, and I believe the suggestion will be carried into effect, that clothing for 100 privates should be sent

to be made up by the master tailor; in time of peace at home that could be arranged. There are many men who are differently made, some are higher in the shoulders, and some more corpulent than the ordinary scale, and in order to meet those requirements, and to save unnecessary alteration, it has been suggested that a greater number of unmade suits should be sent to a regiment.
Do you know of any other army tailor who now uses machinery as you do? - No; I think, from what Mr Dolan stated, they use it for trousers to some extent.
Have you many women and children in your employment? - No children; we have girls and women.
What number? - Perhaps 800.
How many men? - A great many men work out of doors; I have 40 men indoors.
Are the majority of your workpeople females? - Yes.
(*Mr Turner*) I presume you do not include all those girls and women in the 1*l*. a week tariff? - That is the lowest price I pay the men.
What do the women get? - Those that put on the lace that you see on that sergeant's coat can earn from 4*s*. 6*d*. to 6*s*. a week, and those that have the finer portions of the work earn up to 10*s*.

Appendix B

The scale of sizes, in inches, in which uniform tunics and trousers were made in 1858 for an infantry regiment of 800 men.

	Tunics			Trousers		
Height	Number	Chest	Waist	Number	Waist	Leg
5′ 5″	10	36	31	10	31	All 31¼
	10	37	32	10	32	
	15	38	33	15	33	
	10	39	34	10	34	
	5	40	35	5	35	
	50			50		
5′ 6″	20	36	31-32	10	31	All 31½
	30	37	32-34	30	32	
	55	38	32-35	45	33	
	40	39	33-35	45	34	
	20	40	34-36	30	35	
	5	41	36	10	36	
	170			170		
5′ 7″	15	36	31-32	10	31	All 31¾
	30	37	32-34	30	32	
	70	38	32-35	50	33	
	65	39	33-36	80	34	
	40	40	34-37	30	35	
				15	36	
				5	37	
	220			220		
5′ 8″	10	36	31	10	31	All 32
	20	37	32-33	10	32	
	30	38	33-34	40	33	
	80	39	33-35	70	34	
	30	40	34-37	30	35	
	10	41	37	10	36	
				10	37	
	180			180		

5′ 9″	20	38	33-34	15	33	All 32½
	40	39	33-35	30	34	
	20	40	36	20	35	
				10	36	
				5	37	
	80			80		
5′ 10″	5	38	34	15	34	All 33
	10	39	35	20	35	
	15	40	35	10	36	
	20	41	36	5	37	
	50			50		
5′ 11″	5	39	34	5	34	All 33¾
	10	40	35	10	35	
	15	41	36-37	10	36	
				5	37	
	30			30		
6′ 0″	10	40	34-35	5	34	All 34½
	10	41	36-37	5	35	
				5	36	
				5	37	
	20			20		
Total	800			800		

Appendix C

A brief explanation of the nature of, and the operation of, the market in, Bills of Exchange

Genuine Trade Bills of Exchange

Bills of exchange were a frequently used way of providing credit for commercial transactions in the years in which Collie was operating. In its simplest form a bill of exchange was an instrument in writing, by which one person requested another to pay a certain sum of money to him at a specified time.

For example, **A** had supplied goods to **B**, for which **A** wanted immediate payment. **B**, on the other hand, wanted, say, four months' credit, so that he could sell the goods before he had to pay for them. **A** therefore would have drawn a bill of exchange on **B** for the value of the goods, to be paid 'four months after date', and sent it to **B**. The bill, which would normally, but not necessarily, have included some identification of the goods in respect of which it had been drawn, or have included the words 'for value received', would then have been 'accepted' by **B**, who would have done this by writing 'accepted' on it and signing his name on it. He would then have returned the bill to **A,** who would have 'endorsed' it by writing his name across it, and discounted it with his bank.

That is to say, the bank would have advanced to **A** the amount of the bill, less four months' interest (or discount). At the end of the four months the bank would have presented the bill to **B** who would have been liable to pay the amount of it to the bank, rather than to **A** who had sold him the goods in the first place. If **B** was unable to pay the amount of the bill, the bank could have had recourse to **A** who had made himself liable by endorsing the bill to enable him to discount it with his bank.

Sometimes **A**, in the above example, instead of discounting the bill with his bank, might have discounted it with a bill broker (a firm specialising in the discounting of bills). The bill broker would have added his own endorsement to the bill and discounted it with his own bank. In this case, the bank would have presented the bill to **B** for payment, and, if **B** could not pay it, the bank would have had recourse either to **A** or to the bill broker, both of whom had endorsed the bill. The bill broker would have expected to make his profit by charging a higher rate of interest (or discount) to **A,** than his bank had charged him.

The successful operation of the market in bills of exchange was based on trust, since no title to the goods giving rise to a bill passed by way of security; thus the bank or broker who discounted a bill had to depend entirely on his personal knowledge of the drawer and acceptor of the bill. A bank discounting a bill for a bill broker; being at one remove from the parties to a bill, assumed a greater risk.

Accommodation Bills of Exchange

An accommodation bill was a bill of exchange drawn for a fictitious debt, for the purpose of raising money by discounting it. However, to discount an accommodation bill, which pretended to be a genuine trade bill and purported to identify goods, or was expressed to be 'for value received', was a fraudulent act.

Renewals of Bills of Exchange by Succession

Either a genuine trade bill of exchange or, more often, an accommodation bill might be renewed by succession.

To take the example above, if **B** knew that he would be unable to pay the bill at the end of the four months, **A** might agree to draw a new bill on **B** for the same amount, to be paid, say, another four months hence. The same procedure for acceptance, endorsement and discounting would be followed; the proceeds being paid by **A** to **B** to enable **B** to pay the amount due on the original bill at maturity. A bill could be renewed in this way indefinitely. However, what is said above about trust and risk would apply with greater force in the case of the renewal of an accommodation bill.

Appendix D

Memorandum of Agreement entered into between Peter Tait & Co and C J McRae Esq representing the Confederate States Government

Peter Tait & Co agree to supply 40,000, forty thousand Uniforms, viz: Jackets and Trousers, at Eighteen Shillings and Six pence per suit, net Cash; the clothing to be supplied in accordance with the Samples deposited with Major J B Ferguson, of assorted sizes, which will be agreed upon by that Officer, and C J McRae agrees to pay for the Clothing, in lots of 5,000, five thousand suits, as they are completed.

The Cloth for these garments to be inspected at Leeds and the made up clothing at Limerick, by Major J B Ferguson or such person as he may appoint for that purpose. The garments are to be packed in waterproof Bales of 150, One hundred & fifty, each, at a charge of 10/6d, ten shillings and six pence, each Bale. The carriage of the goods to be paid for to such place, on production of the carrier's vouchers, as shall be directed by C J McRae, in addition to the price above named. If shipped at Limerick, no charge for carriage will be made. The Expenses of the inspection at Limerick will be paid for by Peter Tait & Co who hereby agree to give every facility to the Inspector in the carrying out of his duties.

This contract is entered into, in the spirit of good-fellowship, each party hereto being most anxious that it shall be carried out to the entire satisfaction of all concerned, and is to be completed by the 1st of December 1864.

(signed) Peter Tait & Co

Liverpool. 13 October 1864. (signed) C J McRae

Appendix E

A representative timetable of the train and boat services between Limerick and London in about 1866.

Limerick to London

Limerick	22.45pm	12.45pm
Dublin Kingsbridge (now Heuston)	4.30am	17.35pm
Dublin Westland Row (now Pearse)	6.30am	19.00pm
Kingstown (now Dun Laoghaire)	7.00am	19.30pm
Holyhead	11.40am	0.10am
London Euston	18.25pm	6.55am

London to Limerick

London Euston	7.25am	20.25pm
Holyhead	14.05pm	3.05am
Kingstown	18.05pm	7.05am
Dublin Westland Row	18.35pm	7.35am
Dublin Kingsbridge	19.45pm	8.35am
Limerick	1.20am	13.20pm

Notes

Notes to Chapter 1: The Early Years

1 Address by Tait at the Old Wesleyan Chapel, Lerwick. *Zetland Times* 2 December 1872.

2 *Ibid.*

3 John J Graham, *A vehement thirst after Knowledge* (Lerwick 1988) p. 127.

4 Mutual dispositions and deeds of settlement 1841 and 1850. Shetland Archives SC 12/53/11 272 and 276.

5 Abridgements of Registers of Seisins, Orkney & Shetland. Shetland Archives P.R. 19.242, P.R. 20.25 and P.R. 20.63.

6 Viola Tait, *A Family of Brothers* (Melbourne 1971).

7 Tait & Logie v. Sharp. Defences for William Sharp. Orkney Archives SC 11/5/1854/25.

8 Tait & Logie v. Sharp. Orkney Archives SC 11/5/1854/25.

9 Sequestration of James Tait. National Archives of Scotland C5318/7/340.

10 The Independent Chapel of the Congregational Union of Ireland at 6 Bedford Row has long since disappeared. It is sometimes confused with the Primitive Wesleyan Methodist Chapel at 3 Bedford Row, which was converted into a cinema. That building still stands.

11 Sasine in favour of Mrs Barbara Leslie or Tait and Mr James Tait etc. 1854. National Archives of Scotland RS 47/20, fol. LXVIIIr.

Notes to Chapter 2: Tait's Army Clothing Factory

1 Tait, in evidence to the Commissioners appointed to enquire into the administration of the Army Clothing Depots. Reports from the Commissioners, 1859, sess. 2, no. 2577.

2 *Limerick Chronicle*, 5 and 8 April 1854.

3 John Quinn and Peter Tait took an assignment of the premises in Chapel Street by an Indenture dated 31 March 1860 (recited in Memorial 1870 6 205 of Deed of Assignment dated 18 February 1870). Registry of Deeds, Dublin.

4 Terms and Conditions of the Contract for the Supply of Stores to the War Department. 15 July 1856. Parliamentary Paper 362 VII 117.

5 As explained in the Preface, an amount shown in italics within square brackets gives an indication of the sterling equivalent in 2005 of the sum of money which it follows.

Notes to Chapter 3: Government Contracts for Army Clothing

1 Included in a 'Specification etc. for Tunics and Trowsers for Infantry Regiments'. May 1858. National Army Museum.

2 Peter Tait to Sir Thomas Larcom 17 February 1864. National Archives, Dublin, Registered Papers, 1864, no. 12607.

3 Parliamentary Debates 3rd Series CLXXVI, House of Commons 22 July 1864 col. 1960.

4 Submission by the Inspector General of Constabulary 23 May 1865. National Archives, Dublin, Registered Papers, 1865, no. 4927.

Notes to Chapter 4: Cannock Tait & Co.

1 Walter Bagehot, *Lombard Street* (New York 1895) (first published in 1873) pp. 8 and 9.

2 For a full discussion of the history of Cannock Tait & Co. see Frances Twomey's Thesis, *"Cannock's" A Social and Economic History of the Limerick Company from 1840-1930,* of which a copy is deposited at the City Library in Limerick.

Notes to Chapter 5: Clothing for the Volunteer Militia of Canada

1 R J Marrion and René Chartrand, 'Canadian Volunteer Militia Infantry, 1863-1870', *Military Collector & Historian, Journal of the Company of Military Historians,* (Washington, DC), vol. XXXVI no. 3 Fall 1984, p. 123.

2 Parliamentary Papers. Sessional Papers (No. 12). A 1863.

3 *Ibid.*

4 *Southern Chronicle* 30 May 1863.

Notes to Chapter 6: Attempted Revival of the Flax Industry

1 *Limerick Chronicle*, 23 January 1864.

2 Earl of Donoughmore to his agent, SHG Adams, 6 January 1864. *Clonmel Chronicle,* 12 January 1864.

3 William Lane Joynt quoted by the *Northern Whig*. *Limerick Chronicle,* 26 January 1864.

4 Letters addressed to Sir Robert Peel Bt. MP for submission to the Lord-Lieutenant dated 23 March 1864 and 1 April 1865. National Archives of the UK: Public Record Office HO 122/22.

Notes to Chapter 7: Tait and the American Civil War

1 *Llloyds List* reported on 28 November 1862, col. 22, that 'the *Kelpie,* from Limerick to Nassau, had foundered 80 miles East of Nassau; crew saved', and on 8 December 1862, col. 15, that the vessel 'is reported to have been sunk by a collision, 50 miles from Nassau'.

2 Capt Roberts (the assumed name of Capt the Hon Augustus Charles Hobart), *Never Caught. Personal adventures connected with twelve successful*

trips in blockade-running during the American Civil War, 1863-64 (London, 1867).

3 Young v. United States. U.S. Supreme Court. 97 U.S. 39 (1877).

4 *The Times*, 5 August 1875.

5 Court of Bankruptcy, ex parte Adamson, re Collie. *The Times*, 28 February 1878.

6 *The Times*, 10 August 1875.

7 See evidence in Young v. United States. U.S. Supreme Court 97 U.S. 39 (1877).

8 C J McRae to Hon. James A Seddon, 4 July 1864. *The War of the Rebellion* (Washington 1900), Series IV Vol. III pp. 525-529.

9 Randolph Elder & Co., Glasgow. Finished costs and specifications book. Glasgow City Archives UCS 2/73/1.

10 Sir Peter Tait & Ors. v. Alexander Collie & Another. Court of Chancery. Answer of Alexander Collie to the Plaintiffs' Bill of Complaint, 4 January 1871 p. 3 para. 10. National Archives of the UK: Public Record Office C 16/682 pt.1.

11 E P Stringer to James Spence, 9 April 1868. Head of Leisure Services, Sheffield City Council Wharncliffe Muniments 461 in Sheffield Archives. James Spence had evidently induced the Earl of Wharncliffe to join more than one of Collie's joint ventures.

12 James L Tait to Hon. James a Seddon, 15 December 1863. U.S. National Archives and Records Administration. War Department Collection of Confederate Records RG109.6 M437 File T-320 (WD) 1863.

13 Shoddy is inferior cloth, made either from the waste arising from the manufacture of wool, or from the wool of old woven fabric reduced to the state in which it was before being spun and woven.

14 A R Lawton to James L Tait, 19 December 1863. U.S. National Archives and Records Administration RG 109.6 ch. V vol. 18.

15 Tait v. Collie. Court of Chancery. Answer of Collie, 4 January 1871 p. 7 para. 21.

16 Invoice of Quartermasters Stores shipped to Trans:Mississippi Dept. Dated 12 and 29 November 1864. The Center for American History. The University of Texas at Austin. Ramsdell Microfilm Collection reel 209B, pt. 47.

17 U.S. National Archives and Records Administration. War Department Collection of Confederate Records RG 109. 13. 3. M346. Tait & Co., Peter.

Notes to Chapter 8: The Ill-fated Voyage of the 'SS Condor'

1 Randolph Elder & Co., Glasgow. Finished costs and specifications book. Glasgow City Archives UCS. 2/73/1.

2 Alexander Collie to the Earl of Wharncliffe, 6 August 1864. Head of Leisure Services, Sheffield City Council, Wharncliffe Muniments 460A in Sheffield Archives.

3 Hewitt is sometimes confused with Capt. the Hon. Augustus Charles Hobart, who commanded the *SS Don* from quite early in the Civil War

until just before it was captured in March 1864. Later in that year Hobart assumed command of Collie's vessel, the *SS Falcon*. He was in Halifax with the *Falcon* in August 1864 when the *Condor* sailed from the Clyde. Unlike Hewitt, Hobart had no decorations at that time.

4 Sir Peter Tait & Ors. v. Alexander Collie & Another. Court of Chancery. Affidavit of Alexander Collie, 10 January 1871, p. 25. National Archives of the UK: Public Record Office C 16/682 pt. 1.

5 Alexander Collie to the Earl of Wharncliffe, 23 August 1864. Head of Leisure Services, Sheffield City Council, Wharncliffe Muniments 460A in Sheffield Archives.

6 Collie to Wharncliffe, 14 December 1864. *Ibid.*

Notes to Chapter 9: The 'SS Evelyn'

1 *The Cotton Supply Reporter* (Manchester), 1 August 1864.

2 *Ibid.* 1 November 1864.

3 Sir Peter Tait & Ors. v. Alexander Collie. Court of Chancery. Answer of Collie to the Plaintiffs' Bill of Complaint, 4 January, 1871, Balfour Logie, Peter Tait & Co, to Alexander Collie & Co, 26 October 1864, p. 9 para.25. National Archives of the UK: Public Record Office C 16/682 pt.1.

4 Tait v. Collie. Court of Chancery. Answer of Collie, 4 January 1871, p. 10 para. 30. National Archives of the UK: Public Record Office C 16/682 pt. 1.

5 *Ibid.* p. 18 para. 46.

6 *Ibid.* pp. 20/21 paras. 53/55.

7 *Lloyds List*, 25 August 1865 col. 13.

8 *Ibid.* 3 February 1866 col. 29.

Notes to Chapter 10 :An Eventful Year

1 It will be recalled that Tait's London establishment had been opened as Tait Bros & Co. in November 1861 and that a branch had been opened in Alexander Street, Leeds, in about 1865 which remained there until at least 1870.

2 Peter Tait to William Monsell, 7 July 1865. National Library of Ireland Emly Papers, MS 20676.

Notes to Chapter 11: The Hinchy Affair

1 Details of Ellen Hinchy's committal to the City Goal are taken from the *Registry of Criminals Committed to the Goal of the City of Limerick.* 1859 no. 558, 1866 nos. 25 and 349, 1867 no. 137, 1868 no. 26, and 1869 nos. 23 and 94. National Archives, Dublin, Prison Registers 1/24 series.

2 Ellen Hinchy to the Lord-Lieutenant of Ireland, 14 May 1867. National Archives, Dublin, Chief Secretary's Office: Lunatics File H5/1867, by permission of the Director of the National Archives.

3 *Limerick Reporter and Tipperary Vindicator*, 21 January 1868.

4 Family Record Centre RG9/350.

5 *The Times*, 23 July 1860.

6 Queensland State Archives. Emigration Department: passenger list 231 pp. 397 and 398.
7 State Library of Victoria. Australian Medical Pioneers Index.
8 F B Vignole v. R T Tait. High Court of Justice, Queens Bench Division. Deposition of James Tait, 26 July 1877. National Archives of the UK: Public Record Office J 16/07.

Notes to Chapter 12: Caught up in a Mining Speculation

1 Tait to Charles S Still, 26 December 1872. *The Zetland Times*, 6 January 1873.
2 Filton v. Marshall. Court of Common Pleas. *The Colliery Guardian*, 8 December 1866.
3 The surviving papers of the Registrar of Joint Stock Companies relating to the Glamorgan Iron and Coal Company Limited. National Archives of the UK: Public Record Office BT 31/1118/2221C.
4 Marshall v. GICC & Ors. Court of Chancery. Bill of Complaint, 7 October 1867 p. 2 para. 2. National Archives of the UK: Public Record Office C 16/442.
5 Copies of Prospectuses. Guildhall Library, London.
6 Stock Exchange. General Purposes Committee Minutes, September 1865, nos. 253, 258 and 260. Guildhall Library MS 14600/29.
7 Stock Exchange. Listing Application Papers. Guildhall Library MS 18000/23A/1347.
8 *The Mining Journal*, 14 July 1866.
9 *The Times*, 14 and 15 August 1866.
10 See also the case of Penson v. GICC in the Exchequer of Pleas; P J Moore's Answer to the Plaintiff's Interrogatories sworn 11 June 1866. National Archives of the UK: Public Record Office E 1/33/87.
11 Marshall v. GICC & Ors. Bill of Complaint, 7 October 1867, p. 7 para. 12.
12 Court of Chancery. Companies Act 1862 and the GICC. Affidavit of William Hibbit, 1 July 1867. National Archives of the UK: Public Record Office C 31/2102 pt. 2/1770.
13 Marshall v. GICC & Ors. Bill of Complaint, 7 October 1867, p. 9 para. 16.
14 The papers of the Registrar of Joint Stock Companies. Ibid.
15 Court of Chancery. Entry books of Decrees and Orders. Companies Act 1862 and GICC. 2 March 1867. National Archives of the UK: Public Record Office C 33/1127.
16 *Ibid.* 30 July 1867. National Archives of the UK: Public Record Office C 33/1130.
17 Plymouth Estate Records. Glamorgan Record Office D/D Pl.
18 Home Circuit Minute Book. Spring 1867 to Summer 1868. Guildford Summer Assizes before Mr Baron Martin. National Archives of the UK: Public Record Office ASSI 32/20. See also *The Mining Journal*, 15 August 1868, for fuller report.
19 *The Times*, 16 June 1869.

20 High Court of Justice, Chancery Division. Order dated 10 May 1889. The papers of the Registrar of Joint Stock Companies. *Ibid.*

Notes to Chapter 13: Mayor of Limerick

1 Limerick Archives. Corporation Minutes.
2 Limerick Archives. Minutes of Harbour Commissioners, 29 Sept. 1866.
3 Glasgow University Archives Services, William Denny Collection UGD 3/5/0031 Ship no. 106.
4 Limerick Archives. Corporation Minutes.
5 Dr Butler to William Spillane, 10 January 1870. National Library of Ireland Emly papers MS 20677.
6 *The Dublin Builder*, 1 May 1866.
7 John Collie to Mr Quinn, 17 October 1865. *Limerick Chronicle*, 21 October 1865.
8 Limerick City Museum. 0000.1781.
9 *The Times*, 13 February 1867.
10 *Ibid.* 25 February 1867.
11 National Archives, Dublin, Registered Papers, 1867, no. 10794.
12 *The Dublin Gazette*, 5 April 1867.
13 Victoria & Albert Museum, National Art Library Shelf marks A.19(6), A.28(2-15), A.30(1) and A.30(30).
14 The oo (*moho nobilis*), also called the yellow tufted honeysucker, is a bird of the Hawaiian Islands having brilliant yellow feathers.
15 *Limerick Chronicle*, 20 June 1867.
16 Seamus Flynn and James McMahon *IF WALLS COULD TALK: The Limerick Athenæum: The story of an Irish Theatre since 1852* (Limerick 1996).
17 *Limerick Chronicle*, 11 July 1867.
18 C of E Institution. Board Minutes. Guildhall Library, London, MS 12160E/4, minute 430C, 20 September 1867.
19 Chief Registrar of Shipping. Copy Register. Ship no. 54968. National Archives of the UK: Public Record Office BT 108/96.
20 *The Rhyl Record*, 27 September 1866 and 23 May 1868.
21 Chief Registrar of Shipping. *Ibid.*
22 *Limerick Chronicle*, 11 July 1867.
23 *Ibid.* 18 July 1867.
24 Walter Bagehot, *Lombard Street* (New York) (first published in 1873) pp. 154-156.
25 *The Times*, 21 February 1868.
26 *Limerick Chronicle*, 22 February 1868.
27 Limerick Archives. Limerick Corporation Minutes, 24 April 1868.
28 *Ibid.*, 1 October 1868.
29 Mr John Ellard, Town Clerk of Limerick, in evidence to the Select Committee on Parliamentary and Municipal Elections, 4 June 1869. Parliamentary Papers. Government Elections 4. Sess. 1868-1870, p. 275 para. 7181.
30 *The Times*, 20 November 1868

31 This account of the 1868 election in Limerick is based to a large extent on the Minutes of Evidence taken before the Select Committee on Parliamentary and Municipal Elections between 7 May and 4 June 1869. Parliamentary Papers. Government Elections 4. Sess. 1868-1870, pp. 206 to 279.

32 *The Times*, 11 January 1869.

33 Certificate of F A Fitzgerald, 26 January 1869. Select Committee on Parliamentary and Municipal Elections. Parliamentary Papers. Government Elections 4. Sess. 1868-1870, Appendix no. 1 p. 586.

34 Limerick Archives. Limerick Corporation Minutes, 1 December 1868.

35 *The Dublin Gazette*, 8 December 1868.

36 National Library of Ireland, Office of the Chief Herald Ms. GO 109 pp.179/180.

37 John Mahony became Mayor in 1872.

Notes to Chapter 14: Robert Tait: an Illicit Liaison

1 Private Collection.

2 Westminster Police Court. Evidence of Annie Vigil. *Morning Post*, 21 February 1878.

3 *Ibid.*

4 *Ibid.*

Notes to Chapter 15: The Head of a Steamship Company

1 Sir Peter Tait & Ors. v. Alexander Collie & Another. Court of Chancery. Answer of Alexander Collie to the Plaintiffs' Bill of Complaint, 4 January 1871 p.22 paras. 58 and 59. National Archives of the UK: Public Record Office C 16/682 pt. 1.

2 *Ibid.* p. 22 para. 60.

3 *Shipping & Mercantile Gazette*, 15 July 1870.

4 Court of Chancery. Companies Acts 1862 and 1867 and The London, Belgium, Brazil and River Plate Royal Mail Steam Ship Company, Limited (the Steamship Company). Affidavit of Robert T Tait, 16 July 1872. National Archives of the UK: Public Record Office C 31/2654 pt. 2/2141.

5 *Ibid.* Affidavit of David Swayne, 13 July 1871. C 31/2547 pt. 1/ 1927.

6 *Shipping & Mercantile Gazette*, 17 September 1870.

7 Chief Registrar of Shipping. Copy Register. Ship no. 56884. National Archives of the UK: Public Record Office BT 108/14.

8 *Illustrated London News*, 23 November 1867, p.569 and *The Times*, 28 November 1867.

9 National Archives of the UK: Public Record Office FO 123/ 126/160.

10 Alex. Collie & Co. to Tait & Co., 18 December 1867. 'Sixty-fourths of the steamer' refers to the fact that ownership of vessels was always divided into sixty-four shares. Tait v. Collie. Court of Chancery. Answer of Collie, 4 January 1871, p. 24 para.62. National Archives of the UK: Public Record Office C 16/682 pt. 1.

11 Tait v. Collie. Court of Chancery. Answer of Collie, 4 January 1871, pp. 24 to 26 paras. 63 to 66.
12 *Limerick Chronicle*, 21 March 1868.
13 Chief Registrar of Shipping. Copy Register. Ship no. 60855. National Archives of the UK: Public Record Office BT108/15.
14 The surviving papers of the Registrar of Joint Stock Companies relating to the Steamship Company. National Archives of the UK: Public Record Office BT 31/1410/4055.
15 Court of Chancery. Companies Acts and the Steamship Company. Affidavits of William Every and Alexander Howden, 8 November 1870. National Archives of the UK: Public Record Office C 31/2443 pt. 3/2862 and 2863.
16 The papers of the Registrar of Joint Stock Companies. *Ibid.*
17 Court of Chancery. Companies Acts and the Steamship Company. Affidavit of Robert N Fowler, 29 September 1870. National Archives of the UK: Public Record Office C 31/2443 pt. 3/2681.
18 Court of Chancery. Companies Acts and the Steamship Company. Order of Vice Chancellor Bacon at Chambers, 15 November 1870 and Affidavit of William Every, 12 December 1870. National Archives of the UK: Public Record Office C 33/33/1169 and C 31/2444 pt. 2/3228.
19 The papers of the Registrar of Joint Stock Companies. *Ibid.*
20 Post Office (Mail Contracts). Return to an Order of the Honourable the House of Commons dated 16 July 1869. Copy of Contract of 9 July 1869.
21 *Lloyds List*, 26 September 1868, col. 16.
22 Court of Admiralty. Suit no. 4927, 15 June 1869. *The Times*, 17 June 1869.
23 Court of Chancery. Companies Acts and the Steamship Company. Affidavits of Charles T Gitting, 22 June and 8 November 1871. National Archives of the UK: Public Record Office C 31/2546/1670 and C 31/2548/2654.
24 Court of Chancery. Companies Acts and the Steamship Company. Affidavits of Edmund Ayres, 27 June 1871 and of Richard Topper, 19 January 1872. National Archives of the UK: Public Record Office C 31/2546/1721 and C 31/2651 pt. 2/236.
25 Court of Chancery. Companies Acts and the Steamship Company. Affidavit of William Every, 29 September 1870. National Archives of the UK: Public Record Office C 31/2443 pt. 3/2675.
26 The Papers of the Registrar of Joint Stock Companies. Ibid.
27 Court of Chancery. Companies Acts and the Steamship Company. Affidavit of William Every, 7 August 1876. National Archives of the UK: Public Record Office J 4/ 132/2334.

Notes to Chapter 16: Bankruptcy and its Aftermath

1 *The Times*, 29 July 1869.
2 National Archives of the UK: Public Record Office B 5/174 no. 41390.
3 This appears to be the only reference in the records to a firm of this name in connection with Tait.

4 Sir Peter Tait & Ors v. Alexander Collie & Another. Court of Chancery. Re-amended Bill of Complaint, 17 November 1873, p. 7 para. 18. National Archives of the UK: Public Record Office C 16/682 pt. 1.

5 *Irish Times*, 28 October 1869.

6 Tait v. Collie. Court of Chancery. Re-amended Bill of Complaint, 17 November 1873, p. 8 para. 21. National Archives of the UK: Public Record Office C 16/682 pt. 1.

7 *Ibid.* p. 10 para. 25.

8 S Laing to Charles T Still, 25 December 1872. *The Orcadian*, 28 December 1872.

9 Archives of Ashurst, Morris & Co. Guildhall Library, London, Ledgers 2 (1867) to 8 (1883).

10 Church of England Life & Fire Assurance Trust & Annuity Institution (the C of E Institution). Minutes of Directors' Meetings, 20 September 1867 and 9 October 1868. Guildhall Library, London MS 1260D/6 430C and 1260D/7 69F. Royal Bank of Scotland Archives. The National Bank Regular Minute Book 21 nos. 107 and 212.

11 Tait v. Collie. Court of Chancery. Bill of Complaint, 4 August 1870. National Archives of the UK: Public Record Office C16/682 pt. 1.

12 Court of Chancery. Companies Acts 1862 and 1867 and the Steamship Company. Affidavit of William Every, 22 April 1872. National Archives of the UK: Public Record Office C31/2652 pt. 3/1117.

13 Tait v. Collie. Court of Chancery. Answer of Collie, 4 January 1871, p. 34 para. 87. National Archives of the UK: Public Record Office C 16/682 pt. 1.

14 *The Times*, 9 July 1869.

15 *The Times*, 10 August 1871.

16 The C of E Institution. Minutes of Directors' Meetings, 18 January 1871. Guildhall Library, London, MS 1260D/7 297E.

17 Archives of the Royal Literary Fund. Anniversary Documents. British Library Manuscript Collections.

18 *Munster News*, 2 November 1872.

Notes to Chapter 17: An Extraordinary Case of Seduction

1 *Cork Daily Herald*, 25 to 31 March 1871. *The Times*, 30 March 1871.

2 *The Times*, 16 January 1872, 20 and 28 June 1873.

Notes to Chapter 18: The Orkney and Shetland By-election

1 The by-election which followed the death of Frederick Dundas was extensively reported in the local press in both Orkney and Shetland. What follows in this chapter is based largely on these reports.

2 The surviving papers of the Registrar of Joint Stock Companies relating to The Army Navy and General Outfitting Company, Limited. National Archives of the UK: Public Record Office BT31/1785/6755.

3 Report of Royal Commission upon the Administration and Operation of the Contagious Diseases Acts, 1871.

4 *Ibid.* Vol. I p. 3 para. 1.

5 *Ibid.* Vol. I p. 5 para. 17.

6 Court of Chancery. Companies Acts 1862 and 1867 and The London, Belgium, Brazil and River Plate Royal Mail Steam Ship Company, Limited. Affidavit of David Swayne, 13 October 1870 and Liquidators' Accounts, 23 May 1876. National Archives of the UK: Public Record Office C31/2443 pt. 3/2710 and C30/1867.

Notes to Chapter 19: The Laxfirth Estate in Shetland

1 Disposition by James Davidson to Sir Peter Tait. National Archives of Scotland RS 111/39 ff. 160v-163r.

2 *Owners of Lands and Heritages 17 & 18 Vict. Cap. 91 1872-1873* (1874).

3 Bond etc. by Sir Peter Tait to Trustees for the firm of Brown Janson & Co. National Archives of Scotland RS 111/16 ff. 4v-10r.

4 Sir Peter Tait against David Inglis, January 1877. The Sheriff Court of Caithness, Orkney and Zetland at Lerwick. Shetland Archives SC 12/6/1877/3.

5 Petition of Sir Pater Tait and George B Hay to the Sheriff of the Sheriffdom of Caithness, Orkney and Shetland, 1 March 1876. Shetland Archives SC 12/6/1876/16.

6 Bond etc. by Sir Peter Tait to Thomas M Adie. National Archives of Scotland RS 111/26 ff. 129R-138V.

7 *Ibid.* as note 4 above.

8 Disposition by Thomas M Adie to John Robertson junior, 27 September 1880, and Disposition by John Robertson junior to Thomas M Adie, 28 September 1880. National Archives of Scotland RS 111/39 ff. 72R-79V and ff. 79b-83b.

9 Petition of Peter Garrick to the Sheriff of the Sheriffdom of Caithness, Orkney and Zetland, 24 September 1878. Shetland Archives SC 12/6/1878/70.

Notes to Chapter 20: Financial Difficulties in Limerick

1 Church of England Life & Fire Assurance Trust & Annuity Institution. Minutes of Directors' Meetings, 5 November 1873, and 10 June and 14 October 1874. Guildhall Library, London, MS 1260D/8 129b, 188D and 220E.

2 R Bourke to the Local Government Board for Ireland, 30 June 1880. National Archives, Dublin, Registered Papers, 1880, no.15683.

3 W E Foster to War Office, 9 July 1880. National Archives, Dublin, Registered Papers, 1880, no. 16699.

4 *The Times*, 26 December 1885.

Notes to Chapter 21: Constantinople: the Early Years

1 The Archives of the Royal Literary Fund. Anniversary Documents. British Library Maunuscript Collections.

2 What I have written has of necessity been derived from research into a very small part of a very complex subject; for a full study of the financial

affairs of the Ottoman Empire since the middle of the nineteenth century, see Edhem Eldem, *A History of the Ottoman Bank* (Istanbul 1999).

3 1er Décret concernant l'emission du Papier-Monnaie. Publié dans la journal *La Turquie*. Le 16 Août 1876.

4 2me Décret concernant l'emission du Papier-Monnaie. Publié dans la journal *La Turquie*. Le 5 Janvier 1877.

5 Edhem Eldem, *A History of the Ottoman Bank* (Istanbul 1999) Graph 1.6 p. 523.

6 Receipt by Erskine Foster to the Imperial Ottoman Bank, 6 June 1876. Ottoman Bank Archives and Research Centre, Ottoman Bank Archives Miscellaneous files XX-001.

7 Tait v. C S Hanson & Co. Award dated 27 February 1877. Her Britannic Majesty's Supreme Consular Court at Constantinople (the Consular Court). National Archives of the UK: Public Record Office (TNA: PRO) FO 780/79.

8 Ottoman Bank Archives C-J I-044/45 and C-C I-026. Also, for the proceeds of the *havale*, *ibid.* as note 7 above.

9 Sentence no. 435 rendered by the First Chamber of the Commercial Tribunal of the Tidjaret, the Ottoman Commercial Court, 21 October 1882. TNA: PRO FO 195/1424.

10 Tait to H Wyndham, Chargé d'Affaires at the British Embassy, 16 December 1882. TNA: PRO FO 195/1424/M658.

11 Opinion of Hassan Fehmi Effendi 8 June 1877. TNA: PRO FO 195/1424/M683.

12 J H Fawcett to Austin H Layard, 7 May 1877. PRO FO 198/38.

13 Affidavit of Baronak Baronaki, British Embassy dragoman, in the Consular Court, 21 November 1882. TNA: PRO FO 195/ 1489/M179.

14 Notes Verbale from the British Embassy to the Sublime Porte, 1 October 1877, and reply of 8 December 1877. TNA: PRO FO 198/38/306.

15 Tait to R Plunkett, Chargé d'Affaires at the British Embassy, 6 June 1881. TNA: PRO FO 195/1383/M378.

16 Edwin Pears to Austin H Layard, 3 April 1878. TNA: PRO FO 198/38/338.

Notes to Chapter 22: A Diplomatic Incident

1 The Right Hon Austen H Layard had been made a Knight Grand Cross of the British Empire earlier in 1878.

2 Edmund Calvert to Sir Henry Layard, 7 December 1878. Public Record Office (TNA: PRO) FO 195/1155/2238.

3 J d'Akcharoumoff, Chef de la justice militaire de l'armée active russe, 6 December 1878. TNA: PRO FO 195/1185/2239.

4 Calvert to Layard, 9 December 1878. TNA: PRO FO 195/ 1185/2255.

5 Tait to Layard, 10 December 1878. TNA: PRO FO 198/38/ 1123.

6 Sublime Porte to British Ambassador, memorandum 18 September 1880. TNA: PRO FO 195/1327/SP501.

Notes to Chapter 23: Constantinople: the Later Years

1 Tait to J H Fawcett, Consul General and Judge of the Consular Court, 27 November 1879. National Archives of the UK: Public Record Office (TNA: PRO) FO 780/171.

2 Tait to F R Plunkett, 30 May 1881, and Tait to G J Göschen, Especial Ambassador, 19 July 1880. TNA: PRO FO 195/1383/ M358 and FO 195/ 1333/M616.

3 Edwin Pears to Sir Henry Layard, 26 November; Layard to Rassim Pasha, 30 November; and Rassim Pasha to Layard 25 December 1879. TNA: PRO FO 198/38.

4 Bank of Constantinople v. Tait. The Consular Court. TNA: PRO FO 780/ 780/153.

5 Tait to Göschen, 19 July 1880. TNA: PRO FO 195/1333/M616.

6 Earl Granville to Göschen, 29 July 1880, enclosing memorandum dated 22 July in which Mr O'Shaughnessy MP prays for the intervention of the Ambassador on Tait's behalf. TNA: PRO FO 195/1280/M1209.

7 Tait to Hassan Pasha, 12 April 1881. TNA: PRO FO 195/1382/ M208.

8 Tait to Goschen, 15 April 1881. TNA: PRO FO 195/1382/ M208.

9 Tait to Plunkett, 30 May 1881. TNA: PRO FO 195/1383/ M357.

10 Tait to Plunkett, 26 June 1881. TNA: PRO FO 195/1383/ M450.

11 Tait to Plunkett, 29 June 1881. TNA: PRO FO 195/1383.

12 Plunkett to the Foreign Secretary, memorandum 23 July 1881. TNA: PRO FO 195/1347/618.

13 Tait to Plunkett, 4 July 1881. TNA: PRO FO 195/1383/M472.

14 Notes Verbale from the Sublime Porte to the British Ambassador, 18 and 23 August 1881, and Earl of Dufferin to Tait, 25 August 1881. TNA: PRO FO 195/1379/SP159 and SP162, and FO 195/1387/M283.

15 Tait to Dufferin, 7 September 1881. TNA: PRO FO 195/1384/ M688.

16 Tait to Dufferin, 10 September 1881. TNA: PRO FO 195/ 1385/M708.

17 Certificate by which Holder is entitled to Protection, no. 488 for 1886. British Consulate General, Istanbul, British Subjects Registers.

18 Edwin Pears to Tait, 19 March 1884. TNA: PRO FO 195/1489.

19 Sentence no. 435 rendered by the First Chamber of the Commercial Tribunal of the Tidjaret, the Ottoman Commercial Court, 21 October 1882. TNA: PRO FO 195/1424.

20 Tait to the Directors of the Imperial Ottoman Bank, 10 December 1883. Ottoman Bank Archives and Research Centre, Ottoman Bank Archives Miscellaneous files XX-001.

21 Dufferin to Aarify Pasha, 28 December 1882. TNA: PRO FO 195/1419/ SP233.

22 Tait to Dufferin, 1 December 1883. TNA: PRO FO 195/ 1460/M551.

23 Tait to H Wyndham, Chargé d'Affaires at the British Embassy, 28 January 1885. TNA: PRO FO 195/1522/M25.

24 Wyndham to Pears, 14 January 1885. TNA: PRO FO 195/ 1525/M12.

Notes to Chapter 24: The Sale of the Army Clothing Factory

1 Report of the Director of Army Clothing Contracts for the year ended 31 December 1880, p. 7. National Archives of the UK: Public Record Office WO 33/36.
2 *Limerick Chronicle*, 5 March 1881.
3 Report of the Director of Army Clothing Contracts for the year ended 31 December 1881, p.7. National Archives of the UK: Public Record Office WO 33/36
4 Hansard 16 June 1881.
5 *Ibid.* as note 3 above.
6 Companies House. Company no. 18012.

Notes to Chapter 25: Cigarette Maker

1 Certificate by which Holder is entitled to Protection, no. 268 for 1885. British Consulate General, Istanbul. British Subjects Registers.
2 The surviving papers of the Registrar of Joint Stock Companies relating to the Turkish Tobacco Company Limited. National Archives of the UK: Public Record Office BT 31/1785/6755.

Notes to Chapter 26: A Speculative Purchase in the Caucasus

1 Charles Marvin, *The Region of the Eternal Fire: an account of a journey to the petroleum region of the Caspian in 1883* (London 1884) p. 96.
2 *The Times*, 24 December 1888.
3 John Mitzakis, *The Russian Oil Fields and Petroleum Industry* (London 1911) pp 50-51.
4 The Tiflis Treasury to the Poti District Treasury, 6 October 1886. Kutaisi State Archives (KSA) fund 23 case 22 pp. 9-12.
5 The Kutais District Treasury to the Tiflis State Chamber, 7 February 1889. KSA fund 23 case 22 p. 37.
6 Memorandum and plan, 15 October 1883. KSA fund 58 case 504 pp. -13-15.
7 Mountain Area Development Board to the Poti District Treasury, 13 October 1893. KSA fund 23 case 22 p. 77a.
8 Memorandum, 9 November 1892. KSA fund 23 case 22 pp. 61-62.
9 Batoum Notary's Registration Book, entry 2260, 24 July 1890. KSA fund 12 case 38 p. 144.
10 Batoum Notary's Registration Book, entry 1758, 8 June 1890. KSA fund 12 case 38 p. 62.
11 Mountain Area Development Board to the Tiflis State Chamber, 11 December 1893. KSA fund 23 case 22 p. 87.

Index